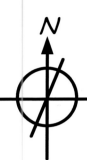

CHARLIE'S CHARTS

of POLYNESIA

The South Pacific, East of 165° West Longitude

Charles and Margo Wood

7th Edition Revision by
Captain Holly Scott and Jo Russell

Published by

CHARLIE'S CHARTS
P&S Marine, LLC
PO Box 352
Seal Beach, CA 90740
U.S.A

Website: www.charliescharts.com   Email: info@charliescharts.com

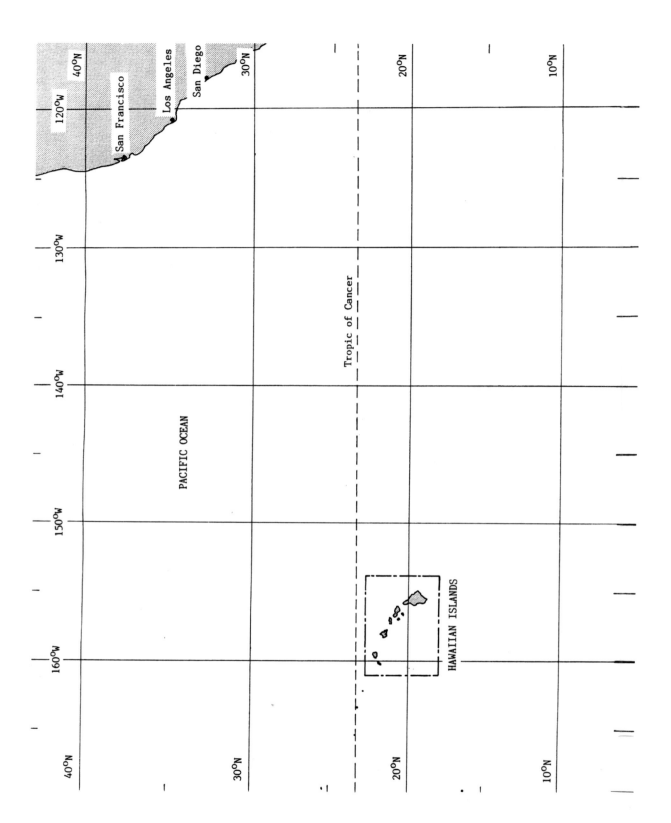

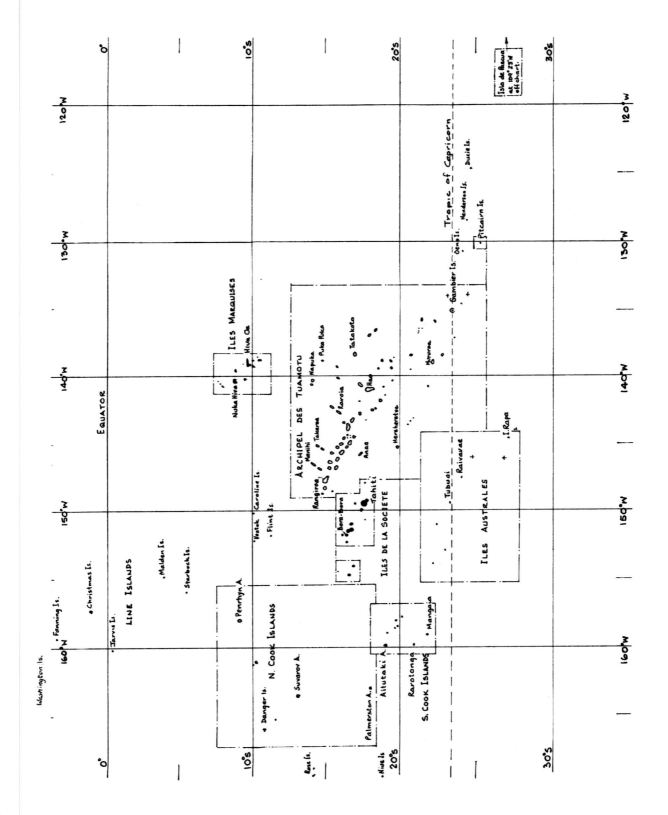

iii

CHARLIE'S CHARTS CRUISING GUIDES

CHARLIE'S CHARTS NORTH to ALASKA

CHARLIE'S CHARTS of the Western Coast of MEXICO

CHARLIE'S CHARTS of POLYNESIA

CHARLIE'S CHARTS of the HAWAIIAN ISLANDS

CHARLIE'S CHARTS of the U.S. PACIFIC COAST

CHARLIE'S CHARTS of COSTA RICA

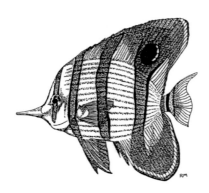

SEVENTH EDITION

US Copyright © 2011 P&S Marine, LLC

All rights reserved.

Published in the United States by P&S Marine, LLC

Wood, Charles E. (Charles Edward), 1928-1987 and Margo Wood (1934 -)

Revision by Scott, Holly (1955 -) and Russell, Anita Jo (1960 -)

Charlie's Charts of Polynesia – 7th Edition

1. Pilot guides – Polynesia   2. Boats and boating – Polynesia – Maps

3. Polynesia – Description and travel

I. Title.

Canadian Copyright © 1983, 1989, 1994, 2000, 2005, 2010   P&S Marine, LLC

US Copyright © 2011 P&S Marine, LLC

Illustrated by Charles Wood and Richard Miller. Seventh edition edits by Holly Scott
Front cover photograph by Steve Snider. Back cover photograph by Mark Mitchell. Remaining
photographs as credited.

PRINTED IN USA   ISBN: 978-0-9833319-0-2

GREETINGS FROM HOLLY AND JO

As the new owners of the Charlie's Charts family of cruising guides, we would like to welcome you to our first effort – the 7th Edition of Charlie's Charts of Polynesia. As cruisers, we have used various editions of Charlie's Charts over the years, and have come to appreciate the simplicity and clarity of the text and sketches and hope you will too.

Charles and Margo Wood began Charlie's Charts in 1982 while cruising down the Pacific Coast of the US and Mexico. They were a big hit with coastal cruisers. After Charles passed away in 1987, Margo took on the task of continuing and expanding the guides. She's ready to go have some fun now and we are honored to have the opportunity to take the next watch on the helm of Charlie's Charts.

Jo and I have been friends for a long time and have discovered that we work well together, whether getting my boat ready for a Mexico cruise, doing deliveries, fixing stuff on each other's boats, anchoring in nasty conditions when you can't hear anything over the wind or building a cruising guide business. She's the sensible-business-brain-computer-savvy one and I (Holly) am the A.D.D.-full-of-crazy-ideas-let's-just-go-sailing one. We make a great team.

There are six different volumes of Charlie's Charts covering the Pacific coasts of Southeast Alaska, all the way down to the tip of Mexico, Costa Rica, Hawaii and the Polynesian Islands. That's a lot of territory to keep up with, so if you're out there and discover something new, please let us know so we can keep our guides up to date. You can always go to our web site www.charliescharts.com to check out the latest updates.

We look forward to sharing your cruising adventures with you through Charlie's Charts. Let us know where you are and what's new. Together, we will continue Charles and Margo's legacy for many years to come.

Sail smart, sail safe and have a great time out there.

As always, thanks for choosing Charlie's Charts!

Holly and Jo...

Jo, Holly and Holly's ubiquitous Diet Coke

A WORD OR TWO ABOUT KARMA

Sailors have always been a superstitious lot, and for good reason. How often have we all wondered what we did to deserve the bad things that happen to us as we are sailing around 'out there'? "Just get me out of this storm in one piece and I'll never throw plastic overboard again!" You know what we're talking about...

So be nice to everybody and everything; other cruisers, the local folks, the wildlife with whom you share the land and seas, our planet and especially your boat. And remember that we print these cruising guides for you so you can cruise with some local knowledge, like having a friend onboard. You will want to share your experiences with other cruisers and mark up your guide with changes and suggestions from cruisers who have been there. Perfect!

However, copying these guides and selling or giving them away is BAD KARMA. You don't need any BAD KARMA, you need good karma. We will be happy to mail a brand new copy anywhere in the world, so just pass along our web information and build up some more good karma for yourself and others while you help us keep the presses rolling here at home.

Navigator's Tip – You've reached *French* Polynesia when there are baguettes in the mail boxes

Holly Scott

ACKNOWLEDGEMENTS

This is like the Academy Awards – there are so many people to thank! First, we want to thank *you* for choosing Charlie's Charts! Of course, Charles and Margo Wood are also at the top of the list. It's mind boggling to begin to understand the amount of work they poured into these books over the years. An extra special thank you to Margo is in order for her patience and guidance as we take our turn on the Charlie's Charts helm and continue her legacy.

Ed and Sharon Cox provided the link for us with Margo in the beginning. Thank you both for thinking of us as a good fit for Charlie's Charts.

As always, we receive and incorporate input from cruisers who note changes while they explore 'out there'. Captain Michael Marquardt and Karen Steinkamp of *S/V Innoey* who have been cruising Polynesian waters for a number of years provided valuable information on changes to navigational aids and other updates. Barry and Sue Swackhamer of *S/V Wind Spirit* forwarded a great deal of useful material covering the Marquesas and Tuamotus. Nick and Jenny Coghlan of *S/V Bosun Bird* sent detailed information and descriptions of the Society Islands, Easter Island and Palmerston Island. The location of a sunken wreck on Bora-Bora was forwarded by Philip and Leslie of S/V *Carina*.

Keith Vial, Commodore of the Niue Yacht Club a/k/a The Biggest Little Yacht Club in the World, provided us with a wonderful update on the new moorings and facilities on the "Rock of Polynesia". While Niue is a bit outside of the boundaries of this guide, it was just too good to leave out and Keith's update made it all the better.

Photos were contributed to the 7th edition by Steve Snider, Keith Vial, Mary Ho, Melinda Young and Betsy Crowfoot. Our thanks go out to them as well.

Captain Denny Emory, Co-founder of OceanMedix.com LLC provided information on Medical Preparedness for coastal cruisers and offshore voyagers.

We've had a great outpouring of logistical support from our wonderful friends and families. Bill Lewis took a day off, brought his truck and helped us pick up the shipment of inventory from Margo. Holly's mom Betty Scott, Rebecca Yeomans, Betsy Crowfoot and Katie Scott have all chipped in to assemble and ship Charlie's Charts as well as helping with editing, layout, and moral support. A special thanks to Barbara Blakey who worked on artwork changes to sketches via remote link from Nova Scotia, Canada.

Last but certainly not least in the technical support department, Robin Stout provided some much needed tutelage on the Adobe CS5 Suite that enabled us to begin our journey to bring the publication of Charlie's Charts into the 21st century.

Holly wants to especially thank her parents Bud and Betty Scott for taking her sailing as a toddler and providing a wonderful life full of boating adventures, love and support. They never once squashed a dream.

And finally, thanks to the late Mary Lester for all the teddy bears and cats.

DISCLAIMER

The word, "CHARTS," in the title of this publication is not intended to imply that these sketches are sufficiently accurate to be used for navigation. They and the accompanying text are meant to act solely as a handy **cruising guide** to assist sailors in identifying and entering passes, harbors and anchorages. With the passage of time, new aids to navigation, marina development and other changes make it inevitable that some of the information may become inaccurate and out-of-date by the time it is used.

The use of current British Admiralty, French or U.S nautical charts is mandatory for safe navigation. **DO NOT USE ANY OF THE DRAWINGS IN THIS BOOK FOR NAVIGATION.** Only the latest edition of charts, pilots and Light Lists for the area covered should be used for navigational purposes. The authors and publisher are in no way liable, directly or indirectly, for any loss or damages to persons and / or property resulting from the use or interpretation of any information within this book.

The coastline of many atolls and islands described in this guide has not been surveyed hydrographically as noted on sketched charts in the Marquesas. Consequently, there could easily be many reefs, shoals and other dangers that are yet to be discovered. Cruisers are cautioned to be vigilant in recognizing and avoiding such hazards.

UPDATING INFORMATION

After new information is obtained and verified it is inserted in each book as an addenda and the same material is posted on our website www.charliescharts.com where it can be downloaded as needed. If you discover a significant change to facilities that would be worthwhile to pass on to fellow cruisers please e-mail us at info@charliescharts.com

Contents

INTRODUCTION

A compulsory pilot in entrance fairways and estuaries meets commercial ships, men-of-war and cruise ships in every port of the world. Dealing with authorities, check-in procedures, provisioning and fitting out is catered for by professional agents with thorough local knowledge. For these services a high price is paid.

Cruisers in small craft, of say less than 60 feet, normally have neither the inclination nor the cruising kitty or need to hire such services. To those who plan their own nautical approach, complete the necessary paperwork, provision and maintain their vessels *Charlie's Charts* are dedicated to provide information, orientation and local knowledge.

This guide is oriented to sailing from North America to the South Pacific. Thus the routes, weather and order of this guide through the islands are given for a westbound journey. However, the guide can be used by those approaching from other locations, though it may not be convenient.

Some general introductory material on important facets of cruising the area is given first. Thereafter, each section describes a particular island group, and includes brief notes on history, weather, winds, currents and other data. These notes are a generalized summary of conditions and are by no means descriptive of what you might actually encounter—that lies with the gods. For additional information refer to the official Sailing Directions, Pilot Charts and other references.

The sketched "charts" illustrate anchorages and the approaches to them and are useful to the cruising sailor. The source material includes nautical charts, maps, other cruiser's comments, and our own material.

The South Pacific is the cruising sailor's dream. The area is politically stable, still cruiser friendly, reasonably free of excessive strict regulations (a matter of opinion), and filled with an intrinsic beauty of land, sea, and weather that make it a paradise for sailors.

Unfortunately, the polluting advance of "civilization" has begun to touch this once idyllic cruising haven. The lagoons adjacent to hotels in Tahiti and Moorea are not as clean as they once were and resorts operating on some atolls are degrading the knife-edge ecologies. In addition, a steady drift of people to Papeete is reducing out-island populations while the birth rate has been rising.

It is a major offshore voyage to get there, to cruise the many islands, and then a major voyage home again. Sailing to Polynesia can be part of a Pacific circuit, a New Zealand hop, or a round-the-world odyssey. In any case it requires a large commitment in time to accomplish it; this is the criterion that does more to separate those who just dream of it from those who do it. Though a rushed voyage to the South Seas and back could be done in three months, enjoyment would be limited with such an itinerary. In fact, taking into account controlling weather conditions, you should plan on up to a year to allow for exploration and maximum enjoyment.

PURPOSE AND LIMITS OF THIS GUIDE

This guide identifies small boat anchorages in the eastern part of South Pacific. It is intended to assist cruisers in their choice of anchorages and to recognize approaches and hazards. Roughly, the area covered is that commonly known as the "Polynesian Triangle," with the exception of the Samoa Islands. Though the Hawaiian Islands are north of the Equator and are found in detail in *Charlie's Charts of the Hawaiian Islands*, they are considered here as part of the South Pacific so the Ports of Entry are included.

This guide helps the cruiser by showing small anchorages in larger scale and detail than most coastal charts. In the case of the South Pacific, the land masses are small, and the special difficulties of navigation in the area mean that there are more large scale charts available, though not as many as one would like.

The sketches are hand-drawn and are not meant to be accurate surveys or to be used for navigation. Nautical charts should be used for all navigational purposes and the sketches herein are intended to provide supplemental information only.

These sketches include information such as land form details in symbolic form, contour lines, depth lines or individual soundings, lights, some navigational data such as leading ranges, etc. In the geographic area covered by this guide, with coral reefs and low-lying atolls, the most important information is often the identification of, and detail of a pass through the reef rather than a specific anchorage. The practice of giving the view from seaward on approaching a coast is useful to sailors although it is disappearing from many current official charts as a consequence of an increasingly technological era.

Details cannot be shown of the complexities of coral heads and shoals once through the reef's pass. Navigation to an anchorage within a lagoon must be done by eye, in the best light, and from as high a position as possible. Thus a sketch might show the detail of an entrance and merely indicate the anchorage across the lagoon. This does not mean a yacht can go carelessly across as if traversing a channel. Passages may involve much maneuvering to thread a route through the coral heads and shoals. The responsibility for safely navigating your vessel through a pass and to any anchorage remains with the skipper, and this guide cannot be held responsible for the safety of a vessel in any way.

If you discover changes in facilities or aids to navigation that would be helpful to cruisers following in your wake it would be appreciated by all concerned if you forwarded the information to us via email at info@charliescharts.com.

PLANNING AND PREPARATION

A South Pacific cruise is an offshore voyage that will last several months. The area is tropical, and inhabited by a warm and friendly people. It is, however, expensive, and much of the region is remote and isolated. Though connected by air and sea to the rest of the world to a far greater extent than previously, there are many deficiencies in the availability of supplies and facilities for repair and replacement of modern yacht equipment. In the regions covered by this guide only Honolulu, Papeete and Raiatea have reasonable facilities. Cruisers can find services further away in Whangarei and Auckland in New Zealand and Suva in Fiji.

Vessels bound for this region must be well found and seaworthy. Your vessel will not only be your home but it will also be your primary means of survival and comfort. Sails and engine should be in good condition, as they are your methods of transportation. Anchors and rodes are essential to the safety of the yacht. Most tropical anchorages are in fairly deep water, and since chain is the best to use in coral waters an anchor windlass is essential. The vessel should be well ventilated, having opening ports and a wind scoop. A cockpit canopy that can be rigged to provide shade and rain protection is necessary.

Since credit cards are useful only in cities, always carry enough traveler's checks (in small denominations) to cover the first major stage of the voyage. ATMs are readily available in large cities. Limited cash should be taken, but it is useful to have some in US currency, for small payments and emergencies. Bank drafts and evidence of funds for transfer are the best way to handle the special demands for financial responsibility of some countries and for renewing funds for the next stage of the cruiser's itinerary.

Replenishing major food supplies is possible in several places including Hilo, Honolulu, Lahaina, Kahalui Bay, Raiatea and Papeete, though small quantities can be obtained in most villages. Supplies in small atolls are expensive and limited; you may be doing a disservice to local inhabitants by purchasing them in quantity. Coconuts, fresh fruits, and produce are available in season.

Water can be obtained in most locations, though amounts available and degree of purity will vary. All water taken aboard should he filtered and treated to ensure purity. Replenishment is best done at ports in the Hawaiian Islands or French Polynesia. Most atolls and small islands collect rainwater for consumption; occasionally it is drawn from a well.

Fuel availability follows a similar pattern. Since supplies of diesel or gasoline at small centers cater primarily to local needs, there may be little left over for visitors. Major towns are the best places for refueling and it is recommended that you carry extra supplies.

Pilot Charts of the North and South Pacific are particularly helpful in planning the voyage. They provide information regarding weather, currents, storm patterns and other factors crucial to the area covered by the cruise.

Items in high demand when trading for fresh produce are 3/8" to ½" rope, whether or not it is used and fishing gear (line, hooks, lures, etc...). These are easy to stow and might even be handy in an emergency.

MEDICAL PREPAREDNESS for the COASTAL CRUISER & OFFSHORE VOYAGER from Captain Denny Emory

Being prepared for a medical illness or injury is an important part of getting ready for any boating activity. Whether day sailing in the bay, making an open water passage or finding oneself in a remote anchorage, being able to cope with a medical emergency may be the most significant factor in contributing to a favorable outcome.

Prior to departure one should evaluate the potential exposure due to distance from or accessibility to professional medical assistance and the level of care that might be available. **A vessel should then be properly outfitted appropriately for that exposure and the extent of the intended cruise or passage.**

Outfitting should include the **appropriate**:
- First Aid Manual
- First Aid Kit
- Emergency Medical Equipment (AED, neck brace / Extrication collar, back brace / emergency stretcher, etc...)
- Prescription Medications (carried in anticipation of need)
- Normal Vessel's Medicine Cabinet Consumables
- Over-the counter pharmacy supplies

To review the spectrum of product options available, check out the **OceanMedix** website at http://www.oceanmedix.com . For further information or advice, contact **OceanMedix** at information@oceanmedix.com or toll-free at 866-788-2642 (307-732-2642 from outside the U.S.A.). Tell them **Charlie's Charts** sent you!

In addition to the outfitting of the vessel, one must consider possible training beyond Basic First Aid and CPR classes. Advanced training courses include First Responder, EMT and certified Marine First Aid.

Have a plan in force to allow for communication with medical personnel if need through the U.S. Coast Guard, a 24/7 tele-medical provider or private practitioner via cell phone, VHF, SSB, satellite....

Thinking through an extraction or evacuation plan to transport an injured or critically ill crew member to a facility capable of providing the necessary level of care may prove to be a valuable exercise.

Preparation, training and experience lead to confidence. In a medical emergency situation this may be the most significant aspect in facilitating a favorable outcome.

ROUTES AND PASSAGE TIMES

The popular routes to the South Pacific are shown on the accompanying chart. From North America, the choices are either to go directly to the Marquesas, or to proceed there from Hawaii or Mexico. Every year numerous vessels arrive from each direction. The choices are shown as (1A), (1B), and (1), (2), or (3).

From Europe or South America, the passage via the Panama Canal, or directly from South American ports, is illustrated as (4). Some cruisers track a route from the Galapagos – Easter Island – Pitcairn – Gambiers and then sail up the Archipelago de Tuamotu to Papeete or go north to the Marquesas. Few travelers today follow the oldest sailing route around the Horn and then head for the Society Islands. The later explorers from Europe and the barks of the last century rounded the Cape of Good Hope, made their easting in the Roaring Forties and climbed up to the South Pacific Islands upon reaching their longitude.

From New Zealand, the passage is either directly to Papeete, or via Rarotonga in the Cook Islands, then to Papeete. Modern vessels can make the windward passage adequately. The older route, sometimes still followed, makes the maximum easting south of, or around latitude 40°S to about 155°W before hauling northward into the trades and then going directly to Tahiti.

Passage times are merely guides based on averaging the past history of many different vessels traveling similar routes. There are many factors that can alter the traveling time therefore times are given only as an aid to planning the voyage. The following table lists an average time for a typical 35 ft. to 40 ft. sailing vessel. Skippers should allow for at least 50% more time providing for unforeseen delays and emergencies.

Route	Departing	Destination	Distance in Nautical Miles*	Average # of Days
1A	Seattle/Vancouver	Hilo, Hawaii	2,400	27
1A	San Francisco	Hilo, Hawaii	2,050	22
1B	Los Angeles or San Diego	Hilo, Hawaii	2,200	23
1	Hilo, Hawaii	Iles Marquesas	2,100	21
	Iles Marquesas	Tahiti	750	7
2	Los Angeles or San Diego	Iles Marquesas	2,850	28
	Seattle/Vancouver	Iles Marquesas	3,650	38
3	Acapulco	Iles Marquesas	2,900	27
3A	Acapulco	Tahiti (via Gambier) Is.)	3,700	38
4	Panama Canal	Iles Marquesas	3,850	40
5	Auckland	Tahiti	2,200	22
	Tahiti	Hilo, Hawaii	2,350	22
	Hilo, Hawaii	San Francisco	2,050	24
	Hilo, Hawaii	Seattle/Vancouver	2,400	27

*Approximate Great Circle distance, not necessarily the actual distance via the route a yacht may follow to avoid the Pacific High Pressure areas.

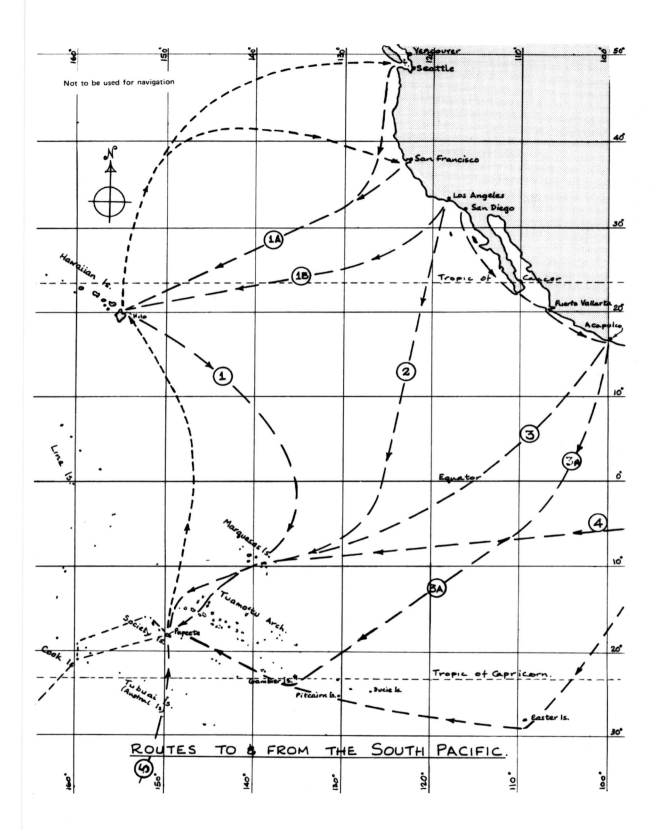

Not to be used for navigation

ROUTES TO & FROM THE SOUTH PACIFIC.

WINDS, WAVES and WEATHER

The main island groups of this guide are within the tropical zone, between the Tropics of Cancer and Capricorn. In this region, the trade winds predominate throughout most of the year, being mainly northeasterly to easterly in the Northern Hemisphere, and southeasterly to easterly in the Southern Hemisphere.

Generally speaking, north of the equator the NE Trades extend above 30°N at all times of the year within the area covered by this guide. They blow stronger during the northern winter, i.e. November to February. South of the equator the SE Trades normally extend at least to 20°S, but in the southern summer, i.e. December to February, they may be dominant as far south as 25°S. The strongest trade winds are experienced from June to September, the southern winter months.

There is an Inter-Tropical Convergence Zone where the two trade winds converge. This area is marked by extensive clouds, squalls and showers with features similar to the doldrums.

The most significant weather factor in these areas (excluding major storms), is the location of the two dominating high pressure areas—the North Pacific High and the South Pacific High, and the intervening tropical low pressure area. The positions of these highs and lows shift in seasonal fluctuation with the sun. Their importance to most sailors arises from the need to avoid the actual high pressure area and find comfortable sailing weather by staying within isobars that offer good winds for passage making. There is an annual, somewhat predictable pattern of movement of the highs, and they are reasonably stable in average seasonal positions. But, there can be considerable actual daily variation in their positions that can be slightly confusing to the skipper trying to plot them from radio weather data in order to determine the vessel's best course.

Within the band of 10° on either side of the equator there is only a very small diurnal variation in pressure, and this is twice daily, 1.5 mb above and below the monthly average. This is helpful to know, because any major change in this pattern, i.e. one exceeding 3 mb from the monthly average, can be taken as a warning of an oncoming tropical depression or major weather change.

The overall, fairly stable weather patterns of this tropical area can be affected by tropical depressions. Among the smaller, slower moving disturbances in the pressure field are easterly waves, i.e. a small drop followed by a small rise then back to normal with the position of this surge moving from east to west. In some cases these develop into closed isobaric systems that become tropical depressions, with winds to Force 7 (33 mph). This is warm tropical air, as there are no hot or cold fronts such as those found at higher latitudes. If they intensify to include winds of Force 8 to 11 (34 to 64 mph) they are tropical storms, and when they reach Force 12 (over 64 mph) they are called hurricanes, typhoons, or cyclones (all terms for the same weather phenomenon).

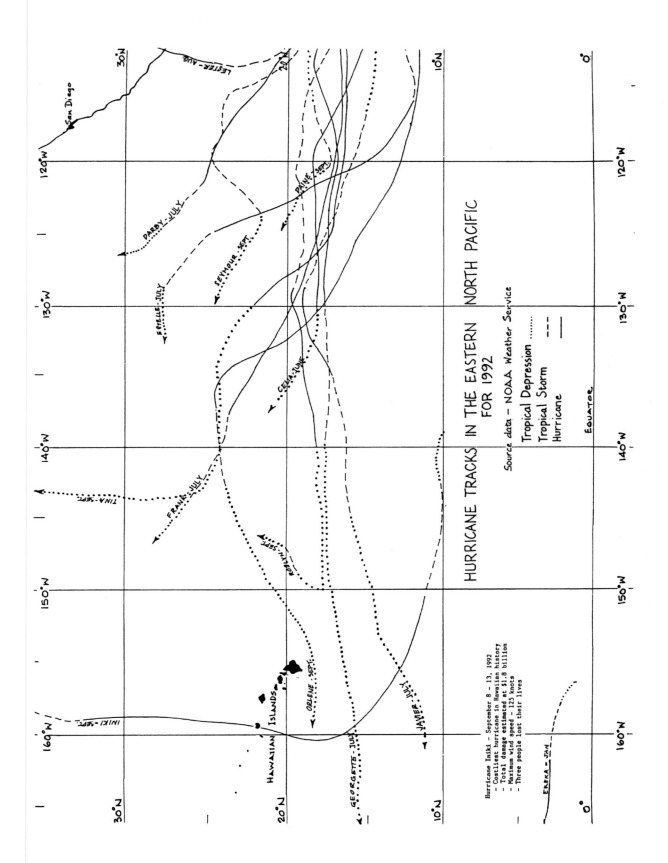

HURRICANE TRACKS IN THE EASTERN NORTH PACIFIC
FOR 1992

Source data - NOAA Weather Service

Tropical Depression ....
Tropical Storm - - - - -
Hurricane _____

Equator

Hurricane Iniki - September 8 - 13, 1992
  - Costliest hurricane in Hawaiian history
  - Total damage estimated at $1.8 billion
  - Maximum wind speed - 125 knots
  - Three people lost their lives

8

HURRICANES and CYCLONES

Major hurricane areas of the Pacific are:

1. On the eastern side of the North Pacific concentrated near the Mexican coast, generally curving northwesterly east of 140°W. A few penetrate further west.

2. On the western side of the North Pacific, generally well to the west of 180° and thus these "typhoons" are not included in this guide.

3. In the southwest corner of the South Pacific, they occur west of 180° and those that occur east of 165°W have been rare in the last 40 years. The following statement referring to Polynesia is excerpted from the Pacific Islands Pilot, Vol. II:

Tropical storms are not frequent in this part of the Pacific, and hurricanes even less so. Parts of this area, however, are notably deficient in observations so that it is quite possible that storms have occurred that have not been reported. Tropical storms are not expected within about 10° of the equator. Moreover, they are not known to have occurred in the southern hemisphere east of longitude 135°W. Otherwise there is no part of this region where there is not some liability for such storms, even though over most of this region they are very rare."

A glance at most charts showing tracks of tropical cyclones and hurricanes supports the above view, and this benign situation has been an attractive feature for cruisers to this area. However, there has been a change in the overall weather pattern of these storms in recent years that might indicate some change in the expected pattern of weather, and it is best to be prepared.

During the last decade, several hurricanes originating near Mexico have traveled westward beyond 140°W. Several have reached Hawaiian waters where they were once rare occurrences.

An even more startling change has been seen in the South Pacific where, as the quotation above shows, cyclones were even less frequent. A number have occurred in the last few years, some originating and passing east of 135°W. Tracks of these storms are shown on pages 7 and 9.

The cause of this change, which is related to the major climatological events occurring recently in many parts of the world, may be the weather phenomenon called "El Nino." This is a vast oscillation of air and water currents across the Pacific, known to have occurred about 10 times in the last 40 years. They are caused by a reduction in the drive of the currents westward, allowing a warming of the water in the eastern Pacific. One theory of meteorologists is that the cloud of dust released by large volcanic eruptions could weaken the heat received from the sun, slowing the trade winds and their associated currents sufficiently to trigger an "El Nino."

As a result of the erratic weather caused by El Nino and La Nina, it was decided to illustrate the hurricane and cyclone tracks from years prior to this period so the frequency and direction of such storms could be seen during normal years. Prudent sailors must be prepared to face severe and unpredicted storms that can occur at any time, but particularly during El Nino and La Nina periods.

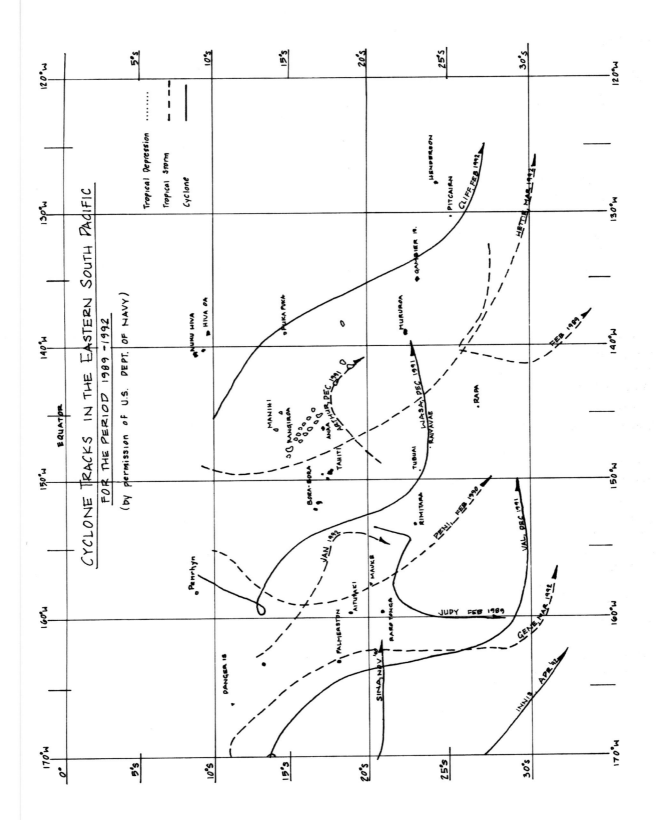

CYCLONE TRACKS IN THE EASTERN SOUTH PACIFIC
FOR THE PERIOD 1989-1992
(by permission of U.S. DEPT. OF NAVY)

10

CURRENTS

The influence of the trade winds causes the oceanic currents in these tropical regions to flow westward across the Pacific forming the North and South Equatorial Currents. They are not equally spaced along the equator. The South Equatorial Current extends a few degrees north of the equator and between it and the North Equatorial Current is a region of the east-flowing Equatorial Counter-Current.

The limits of the counter current can be fairly firmly fixed at times, the southern edge being about 4°N Latitude all year, while the northern edge varies between 8°N and 10°N. However, the boundaries of the main equatorial currents are less defined and they tend to decline into variable currents as the latitude increases.

The North Equatorial Current moves at a fairly uniform rate of about 1 knot. The counter-current is also fairly steady at about 1 knot, but cannot always be assumed as running constantly easterly. The South Equatorial Current is less predictable. Rates of 1 knot are frequently exceeded and 2 to 3 knots have been noted. East of 136° West longitude some rates exceed 3 knots.

The general set of a current can be disturbed by an island group, often by being deflected and accelerated in its vicinity. In the Tuamotus, in particular, the currents can be irregular and the greatest caution and care should be exercised in approaching and passing through the area. Navigators in these waters should allow for a 1- to 2-knot current. The more open oceanic areas near the Society Islands and the Cook Islands have a steady westerly set and a rate of about 1 knot. The most common direction of swell in this area is southwesterly, driven by the great winds and seas of the Roaring Forties. When this swell is heavy and it meets the strong outgoing currents from the atoll passes, it usually culminates in steep, heavy rips and tidal races at the entrances to coral reef lagoons.

NAVIGATION IN CORAL WATERS

Approaches

In the Tuamotus, the sides of the reefs tend to be submerged or awash. They also constitute a lee shore because of the swell set in motion by the powerful storms of the Southern Ocean that crash heavily on the reefs. It is a good idea to approach these atolls to a point 25 to 30 miles north of the destination, provided no other atoll or restriction is in the way. The ideal approach is to arrive at dawn, double check your exact position, and then allow a daylight approach to the destination. A vessel can heave-to, drift, or use shortened sail to maintain a position well off the destination and wait for dawn rather than press on in the dark. This procedure should be followed whether passing through atolls or approaching an anchorage.

Navigation in these waters requires special care because the Tuamotus are very low; the height of a coconut palm on an atoll will rarely exceed 50 feet. From the deck of a yacht this means your horizon is not more than 3 miles away and for even the tops of the palms to be visible you may be as close as 7 or 8 miles. The high volcanic islands are visible much further away; a normal assumption for visibility is 20 to 25 miles, but in good conditions Tahiti can be seen 60 miles away and Hawaii, 100 miles. However, atmospheric and weather effects can drastically reduce visibility. Clouds and mist regularly obscure Tahiti's peaks, and it is astounding that you can sometimes be only 20 to 30 miles from the 13,700 foot peak of Mauna Kea when it is hidden behind a light cloud and you seem to be sailing into an open ocean.

It is difficult to identify atolls because the palm-capped motus are similar in appearance. A combination of confidence in one's navigation and knowledge of the position of the atoll's perimeter or a glimpse of a village or other unique feature add up to a tentative identification. Sometimes long-lasting wrecks offer confirmation. It is often difficult to identify a pass into a lagoon and not all gaps between motus are navigable. An atoll must be positively identified before you can determine the location of a pass.

Running the Passes

The best time for entry through deep channels, assuming calm weather, is at slack low water. At this time reefs and shoals awash are readily seen and the channel is generally more clearly defined. Furthermore, if you should go aground a rising tide will float the vessel free, although tidal variation is low.

Entry should not be attempted when a strong current is opposing the vessel's direction of travel, especially with an under-powered auxiliary motor with a low maximum hull speed. Strong currents are evident by breaking seas and rips that occur outside the entrance to a pass. Before entering a pass it is best to wait for slack water, or the beginning of the change to flood (as indicated by calmer sea conditions). Once within the entrance to the pass, turbulence diminishes and conditions improve for vessel and crew alike. It is necessary to maintain speed for control, especially when going with the tide and this results in rapid progress over the bottom. Since errors in judgment can result in damage it is better to err on the side of caution. Have the anchor ready to allow a quick drop in an emergency.

Estimating Slack Water

Tidal effects are small in the Tuamotus. The tides are predominantly diurnal and an amphidromic point (node where tides are almost negligible) is assumed in tidal calculations to be near Tahiti where spring tides are only about 8 inches. In some waters covered by this guide tidal currents can reach as much as 8 knots and when combined with an opposing wind, dangerous seas can be created.

It is essential to use a current edition of NOAA Tide Tables for Central and Western Pacific Ocean or the equivalent British or French publication. A formula, available from the Sailing Directions (Planning Guide), South Pacific Ocean (Appendix Atlas) suggests that the minimum current is most likely to occur one hour after low tide and one hour after high tide as specified in the Tide Tables.

The estimated time of slack water could be altered by heavy southerly swells or strong prevailing winds. These cause an increase in the flow of water over the reef, which can alter the incoming and outgoing streams, even to the extent of sometimes maintaining a continuous outflowing stream for a considerable period of time.

Navigating by Eye

Once within the reef areas, the best piloting is accomplished by eye. The higher the position of the lookout the better and the sun should be behind the observer or overhead (not in front). The best times are from about 2.5 hours after sunrise to 1 hour before local noon when heading in a westerly direction, and the reverse (1 hour after noon to 2.5 hours before sunset) when heading in an easterly direction. The quadrant of visibility is altered by the northerly or southerly position of the sun in relation to the observer.

The best position for conning on most vessels is at the first spreader. Since the lookout may spend some time looking ahead, gear should be arranged so that it is easy to get aloft and stay for some time. Ratlines on the lower shrouds enable a member of the crew to climb to a perch on a spreader, or for short passages to go up several feet. Ratlines may consist of rope lashed by seizing to the shrouds, or they can be oak strips clamped to the shrouds. Rope ratlines are easy to make, climb, and have less windage, but they are tiring to stand on for long periods as they sag and cut into the feet. A convenient perch made of oak can be placed part way up the shrouds.

Considerable glare is reflected off the ocean. Sunglasses prevent eyestrain, and fatigue and make it easier to see underwater obstacles. Polarized sunglasses assist in making bottom features appear more defined. The choice of tints should help reduce ultraviolet and infrared rays, but should not alter color perception.

A hat or visor also helps to block out unwanted glare and make conning easier. In tropical waters the heat of the sun on the head can be intense.

Visually identifying depth:
A flat, glassy calm is unsatisfactory for good conning since it is difficult to penetrate the surface glare; a slight ripple makes viewing easier. Perception continues to be good even with some wave action, unless there are whitecaps or the surface is quite disturbed. Color is a good indicator of water depth.

Dark Blue or Green	Deep Water
Lighter Blue or Green	More shallow but safe for most vessels
Whiter	Six feet or less
Pale White	Less than one foot
Brown or Purple	Coral Heads
Yellow to Brown*	Reefs

*These colors signal danger and should be avoided, though it is often difficult to judge the true depth over coral heads. If a passage exists it is safer to thread a path following the clearer water.

The type of bottom and the amount of cloud overhead can affect conning. White sand bottom is the best for viewing. Black volcanic sand or olive green lava sand or rock can greatly reduce the amount of light reflected and reduce visibility. Clouds also cause similar effects as they cast shadows, so that when looking ahead to identify a reef, a cloud's shadow can be misleading. Shadows from clouds can darken the apparent water color and alter depth perception. The light becomes flat and colors weaken, sometimes to the extent that all ability to navigate by eye is lost.

Coral barrier reefs and atoll reef perimeters tend to be sharp in edge and outline, so that sometimes there may be deep water fairly close to them. On the other hand, uneven bottoms with many large spherical coral growths reaching toward the surface occur within some lagoons and reef zones, forming the most dangerous type of contours through which to find a passage. However many sailing vessels, often without power, have passed through coral waters without instrumentation other than the eyes of crew and a lead line.

Markers and Buoys
Buoyage systems are not standardized around the world, so sailors must face the need to keep alert for changes when traveling. Where there is a passage within a reef, then the notional "port" to which vessel is "returning" will always be approached in a counter-clockwise direction. This means that on entering a pass, if you are turning starboard (right or counter-clockwise) then you continue to keep the red beacons on your port side (i.e. island side) but if turning to port (clockwise) on entering the lagoon then you will put the red beacons on your right (starboard or island side). To know when you have completed transit of the pass and are inside the reef there is always one, initial cardinal marker (yellow and black) to mark the transition from markers within the pass to markers within the reef. French charts, C-Map and other electronic charts indicate the notional direction to your port of destination with a large arrow in French Polynesia the **IALA System A** of aids to navigation is used and is illustrated in Appendix II. In addition there are special topmarks in use depending on whether you are offshore or within a lagoon. The standard can, T-shaped, vertical up-cone and diamond shapes are used at reefs as they would be for normal seaward approaches. In addition, once within the lagoon, the landward sides are marked by a red hemisphere (with the flat diameter downward) placed on a yellow and red barred spar; the reef side by a downward pointing cone (triangle), also on a yellow and red barred post. However, in many places in French Polynesia, these special marks or beacons, and the regular ones, are sometimes worn or appear unpainted and the colors indistinguishable. The shape of the topmark—if still in place—can be identified.
<u>Warning</u>: **Beacons and markers mentioned in this guide and other sources are sometimes missing.**

Barrier Reef and deep water around Raiatea

Katie Scott

Barrier Reef and shallow water around Raiatea

Katie Scott

14

Alaska Eagle moored to the quay in Papeete

Evening outrigger canoe practice

Some major ports in this area have lighted ranges or colored sector beacons to indicate the correct approach through the pass. In Papeete, a pair of well-lit ranges mark the route through the pass and toward the quays. The green occulting (3) lights on red and white banded pylons have a white topmark for daylight use. The sides of the pass are marked by lit buoys.

Colored sector beacons mark the entry to Moorea, Fare (Huahine), Bora-Bora, Baie Taiohae (Nuku-Hiva) and Autona (Hiva Oa). The bearings of each harbor light differ but they are arranged so that green is on the right of the correct white sector and red is on the left.

In the Hawaiian Islands the U.S Aids to Navigation System is used and is shown in Appendix III.

TRANSIT OF VESSELS IN THE VICINITY OF CERTAIN AIRPORTS

To prevent collisions between masts of sailing vessels and jumbo jets landing and departing from Chenal de Faa'a near Papeete and in the vicinity of Raiatea Airport certain restrictions have been put into place as follows:

Papeete, Tahiti, Chanel de Faa'a: The runway at the international airport has been enlarged to cope with Airbus 300 and Boeing 757 airplanes. The skipper of a vessel with a mast height of more than 15 ft. planning to transit Chenal de Faa'a in either direction between Papeete Harbor and the Taina / Maeva area must call "Papeete Port Control" on International VHF Ch 12 when reaching a boundary line marked with yellow buoys and a large sign in French and English. After the skipper has requested permission to traverse Chanel de Faa'a, a response in French or English will be made. Papeete Port Control will tell the captain to stand by while a call is made to the Air Traffic Control Tower to determine if heavy air traffic is expected. After clearance with the air traffic controller Port Control will call the vessel with instructions.

The best time to transit Chenal de Faa'a is around noon when there is little international air traffic. From about 5 a.m. to 7 a.m. there are numerous international flights departing making this the least desirable time to approach the restricted area because of necessary delay.

Raiatea Airport: A regime similar to that established when transiting Chanel de Faa'a near Papeete has been implemented in the vicinity of the Raiatea International Airport. When crossing the imaginary extended runway line of the airport a vessel of more than 15 ft. in height must call Raiatea Airport Control on VHF Ch 16 and request permission to cross the flight path. This affects all boats heading from the eastern estuaries to the Raiatea Carenage area and vice versa. Vessels passing through the eastern fairways proceeding north to Tahaa are not affected.

PLACE NAMES

The spelling of place names used in different references varies considerably. An attempt has been made to use the spelling practiced in each area described while at the same time providing spelling used on nautical charts and other references. The use of the local name provides the reader with the words used within the country being visited so that communication with residents will be facilitated. For example, the French word "baie," meaning "bay" is used in French-speaking areas while the word "bay" is used in English-speaking countries.

Charts and Official Publications

Since World War II, hydrographic departments have made continued efforts to chart the world. South Pacific sailors owe special thanks to the French Naval Schooner "*Zelee*" which made lengthy trips surveying the dangerous waters of the Tuamotus and was a familiar sight in Tahiti.

The selection of charts is an individual one and with many choices, cruisers should consider the advice of a chart dealer carefully.

U. S. DMA (Defense Mapping Agency) charts and publications are good, and marked in familiar terms to North American sailors who are gradually learning metric measurements. They vary considerably in size and are printed on thin paper stock. Charts for US waters that include Hawaii are produced by NOAA (National Oceanic and Atmosphere Administration) and thus are numbered differently. Both are available from marine supply stores carrying charts.

British Admiralty charts and publications have advantages for waters outside the US. They are uniform in size and printed on heavy paper stock. French charts are the most detailed for French Polynesian waters and many areas have been updated. They use metric measurements and tend to be a little less expensive than British Admiralty charts.

CHARTS and SAILING DIRECTIONS

A list of charts follows. Choices must be made depending on individual itineraries.

Pacific Ocean
    *BA 4002 (Coverage of a large area, good for planning)

Iles Marquises (Marquesas Islands)
    DMA 83207   Nuku Hiva
    French 7352   Nuku-Hiva and details of its bays (Recommended choice)
    French 7353   Ua-Pou and Ua-Huka
    French 7354   Fatu-Hiva and Details of bays in Hiva-Oa and Tahuata
    French 7355   Hiva-Oa, Tahuata and Mohotani
    *BA 1640   Plans in the Iles Marquises

Archipel des Tuamotu (Tuamotu Archipelago)
    DMA 83022   Ile Makemo to Ile Tatakoto (OMEGA)
    DMA 83023   Tahiti to Rangiroa and Makemo (OMEGA)

Iles Gambier
    DMA 83251   Iles Gambier

Iles de la Société (Society Islands)
    DMA 83021   Manuae to Tahiti (OMEGA)
    DMA 83382   Approaches to Tahiti & Moorea
    DMA 83383   Moorea
    DMA 83385   Port of Papeete
    DMA 83392   Iles de la Société - Iles Sous Le Vent: Plans of Manuae, Maupihaa, and
                 Mote One
    DMA 83397   Bora-Bora
    French 6002   Bora-Bora (Recommended choice)

Cook Islands
    DMA   83425   Islands and Anchorages in the Cook Islands
    *BA   979   Other Cook Is. Anchorages: Rakahanga, Manihiki, Danger Is.
    NZ   845   Suwarrow Island
    NZ   945   Tongareva or Penrhyn Island

Hawaiian Islands
    NOAA   19320   Island of Hawaii
    NOAA   19324   Hilo Bay
    NOAA   19348   Island of Maui, Approaches to Lahaina
    NOAA   19347   Channels between Molokai, Maui, Lanai, and Kahoolawe
    NOAA   19381   Kaui
    NOAA   19383   Nawiliwili Bay

Sailing Directions
    SD 126 Pacific Islands (Enroute), Current Edition
• British Admiralty Charts
Tide Tables - Central and Western Pacific Ocean

FORMALITIES

Each country covered by this guide has its own entry requirements, but there are some courtesies common to all.

Entry Procedures

While visiting a country, yachts should fly a courtesy flag of the country at the starboard spreader. At the same time, a vessel should fly its own national ensign at the stern. Flag etiquette requires that the national ensign be hoisted at sunrise and lowered at sunset.

On first entry into a country, the yellow quarantine or "Q" flag should be hoisted under the courtesy ensign of the country being visited. This should be done whether the officials board a vessel for clearance, or the skipper goes ashore to inform them of the vessel's arrival. As soon as a vessel is cleared the "Q" flag can be taken down and need not be hoisted again while in that country.

Officials from Customs, Immigration, Health, Agriculture, Police and the Harbormaster or Port Authority may be involved in the vessel's clearance. In almost all countries an attempt is made to streamline the procedure. The crew and the vessel must be cleared first for health, then by Customs, Immigration, and Agriculture before any person other than the Captain can go ashore. In some ports, especially in the Marquesas, crew trips ashore are not restricted until entry has been completed. Detailed information is given on the following pages by country.

The documents that must be aboard include:

For the Vessel	*For Each Person*
Boat Registration or Documentation	*Individual valid passports*
Crew List	*Visas or Tourist Permits (as required)*
Outward bound clearance from the last port	*Onward airline tickets or funds to cover such bonds as are required*
De-ratization certificate (in certain areas)	

The Customs inspector has the right to search the vessel to determine if it carries arms, contraband, or other prohibited items. Customs officers in French Polynesia are carrying out more rigorous inspections of vessels than have been done in the past. Every firearm and piece of ammunition must be declared at the first Port of Entry. Harsh fines are levied for undeclared firearms. Customs Officers in Papeete may seal the firearms on board when such action is feasible, depending on the yacht's facilities. If this is not possible a note is made on your entry declaration. If you put your boat on the hard and exit the country you must surrender your arms. They are kept in custody for up to 4 months at the end of which time you must collect the weapons and leave the country immediately.

Anchor or moor in areas designated for entry purposes. The skipper should report the vessel's arrival by radio or shore telephone to the Harbormaster or controlling port authority (who may be the local gendarme). He will tell you how to get in touch with the other authorities in correct order or he may do this for you. To avoid overtime charges, entry should be made during normal working hours, Monday to Saturday. Note: The time zone in the Marquesas is one half hour earlier than in the rest of French Polynesia, i.e. Z-9H30M.

Departure Procedures

It is prudent to inquire about departure procedures when you check into the country to avoid surprises that may delay your departure. Typically, you will first clear with the harbormaster and pay moorage bills. Secondly, clear with Immigration and retrieve passports; collect weapons from the Police (these are generally returned to you only within an hour of departure), and lastly, clear with Customs and obtain the outward bound clearance (Zarpe or Permis de Sortie) to be used for entry at the next country. If unable to depart within the hour, inform Customs and remain aboard. They may extend your period of stay; if the delay becomes excessive you may be required to re-enter.

SPECIAL REQUIREMENTS

French Polynesia

The entry system has been made flexible so that it suits down-wind travel routes for yachts. It is necessary to report to the local gendarme in any island group before cruising elsewhere. Although Papeete is the only true Port of Entry for French Polynesia, informal entry can be made by reporting to the local gendarme at the following subsidiary Ports of Entry:

The Marquesas - Baie de Taiohae (Nuku Hiva), Fatu Hiva, Atuona (Hiva Oa) and Hakahau (Ua Pou)

The Tuamotu / Gambier- Tiputa in Rangiroa and Rikitea in Mangareva

Society Islands - Uturoa in Raiatea, Fare in Huahine, Vaitape in Bora-Bora and Afareaitu in Moorea.

Iles Australes - Mataura in Tubuai, Moerai in Rurutu and Tairua in Raivavae

Entry procedures into French Polynesia are ever changing. Be sure to research the latest requirements before you depart for the Islands. A good source of information and a simplified way to enter French Polynesia is via the Pacific Puddle Jump. This is a very loosely organized list of vessels cruising from the west coasts of the Americas, on no particular schedule, all arriving to celebrate their crossing in Tahiti. Entry procedures for vessels registered in the event have simplified entry requirements and the required bond has been waived in some cases. Visit www.pacificpuddlejump.org/longstayvisa.html for the latest information and to register for the event.

Another source of current information on changes in entry procedures, anchorages and weather conditions are the nets on SSB and HAM radio. SSB Radio nets include:

Russell Radio - Weather and daily check-in at	04:00 GMT on 12353
	04:30 GMT on 12359
Coconut Net - Weather and daily check-in at	18:30 GMT on 12353
If this station is occupied, use 12356kv on USB.	

All aboard a vessel must have a valid passport that will not expire during the term of your visit. Non-EEU citizens must also have an outbound air ticket or deposit a bond in a bank on arrival equal to the cost of air fare to the country of origin. Bonds can be returned at Papeete or at a bank in the island from which departure is taken. Banks charge a fee for processing the bonds. By notifying the bank ahead of time they will refund the bond in the currency that was deposited with them. Verify that there is a branch of the bank where the bond was deposited on the island from which departure is intended, usually Bora-Bora, the last port in the west.

Visitors Permits valid for 3 months are granted to citizens from ECM/EEU, Austria, Finland, Norway, Sweden and Switzerland. An extension for another 90 days can be applied for after 60 days by writing to Haut Commissariat/DRCL, Rue Jeanne D'Arc, BP 115, Papeete, Tahiti. Visitors Permits valid for 30 days are granted to citizens of New Zealand, Japan, Singapore and some eastern European countries. A 3-month extension may be applied for by writing to the above address. After receiving the 3-month extension you can apply for another 2-month extension, giving you a total of 6 months, equal to the time allowed cruisers from ECM/EEU nations.

Citizens of Canada and the United States may obtain a visa from a French Consulate outside of Polynesia that is valid for 90 days from the date it is issued; extensions are not allowed. You must buy a US$24 stamp at the post office for each passport when obtaining a 90-day visa. If you wish to remain for more than 90 days it is necessary to obtain a Carte de Sejour (Temporary Resident Card) from a French Consulate. Applicants must explain the reason for the visit, provide information on plans and submit proof of financial independence. The Consulate will forward your request to the High Commissioner in Papeete who will accept or deny your request. Allow about two months for a decision to be made on the application. Cruisers arriving in French Polynesia without a visa are issued one for a 30-day stay, with no extensions of time allowed in French territory.

The **captain** is responsible for the crew's bonds and completion of entry requirements. There isn't a standard form for a crew list but one should be prepared listing the date of arrival, last port of call, name of each person aboard and their position, date of birth, nationality and passport number. Prepare at least 4 copies of this information. All crew changes and boat moves from Papeete (further than Moorea) must be reported to the Maritime Office of Immigration/ DICILEC.

Boats may stay in French Polynesia for 1 year without being subject to duty/taxes provided the boat is on the hard while you are absent. The "year" for tax purposes does not include time on the hard. Taxes are calculated on the value of the boat and range from 19% to 29% depending on the country of origin. If you wish to extend the stay for a maximum of 6 months or obtain further information write (in French) to: Service des Douanes, Centre de controle de la Navigation de Plaisance, BP 9006 Notu Uta, Papeete, Tahiti, French Polynesia.

The vessel can be **put on the hard** for 6 months during the cyclone season (November 1 - April 30), sailed for 6 months and hauled again. Favorable reports have been received by cruisers who stored their boats at Raiatea Carenage Services, telephone (689) 66-2414. Their substantial cradles reduce but do not eliminate the risk of cyclone damage. Storage is also available in Papeete and monthly charges vary from US$350 to $500 per month for a 34 foot vessel.

When arriving in Papeete within 21 days of visiting Fiji, Tonga, Samoa, Cook Islands, and Central and South American Pacific areas, the yacht may be **fumigated** by the Port Authorities to prevent the introduction of the Rhinoceros beetle. It is best, therefore, to anchor out from the Quay on first arrival and clear all formalities before tying up at a moorage. No special **inoculations** are required other than one for yellow fever if the vessel is arriving in Polynesia within 14 days of leaving, or transiting infected areas. It is advisable to have a polio booster, tetanus inoculation and a gamma globulin inoculation for protection against hepatitis A. Filariosis (elephantiasis) and Dengue Fever are mosquito-borne diseases prevented by using mosquito repellent or covering up when ashore in mosquito plagued areas, securing all openings with fine mosquito netting and anchoring well offshore. There are several excellent hospitals in Papeete and some smaller medical centers in the outer islands.

After a **pet** has spent 6 months aboard the vessel In French Polynesia you may take it ashore. There is no quarantine station in French Polynesia. It will be confined to the vessel in Polynesia for 6 months, counting from the date of departure from your last port. Customs will advise you to contact the veterinarians at "Service de Developement Rural." If departing the country by air, you can take the pet but check with "Developement Rural" again and they will take the pet(s) to the airport. The pet can "re-enter" if you apply for re-admittance two to three months before departure and send the pet to the Noumea quarantine station in New Caledonia where it must stay for one month before being shipped to Tahiti. The total cost per pet is about 6000 French francs (not CFP).

There are no restrictions on the **importation of equipment** to French Polynesia as long as you are "yacht in transit." Goods can be ordered from Downwind Marine in San Diego (Telephone 619-224-2733, Fax 619-224-7683) or West Marine's International Branch (Fax 831-761-4020) and have them shipped via UPS or DHL to the California Branch of Danzas Forwarders to be delivered to the Danzas Papeete Branch. Make certain that a pro forma invoice is enclosed with the shipment so questions from Customs can be answered by the carrier. It is advisable to make arrangements ahead of time in the Papeete office with Mrs. Keller-Proia, a very helpful lady who is fluent in English, French and German.

There are **new regulations for a limited visit** to certain areas without having to check in at Papeete. Those cruisers who want to visit only the Marquesas and the Tuamotu may check in and out at the Gendarmerie at Baie Taiohae on Nuku Hiva. Crews who paid the bond can receive a refund from the same office. It is reported that the same procedure is possible in Raiatea at the Gendarmerie.

Cruisers who prefer to have paperwork handled by a local representative may secure the services of Pascuale who charges US$70 for his expertise. For information check the website at www.oceantahiti.com

The Cook Islands

The official Ports of Entry are located on the islands of Rarotonga, Aitutaki, and Penrhyn. Adjust your arrival so as not enter the Islands on a Sunday when the offices are closed and high additional charges are levied for clearance. In Rarotonga all yachts must clear at Avatiu Harbor, flying the Q flag and remaining at anchor outside the small harbor. If the vessel is arriving from Tahiti, Fiji or areas considered infected by the Rhinoceros beetle it will be searched and/or fumigated. Similar procedures are followed at Aitutaki.

Temporary visitor permits given after completing clearance allow a 31-day stay for the yacht and crew. Extensions are available only in Rarotonga and are granted on a monthly basis for a maximum of 5 months.

Fees amounting of about $15 per passport are charged for the permit. Evidence of financial ability may be requested in the assessment of this extension. Tourists arriving by air must have a valid return or on-going ticket and confirmed accommodations before arrival.

This is a healthy part of the world and no special inoculations are required. There is an excellent hospital in Rarotonga and smaller medical facilities are on some of the other islands. Firearms must be declared and will be impounded. The importation of firearms, cartridges and fireworks is expressly prohibited. To prevent the spread of disease, fruit and meat will be confiscated so do not arrive with a lot of fresh supplies. Good local fruit is available.

Outstanding fees are collected by Immigration officials when outward clearance is given. Yachts arriving from Aitutaki or Rarotonga should clear out of the country at those ports, rather than Palmerston. Showers, toilets and potable water are available dockside. Upon leaving the Cook Islands there is an exit fee of NZ$25 per adult and NZ$10 per child (2 – 11 years). Overtime is charged before 0800 and after 1600 on weekdays, and all day during weekends and public holidays.

The Hawaiian Islands

All yachts, including US vessels, must enter the Hawaiian Islands at one of the following Ports of Entry: Hilo or Honokohau on the Island of Hawaii, Kahului on Maui, Honolulu on Oahu, or Nawiliwili on Kauai. Paperwork can also be completed at Ko Olina Marina on Oahu.

Procedures for entry and for leaving the Hawaiian Islands are essentially US standard procedures, but handled in a more detailed and consistent manner than on the mainland. It is important for all cruisers (including US citizens) to have a current passport.

Entry into United States occurs as soon as you have anchored or moored alongside and are in US waters. A vessel may not anchor at any place other than at a Port of Entry before completing official entry procedures. Considerable fines are imposed for violations. After entry, no person who is aboard can go ashore except for the skipper, or his representative, who reports the vessel's arrival to the Customs office. The skipper must return to the vessel immediately after reporting. There may be some variation in how rigorously these regulations are enforced.

The Office of Homeland Security will inform the other departments - Immigration, Agriculture, and Health and they will arrive to board the yacht. Generally the Office of Homeland Security officers handle immigration and health requirements at the same time. In Hawaii the forms and papers are the same for small and large vessels and those used on the US mainland. For US citizens the immigration procedure is simple and brief. All other persons except Canadian citizens are considered aliens and must have valid passports, with visas, where applicable. Complete requirements for entry into the US can be obtained from the nearest US Consulate, and visas obtained for citizens of those countries where the need applies. It is important for the skipper to realize that he is responsible for any alien crew member and he must ascertain that they have proper papers for entry or the skipper could be charged with aiding an illegal entry.

Agriculture is concerned with meats, citrus fruits and vegetables being imported. Most yachts have few problems in this regard since most boaters use all their fresh provisions enroute. There is a strictly enforced quarantine for pets. They are put into quarantine at the Animal Quarantine Center in Honolulu for 120 days. Shipping costs and daily charges must be paid in advance by the pet's owner. Pet owners who leave Hawaii before the 120-day period has elapsed may apply for a refund of the unused balance.

The United States has reciprocal agreements regarding permission to cruise in territorial waters, provided that normal entry procedures have been followed. The countries include: Argentina, Australia, the Bahamas, Canada, New Zealand and Germany. Cruisers on vessels from these countries are issued a cruising permit, valid for 12 months, which allows the yacht to travel in specific waters. The skipper must notify the Office of Homeland Security by telephone for any movement of the vessel, even in the same port or marina. Heavy fines are levied for disregarding this regulation. Vessels from other countries may not cruise in local waters but must make a formal entry and clearance only from designated Ports of Entry.

Firearms possessed by US citizens must be declared and registered in Hawaii even though they may be licensed in your own state. Permits for firearms are issued by the police. Aliens may not possess a firearm in US territory unless previously authorized by the Bureau of Alcohol, Tobacco, Firearms and Explosives.

To protect against unwarranted Customs duties, keep photocopies of receipts for items aboard the vessel such as cameras, navigational instruments and equipment so that proof of the country of purchase is readily available. If this is not done, you may be liable for a customs assessment on any item not clearly identified, and a duty may be charged prior to recovering it by application to the Customs Department.

When leaving the Hawaiian Islands, whether continuing to the US mainland or proceeding elsewhere, all vessels must clear with US Customs and obtain an "Outward Bound Manifest." It is important not to neglect this procedure, as failure to do so may cause the vessel to be subject to seizure when it arrives at the next port without having been properly cleared.

Pitcairn Island
There are no entry formalities for Pitcairn Island and all visitors are welcome. No health restrictions exist, but as the people are isolated, it is unwise for any yacht with an illness aboard or which has had recent contact with a major disease, to land and spread anything that may be potentially infectious.

Radio communication is possible with the island to inform them of your plan to visit, and thus to make arrangements to be landed by the Pitcairn surfboat. Attempts should not be made to land in rough weather using the vessel's dinghy. Lastly, when leaving, do not forget to thank these generous people for their hospitality by performing some community service, or by leaving useful material such as rope, blocks, clothing or school supplies. Please DO NOT leave ammunition or alcohol. .

Easter Island
The Armada prefers that vessels arriving from mainland Chile or Robinson Crusoe Island NOT clear immigration and customs before departure for Easter Island as they consider this an "internal" passage. As long as notification is made by radio, prior anchorage in locations other than Hanga Roa should be possible.

PROVISIONING

Since groceries in French Polynesia (except for some fresh produce and meat) are shipped to the islands from various countries and are subject to high French tariffs, prices are approximately twice that found in North American supermarkets. Consequently, you should provision with as many non-perishable foods and paper products as is convenient before departure as well as fresh produce, baked goods and meat for as long as they are likely to be edible. Unsliced bread will last 2 or 3 weeks if it is wiped with a vinegar-soaked cloth and allowed to dry prior to storing in a plastic bag in a cool location. Mayonnaise will keep well if germs are not introduced into the bottle, so shake out the desired amount rather than scooping it out even with a sterile spoon or knife.

In French Polynesia groceries are found in general stores called magazins. Here you can find anything, from aspirins to pareus (a colorful rectangular piece of cloth that can be tied in various ways to create a "pants" for men or a "dress" for women) to flashlight batteries to baguettes (long traditional French bread which has no preservatives and is of excellent quality). Rice is widely available and as it keeps well without deteriorating it is a basic staple for cruisers. Bring some tasty recipes along, using rice as well as a variety of spices and be prepared to improvise. If you see an item you want to buy but it seems pricey, don't put off purchasing it for it may not be available at other locations.

Locally grown fruits such as sweet (green) oranges, limes, lemons, and coconuts are widely available and are reasonably priced. A treat that shouldn't be missed is pamplemousse, a sweet and juicy fruit that resembles a large grapefruit. Bananas are a treat but once they start to ripen they tend to do so all at once. Take care to hang them in such a way that they don't become bruised as once this happens deterioration occurs quickly. Plantains resemble large bananas but must be cooked prior to eating. Taro root can be cooked like potatoes.

By including breadfruit in your diet you can create meals that will have a local ingredient. Since mashed breadfruit seems to be a tasteless mush it needs flavoring or a savory accompaniment to be palatable. The following recipes have been developed by Pauline Dolinski of the yacht *Syrena*.

Breadfruit Chips
Peel about 1/4 of a medium firm breadfruit and cut into thin slices about 5cm (2 inches) long. Discard the small dark seeds. Drop as many as will float freely in hot oil about 5cm (2 inches) deep. Stir and turn until golden

brown. Remove and drain on paper towels. Salt and pepper to taste. Eat as you would potato chips. If well sealed after cooling they will keep for a few days.

Breadfruit Pancakes

Scoop well ripened, soft breadfruit away from the skin and mash it into a bowl. Add flour until it is firm enough to hold together. Drop into hot oil, flattening it with the back of a spoon to make a pancake. When golden brown, flip it over and finish cooking.

Breadfruit Fritters

Mash about a cup of soft, raw breadfruit into a bowl. Add an egg and mix in flour until it will hold together well. Drop by teaspoon into hot oil. Drain and serve with salsa or ketchup.

Breadfruit Salad

Boil and chill 4cm (2 inch) chunks of breadfruit. Add mayonnaise, 1 tsp. lemon juice, 1 tsp. mustard, garlic salt and chopped onions. Serve like potato salad.

FISH POISONING (CIGUATERA)

A hazard of eating fish caught near coral atolls in parts of Polynesia is poisoning from those containing the toxin that causes ciguatera. No satisfactory explanation of the source and reasons for accretion of the toxins in particular fish has been determined. It appears to be related to the base of the tropical food chain, i.e. some of the algae, fungi or corals that are eaten by some fish. Another possibility is that food is chemically altered within the fish and becomes toxic. Added to the mystery is the fact that a particular species of fish is toxic near one atoll but the same fish in a nearby atoll may be unaffected while other species may be the culprits.

Though the source of the poisoning is unknown, some major facts are known:

1. This problem is present only in certain coral areas, and never occurs where the water temperature is below 68°F.

2. Pelagic fish, such as tuna, bonito and mahi-mahi, are seldom toxic, whereas, many species of reef fishes can be infected.

3. The toxin accumulates in affected fish and humans so that the larger the fish the more likely it is that it has accumulated enough toxin to be dangerous. In Polynesia, barracuda are not eaten, and selling them commercially is prohibited in the market place. Because smaller fish tend to be safe to eat, local fishermen usually keep only small grouper or other food fish measuring 15" or less. It is important to remember that size alone is not a foolproof protection against poisoning if the fish are taken from a particularly toxic lagoon. Checking with the local people will help identify which fish are most likely safe and which are most likely to be infected.

Symptoms - Between a few minutes to a few hours after eating a poisonous fish a tingling numbness (pins and needles sensation) around the mouth and nose and sometimes in the hands and feet is experienced. Contact with cold water intensifies the feeling until it resembles mild electric shocks or a burning sensation. Be aware that these symptoms may intensify. If they do, then soon after, vomiting and acute diarrhea may be experienced, together with aching joints and muscle pains, especially in the legs. Itching that gets no relief from scratching may also occur. The affected person will feel cold and weak; the pulse will slow and blood pressure drop, occasionally to the point where hospitalization becomes necessary. Later effects may include continued numbness and loss of skin on the hands and feet.

These symptoms may continue for variable lengths of time, possibly depending on the amount of toxin ingested or accumulated. The person infected may have already ingested small amounts from other fish without apparent ill effect until a particular dose triggers the reaction. This is why Polynesians, whose diets include a substantial amount of fish, will sometimes suffer severe reactions after a meal that doesn't affect others at the same meal.

Except in cases of low resistance or of a massive toxin intake, fish poisoning is not usually fatal. With rest and proper treatment, the patient will recover in a few hours or perhaps days. Severe cases may take weeks or even months for a full recovery.

Treatment - This should be treated as an emergency and a doctor should be seen as soon as possible. Vomiting should be induced in order to void toxic material in the stomach. This may be accomplished by drinking salt water, syrup of ipecac or putting a finger down the victim's throat.

Epsom salts or sodium bicarbonate may help in neutralizing the poison, especially if some of it is of the scombroid type or due to spoiled fish. Strong allergic reactions may need the use of anti-histamines, which should be carried in every ship's medicine chest. They may be taken orally or for faster results, by intra-muscular injection. If any crew member has known allergies, it is incumbent on them to always alert others on the crew as well as bring their own adequate supply of antihistamine medication (i.e. Benadryl, Epi-pen, etc.), as these may provide the necessary crucial time to seek appropriate medical attention to a serious allergic response.

If the respiratory system is affected, efforts should be made to keep the patient breathing using artificial respiration. Adrenaline may be needed as a heart stimulant but is not advisable if the victim has heart problems. Strong pain relievers, or even morphine, may be needed for severe pain, but should be given only with a doctor's advice.

The victim should have plenty of rest and avoid eating fish or highly seasoned food until recovery is complete.

Prevention - The only foolproof prevention is abstinence from eating fish. But with caution and good judgment you can enjoy some fish following the precautions listed below.
1. If fish intake is to be limited, eat only pelagic fish (those which swim offshore)
2. Do not eat reef fishes more than 15" long or weighing more than 2 lbs.
3. Local advice should be obtained regarding "safe" fish to eat. Fish should not be eaten if there are any reports of poisoning in a certain area.
4. The liver and viscera are the most heavily contaminated; hence cleaning fish immediately after being caught helps to reduce any poisons present.

Cigua-Check™ is a recently developed test kit which is intended to indicate the presence of ciguatoxin in a fish. It costs about US$20 for a kit containing 5 tests and has a shelf life of 6 months. The testing process takes 70 minutes. For information about this product phone Oceanic Test Systems, Honolulu HI at 808-539-2345.

OTHER HEALTH CONSIDERATIONS

Puffer fish are highly poisonous and those eating it have a mortality rate of 60%. Though Japanese gourmets delight in flirting with death and consider it a delicacy, **this fish should not be eaten**. Herring and mullet in certain parts of the Pacific contain some poisons; local advice is worthwhile.

Filariosis (elephantiasis) is on the increase in French Polynesia. Clinics in Atuona, Hiva Oa and Papeete provide medication (pills) which give protection from this illness for six months.

Staph infection often results from scratches on coral, gravel, etc. To stop infection the cut must be washed regularly for at least two weeks with hydrogen peroxide or betadine, followed by application of an antibiotic cream.

Sunburn and insect bites can be painful and irritating however the long-term effects of exposure to the sun's rays can have more severe and lasting consequences. To prevent damage to the skin from exposure to the sun's direct rays as well as reflections from the water, a thin coat of zinc oxide ointment provides 100% UV protection. A hat and thin, long-sleeved shirts are partially protective but some UV rays are able to penetrate any light material. Insecticides containing Deet™ are highly recommended as a deterrent against insect bites but some people suffer a reaction to this ingredient. To avoid direct contact with skin, apply a coat of zinc oxide or sunscreen and wait for half an hour before applying the insecticide.

COMMUNICATIONS

There are several choices of ways to communicate available to cruisers.

1. A Ham operating license provides a wealth of information and extensive possibilities for communication for cruisers. The **Pacific Seafarer Net** www.pacsea.org/ a group of dedicated ham operators from Washington to California, Hawaii and New Zealand provide daily contacts and medical and emergency services for cruisers by SSB voice radio. The position reports are fed into the Pangolin™ net where friends at home may view positions and weather conditions via http://www.pangolin.co.nz/yotreps/reporter_list.php The daily net begins at 03:00 UTC (GMT/Z) on 14.300 USB kHz with an informal 25 minute 'warm up' session to exchange news, answer questions and solve problems. Next follows the Roll Call where cruisers are called on to report their position and local weather. Cruisers with a ham license may report by email to: rollcall@pacsea.net The information is similarly fed into the Pangolin™ system. Pangolin™ is a customer service system operated by the Xaxero Weather Fax and Nautical Almanac Company located in New Zealand.

2. Cruisers may join the **AIRMAIL** system, a worldwide free Ham email (WINLINK) system that gives access to email ashore via SSB radio and a decoder (PTCIII) plus PC laptop, for PACTOR. Information can be obtained from www.winlink.org/GetStarted You may not conduct business through the Airmail system.

3. **SAILMAIL** works via SSB radio and is faster and does not require a Ham license nor does it have the restrictions on business communications of WINLINK.

The computer/receiver hardware is the same as for WINLINK and the cost for an account is US$200 per year. Additional information is available at http://www.sailmail.com/

4. An **Iridium** satellite phone linked to a laptop is a practical, highly reliable alternative / supplement to Ham or SSB, for sending and receiving e-mail, or weather information (including grib files and navtex) and for voice call-in or receiving / sending text messages.

A NATIONAL HOLIDAY – BASTILLE DAY

In recent years the French significance of festivities in July has been very much downplayed. It is just a coincidence that Bastille Day falls in the middle of the month of festivities known as the Heiva. Papeete is the focus of these celebrations, and the city is awash with performers of every age gathering for a marathon of dance competitions, singing and partying. Preparations and rehearsals begin a year in advance for the annual competition and winners in each event are feted as celebrities. Another exciting and colorful event are the canoe races around the island of Tahiti.

It is recognized in far-flung island villages of the Marquesas with the construction of a bamboo stage where costumed performers sing and dance to ukuleles, guitars and spoons backed by the reverberations of powerful drums. The intricate and artistically designed tattoos of the Marquesan dancers with their own historic connection add a unique flavor of intrigue and mystery to the joy and enthusiasm of their performances. However these fun-loving people don't need a calendar date to dance and sing—they will gladly put on a performance even if it's only to welcome the arrival of the *Aranui*, the supply ship from Papeete that calls about once per month. Life is a happy dance and Papeete is far away.

ILES MARQUISES (MARQUESAS ISLANDS)

The Marquesas have a NW/SE orientation between 8°S and 10°35'S latitude and between 138°25' W and 140°50'W longitude. Ten islands and numerous rocks and islets compose the group which has an area of 1,418 square miles (3,672 square kilometers. The southern group is comprised of Fatu Hiva, Mohotani, Tahuata, Fatu Huku and Hiva Oa (the largest). The northern group consists of Motu One, Hatutu, Eiao, Ua Huka, Ua Pou and Nuku Hiva (the largest). These high, volcanically formed islands have steep, black, cliff-edged coasts indented by many valleys. Their sharp outlines are generally clearly visible from at least 20 miles at sea making them a navigator's ideal landfall.

The Marquesas are the northernmost group of islands forming part of French Polynesia and they have their own distinctive setting and style. The total population is about 6,000, the descendants of proud and warlike Polynesian tribes that once numbered approximately 100,000 when Captain Cook visited the islands in the eighteenth century. Sadly, after this time the indigenous population was decimated by western contact and diseases brought from Great Britain and Europe.

The earliest inhabitants are believed to have migrated from Melanesia sometime between 1 – 20 AD. The population multiplied and the culture reached its maximum development from 1400 - 1790 AD. The first European to visit the islands was a Spanish navigator, Alvaro de Mendana in 1595 who named the islands. They were claimed by France in 1842.

Weather
The islands lie within the trade wind belt. The winds are predominantly northeasterly 80% of the year but swing east and southeast during the rainy periods. The rainy season begins in March and continues through October. Southern tradewinds are not as steady as those in northern latitudes and tropical storms and hurricanes are very infrequent. The wind can be dramatically disturbed in the vicinity of the high, steep islands causing frequent squalls and thunderstorms.

The Marquesas have a sub-tropical climate with daytime temperatures averaging 86°F throughout the year. The humidity is higher for two to three months in the middle of the year averaging 80% and annual rainfall varies between 40 to 120 inches.

Currents
The South Sub-Tropical current passes through this region, generally moving in a westerly direction. The capes and points of the main islands alter currents slightly in their immediate vicinity, as do periods of strong winds.

Clearance and Travel Notes
The administrative center of the area is at Baie Taiohae on Nuku Hiva, but entry can also be made at Atuona on Hiva Oa and at Hakahau on Ua Pou. Fly the Q flag on arrival and report to the gendarmerie. After a vessel has cleared to leave it is illegal to stop at other anchorages.

Because of weather considerations in the Northern Hemisphere most vessels make the trip to the Marquises in the period from March to May. Cruisers tend to leave the Marquesas for Tahiti or the Tuamotu at or near full moon. This should give the benefit of bright moonlight for the critical period of passage near the Tuamotu, but squalls which are typical at this time sometimes negate any advantage the full moon can have.

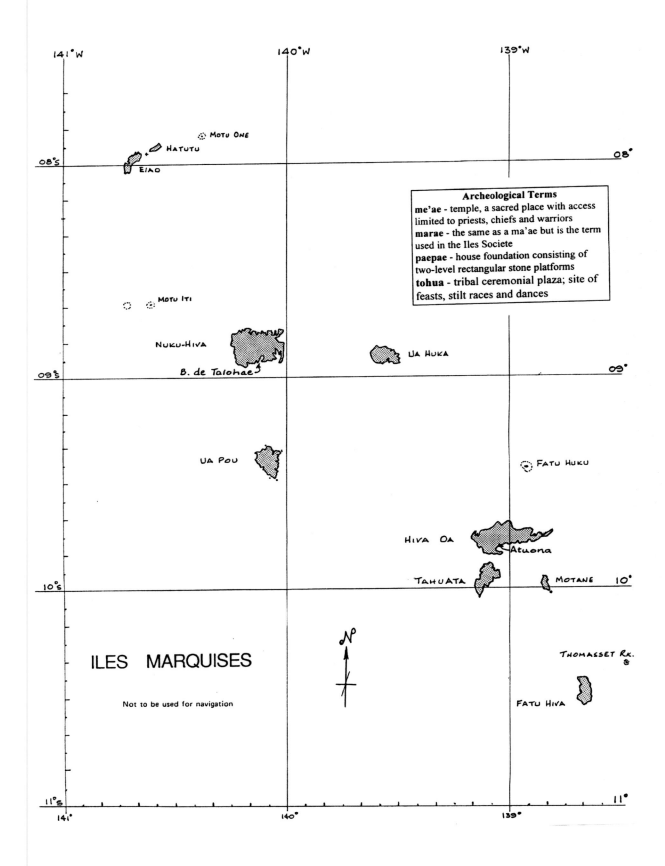

141°W   140°W   139°W

⬭ Motu One

Hatutu

08°S   08°

Eiao

Archeological Terms
me'ae - temple, a sacred place with access limited to priests, chiefs and warriors
marae - the same as a ma'ae but is the term used in the Iles Societe
paepae - house foundation consisting of two-level rectangular stone platforms
tohua - tribal ceremonial plaza; site of feasts, stilt races and dances

Motu Iti

Nuku-Hiva   Ua Huka

B. de Taiohae

09°S   09°

Ua Pou   ⬭ Fatu Huku

Hiva Oa

Atuona

Tahuata   Motane

10°S   10°

N

ILES MARQUISES

Thomasset Rk.

Not to be used for navigation

Fatu Hiva

11°S   11°

141°   140°   139°

FATU HIVA (FATU-HIVA, FATUIVA or FATU 'IVA)

The southernmost island of The Marquesas, Fatu Hiva lies about 35 miles south of Hiva Oa. With its heavy rainfall and lush vegetation, it is the most beautiful island in the Marquesas. Featured in Thor Heyerdahl's book of the same name, it is the only island without an airstrip and is therefore the most unspoiled. The central range of mountains runs north to south, reaching 3,150 feet at the south end. The eastern side is steep, precipitous and pounded by heavy surf. Only on the western lee side, are there useable anchorages. The most practicable anchorage for small vessels is Baie des Vierges.

From a sailing standpoint Fatu Hiva is the first logical stop in the Marquesas. It has been reported that some cruisers have stopped at the island and then continued in a northwesterly direction to visit other islands without running into problems with official authorities. The local police do not belong to the Police Nationale or Gendarmerie Nationale and these forces alone have the authority to register arrivals and report them to headquarters in Papeete. For many years cruisers arriving in the Marquesas have been required to enter at specified locations before proceeding elsewhere and <u>officially these regulations have not changed</u>.

This is the only island where tapa cloth (produced from the inner bark of trees) is still being made. This time-consuming process is interesting to observe and several of the crafts-women are pleased to demonstrate how it is done. The source of the bark determines the color of the tapa cloth; off-white bark comes from the mulberry tree, medium brown is from the breadfruit tree and dark brown comes from the banyan tree. Because many cruisers visit this bay, the inhabitants have become market-wise, demanding realistic returns for their tapa.

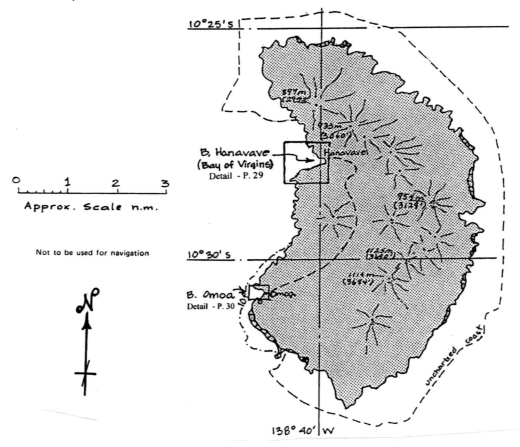

Approx. Scale n.m.

Not to be used for navigation

Baie Hanavave / Baie des Vierges (Bay of Virgins)*

This incredibly beautiful bay lies about 2.5 miles SSE of Pointe Teaitehoe, the northern end of the island. The rocky spires near the head of the bay are the most noticeable feature. On either side and beyond are dark green cloaked, steep-sided mountains creating a spectacular view that is made more dramatic when highlighted by the setting sun. It has a 0.5 mile wide opening which narrows to a beach at the head of the bay. The bottom is steeply sloping and the 10 fathom curve is well within the bay. Though swells are tolerable, gusty winds sweeping down the steep slopes can cause a vessel to drag. In archaic Marquesan, Hanavave means "strong surf bay," a name that is most appropriate at times.

The bay is entered by lining up a steep pinnacle rock on the north side with a whitish peak halfway up the slope behind. Small vessels can then proceed toward the head of the bay to anchor in 6 fathoms, good holding mud and sand. At the north end of the beach is the village of Hanavave where landing can be made at the concrete wharf at the north end of the bay. A breakwater protects the wharf making it an easy landing place. The village is famous for its many graceful outrigger canoes which are used for fishing and visiting Baie d'Omoa.

About an hour's walk behind the village, is a spectacular 200-foot waterfall, or you may take a hike to Omoa, about 10 miles distant, which takes 4 to 5 hours. Along the way orchards of cashew trees and noni plantations can be seen. Beyond the highest part of the trail and when in season, windfall mangos provide a tasty snack. Look for them where the road is covered with a blanket of dried mango seeds. Water in the former swimming hole in the river is polluted and should not be considered safe for swimming.

*It has been rumored that the bay was originally named "Bay des Verges" (Bay of the Phalli) by early explorers because of the shape of the rocky pillars. Supposedly the missionaries disapproved, and inserted an "i" making it "Bay des Vierges" which translates to Bay of the Virgins.

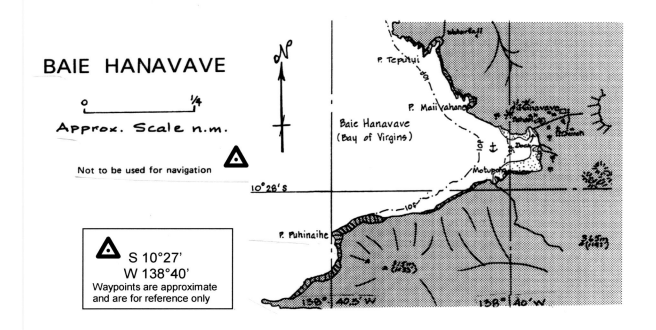

30

Baie Omoa

This bay, 3 miles south of Baie des Vierges, lies between Pointe Matahumu in the north and Motutapu, a dark, rocky 100 foot spire to the south. Beyond the head of the bay is a conspicuous slender pinnacle, Pierre Bonhomme with a height of 336 feet. To enter the bay steer 095°T for Pierre Bonhomme.

Anchorage in about 6 - 7 fathoms may be taken when the northern entrance point of the bay bears north. This bay is not well suited for small vessels as it is uncomfortable due to swell and poor holding. In addition, strong winds affect the bay and heavy gusts sweep down from the mountains. Landing is possible on a slippery concrete dock where the swell makes this a difficult and sometimes dangerous operation. Alternatively, if conditions permit, landing can be attempted on the northwest point or in the southeast corner of the bay, near the village.

Near the chapel there is a good museum that is well worth visiting. A few petroglyphs may be found in the vicinity.

Occasionally it is possible to trade for tapa, wood carvings or other crafts. In addition to being items of interest for trading, the following may also be used as gifts: small bottles of perfume, sunglasses, fishing gear, toys, earrings for pierced ears, hair clips, tools or T-shirts. An indication of the wide-ranging influence of television is the fact that figurines of well-known landmarks such as the Eiffel Tower, Statue of Liberty and London Bridge are prized trading items in these remote islands.

BAIE OMOA

Approx. Scale n.m.

Not to be used for navigation

S 10°40'
W 138°41'
Waypoints are approximate
and are for reference only

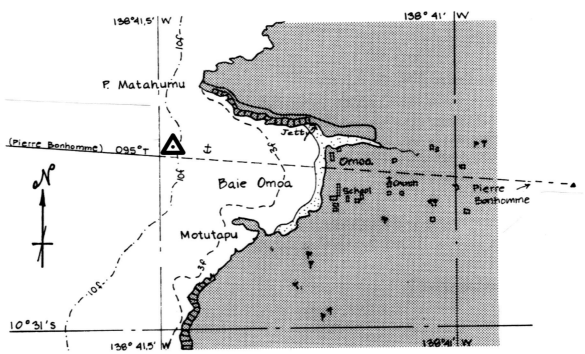

TAHUATA (Santa Christina Island)

This island is south of Hiva Oa across the 2.5 miles width of Canal du Bordelais. Here, as is normal in narrow passages between high islands, the wind and sea are usually more intense. A 2 - 3 knot westerly current is typical in this passage unless there have been several days of westerly winds. The center of the island is a 1,500-foot mountain chain, radiating out in steep ridges and valleys to the coast. It is well worth sailing around the island to see the rugged southern coastline and its spectacular scenery. The principal villages of Vaitahu and Hapatoni are on the west coast. The population of the island is about 600.

TAHUATA

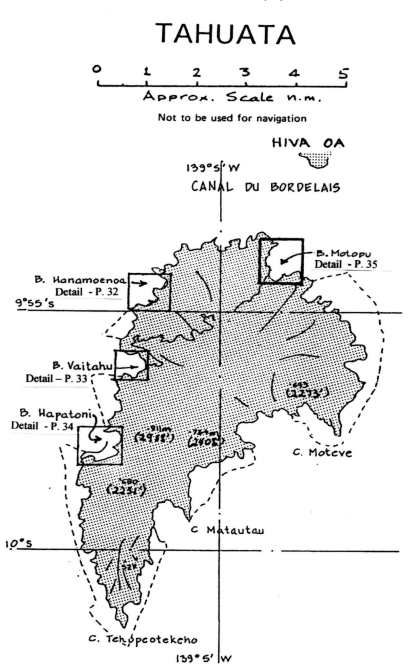

Approx. Scale n.m.

Not to be used for navigation

HIVA OA

139°5′ W

CANAL DU BORDELAIS

B. Motopu
Detail - P. 35

B. Hanamoenoa
Detail - P. 32

9°55′S

B. Vaitahu
Detail – P. 33

B. Hapatoni
Detail - P. 34

·643
(2173′)

·911m
(2955′)

·731m
(2408′)

C. Moteve

·680
(2231′)

C. Matautau

10°S

·328

C. Tchopeotekeho

139° 5′ W

Baie Hanamoenoa (Hana moe noa)

This is the most popular anchorage on Tahuata. It is 2 miles NNW of Baie Vaitahu and is the third sandy bay visible after coming around the corner from Atuona. Anchorage may be taken in the middle of the bay in 5 fathoms, good holding sand. The clear water provides excellent diving and shelling although the beach has many nonos. Eric Hiscock rated this as one of the three most beautiful anchorages in Polynesia.

Several cases of ciguatera have been reported as a result of eating fish from the bay.

BAIE HANAMOENOA

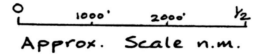

Approx. Scale n.m.

Not to be used for navigation

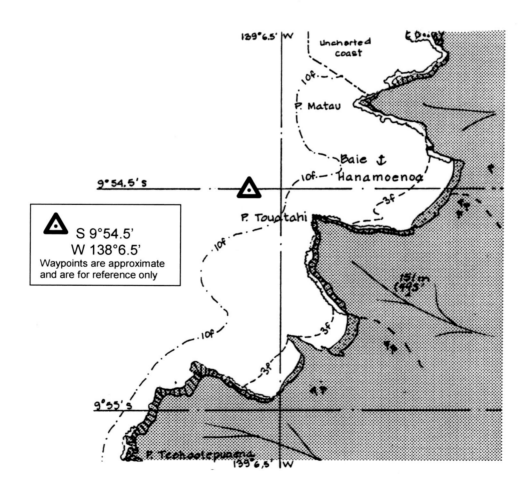

S 9°54.5'
W 138°6.5'
Waypoints are approximate
and are for reference only

Baie Vaitahu

Situated 2 miles SSW of Hanamoenoa is Viatahu, the largest village on the island. As an anchorage the bay has some shortcomings. Though protected from the prevailing winds, it is fairly open and has such a steeply sloping bottom that it does not provide dependable holding. Squalls blowing over the mountains into the bay may cause dragging, so set two anchors off the bow. Northerly winds and swell can also make the anchorage untenable. Landing can be difficult on the beaches and may have to be made at the concrete wharf.

The town has an infirmary, radio station, telephone, post office and a small museum well as several sights of interest in the village. A monument in the center of the village proclaims the true Marquesan name for the islands – Fenua Enata (Land of Men). Eglise Sainte Marie de L'enfant Jesus, a Catholic church built near the shore, was built in commemoration of the 150th anniversary of the arrival of Catholic missionaries to the islands. The structure has been designed to artistically combine local wood with discarded stones used as ballast for 19th century trading ships. A beautiful stained glass window graces the altar. Several archeological sites can be visited in the valley beyond the village. Bone carvings are sold and tattoos can be obtained at a studio near the church.

Viatahu has been the site of several historic occurrences in the past. It was here that the first European visitors disembarked: the Spaniard Mendana in 1595 followed by James Cook in 1774. In 1842 Admiral Dupetit -Thouars signed the treaty linking the archipelago to France.

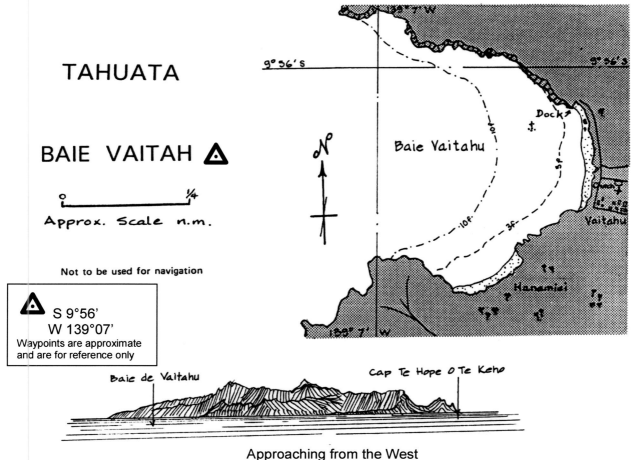

Approaching from the West

Baie Hapatoni

This beautiful bay 1.5 miles south of Baie Vaitahu, is the southern part of a double-lobed indentation between Pointe Fakaua on the north and Point Vaioteoho on the south. The village of Hapatoni is one of the friendliest and most attractive in the island group. The villagers welcome visitors with a sincerity that is heartwarming. Landing at the concrete wharf can be difficult when surf is present and care must be taken to avoid an accident. When the sea is calm excellent snorkeling can be enjoyed in the shallows near the dock.

The anchorage area is directly off the village; it is quite deep, sometimes rolly, and has many coral heads on which the anchor can be snagged. The tree-lined road through the village leads to a large and recently restored archeological site consisting of huge stone platforms (maeae) near a Christian cemetery. Handicrafts sold in the covered marketplace adjacent to the bay include beautifully carved wooden bowls, necklaces and replicas of javelins. Also for sale are bottles of locally made fragrant coconut oil scented with sandalwood (Pani Puahi).

Baie Hanatefau

This uninhabited bay is the next bay to the north, separated from Baie Hapatoni by rocky Pointe Matautu. It is a better anchorage and has some of the best snorkeling in the Marquesas with good visibility and excellent coral formations.

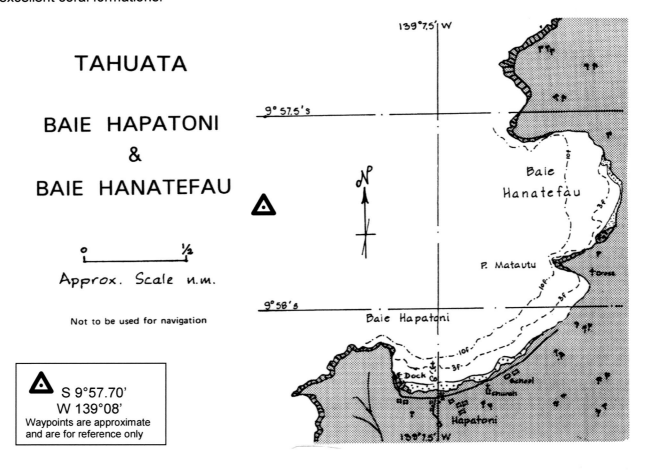

TAHUATA

BAIE HAPATONI
&
BAIE HANATEFAU

Approx. Scale n.m.

Not to be used for navigation

S 9°57.70'
W 139°08'
Waypoints are approximate
and are for reference only

Baie Motopu

Situated southeast of the northern extremity of Tahuata, Baie Motupu is an open bay entered between two points bordered with steep, rocky cliffs. Point Paona divides the shoal areas at the head of the bay in two. Avoid the shoal patch almost awash located a short distance northeast of Point Paona.

Rolly anchorage may be taken in 6 - 7 fathoms, sand and coral. Cruisers seldom visit the bay and a stop-over would no doubt be met with a warm welcome.

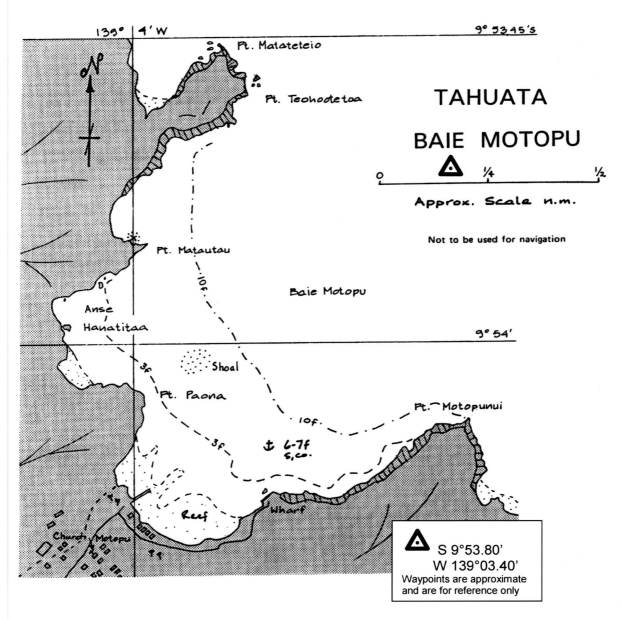

HIVA OA (Dominica Island)

Hiva Oa, the largest of the Marquesas, is the main island of the southern group of four islands of this archipelago. It lies east-west, and the land falls to the indented coastline from a central ridge of high mountains reaching 3,500 feet at the eastern end. Much of the coast is composed of steep cliffs. A westerly current is often found along the southern coast of the island. Pointe Teaehoa stretches to the south forming a large bay, Baie Taaoa (also called Baie Vipihai or Traitor's Bay). At its northern end is a smaller bay, Baie Atuona and the **Port of Entry** of Atuona. South of Hanakee, Baie Taaoa is open to the prevailing winds and seas. Several bays along the northern coast can be used as anchorages. The current generally sets westward along the southern coast.

Baie Atuona and Baie Tahauku are two adjacent bays indenting the northern part of Baie Taaoa, otherwise known as Traitor's Bay. They are separated by a small rocky point, Pointe Feki, on which there is a light. Between Pointe Feki and Ilot Hanakee to the south is the open bay of Atuona (Traitor's Bay). A somewhat rolly anchorage may be had within the mouth of the bay in 8 to 10 fathoms. Cruisers can no longer anchor in the protection of the breakwater (and Med-tie to it) as this is reserved for local fishing vessels. Plenty of space off the breakwater must be left for freighters and passenger ships to maneuver in an arc when docking at the wharf.

The largest town on Hiva Oa is Atuona where entry permits for the Marquesas can be obtained at the gendarmerie located downtown. With a population of over 1,500, Atuona is the administrative center for the southern Marquesas. It has a radio station, bank, hospital, church, bishopric, hotels and restaurants. You can use a credit card any weekday to purchase a bond at the bank. International telephone calls and faxes may be sent from the post office. In addition to water and various groceries, beef and excellent goat meat are available at stores in the town (closed from 1130 to 1430). Fresh fruit and vegetables are usually difficult to find, but on the road west of the village there are some market gardens that may sell produce in season. The airstrip, with connections to Tahiti, is on the plateau north of the village.

The French artist, Paul Gauguin lived in Atuona. He and Jacques Brel, a songwriter, are buried in the Calvary Cemetery, on a hill overlooking the bay, about a one-hour walk from town. The Gauguin Museum features copies of his art and various memorabilia.

It is a one-hour hike to the site where Jacques Brel planned to build a house (Belvedere). Here, a memorial in his honor has been erected where the view of the town and bay is spectacular. In addition several sights of interest are in the vicinity, in the valley behind the anchorage where petroglyphs can be seen or by walking or hitchhiking to the village of Taha'a (5 miles west of Atuona) where you can find a tiki and some paepaes.

Baie Tahauku is immediately to the east of Pointe Feki. A breakwater near its mouth greatly reduces the effect of the swell, though backwash effects do occur and it can be a rolly anchorage. Anchor in 5 fathoms, good holding sand, northeast of an imaginary line extending seaward from two yellow crosses on the western shore. Landing can be made at either the steps or the wharf, where showers are available. Spring water found between Mobil and the breakwater is better to drink than river water between Mobil and the shower. The head of the bay is shoal and swimming is inadvisable because of the large shark population.

ILES MARQUISES
ILE HIVA OA

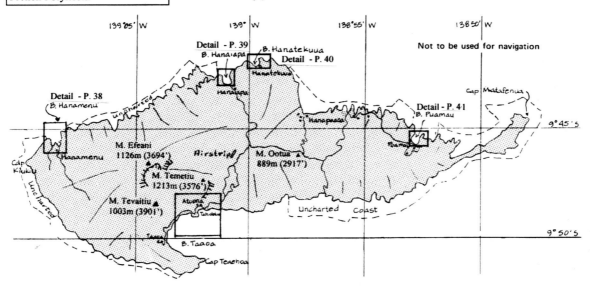

Not to be used for navigation

BAIE TAAOA
(Traitor's Bay)

BAIE ATUONA
&
TAHAUKU

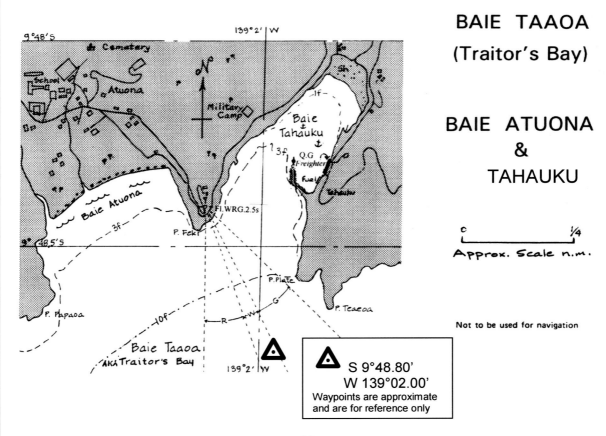

Not to be used for navigation

S 9°48.80'
W 139°02.00'
Waypoints are approximate
and are for reference only

38

Baie Hanamenu (Hana Menu)

A double-lobed indentation is at the northwestern end of Hiva Oa, between Point Kaunakua (Point Gaussin) on the east and Point Matatana (Point Bonnard) on the west. The bay is divided into two by the steep-sided peninsula terminating with Point Matahau, which is marked with a steep, massive dark rock, Grosse Tour, 368 feet high. Anse Tanaeka (Hanaheka), the western bay is shallow and open. Baie Hanamenu is the eastern bay. It is deeply indented with steep, almost overhanging cliffs on the western side and on the east are the slopes of a mountain ridge. The head of the bay is shoal with a lovely beach and a coconut palm plantation beyond.

Vessels may travel well into Baie Hanamenu, anchoring toward the head in about 6 fathoms, sand bottom. It is a good idea to buoy your anchor to assist in retrieving it in case sunken tree trunks on the bottom foul the vessel's anchor. Northerly winds make the anchorage rough and squalls may sometimes be felt off the steep walls. A strong onshore breeze often comes up in the afternoon, making landing through the surf difficult. Wild pig and cattle hunters occasionally visit the bay. The small village of Hanamenu at the head of the bay has no facilities but water reported to be of excellent quality is available from the stream at the eastern end of the beach.

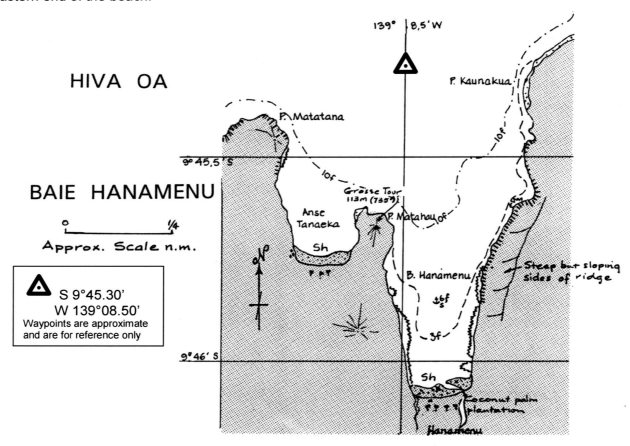

Baie Hanaiapa

Located on the north coast of Hiva Oa, Baie Hanaiapa is between Pointe du Dome on the east and Pointe Jouan on the west. Excellent protection from easterly winds and anchorage in 7 to 10 fathoms, good holding sand can be taken in the middle of the bay. Do not proceed far into the bay as some coral is scattered about and a very shallow spot extends northwest of the little peninsula extending from the head of the bay. This is the best anchorage on the north side of the island.

A rough concrete wharf on the east side of the bay is joined to the village of Hanaiapa by road which leads on to Atuona and Puamau. The tiny village stretches for more than half a mile and the luxuriant variety of lush vegetation and colorful flowers make visiting it a treat. A well-kept paepae is featured in the center of the village. The harvesting of copra is the mainstay of people in the area. The copra-drying sheds with their removable covers attest to the showers frequently experienced.

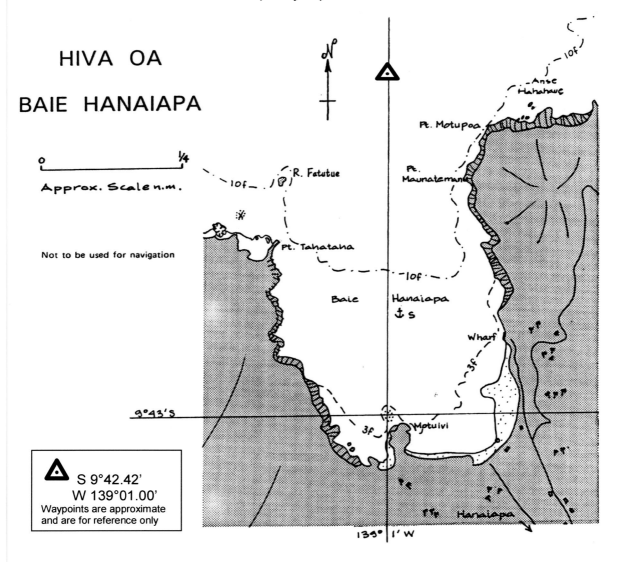

S 9°42.42'
W 139°01.00'
Waypoints are approximate
and are for reference only

Baie Hanatekuua

Baie Hanatekuua is five miles west of Pointe Mautau. The French Hydrographic Service states that a vessel may find suitable anchorage about 800 feet from the northeastern point of the bay when it has a bearing of 054° on the high part of the point or closer to the coast in 5 to 6 fathoms, sand. There are no facilities at the small village of Hanatekkuua.

HIVA OA
BAIE HANATEKUUA

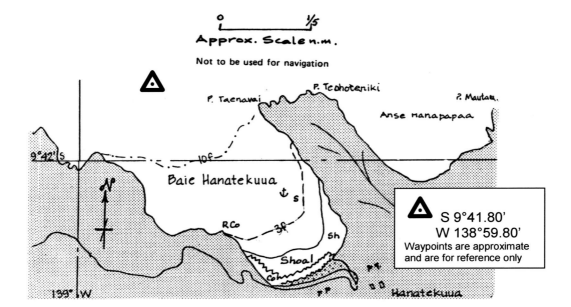

Not to be used for navigation

S 9°41.80'
W 138°59.80'
Waypoints are approximate
and are for reference only

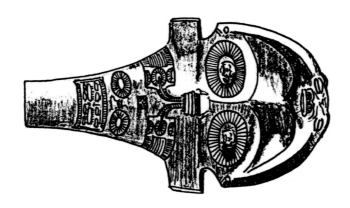

MARQUESAN WAR CLUB

Baie Puamau

Open to the northeast, Baie Puamau is between Pointe Mataai on the west and Pointe Obelisque on the east. The hill on this point is surmounted by a natural obelisk composed of two vertical rocks separated by a fissure. Two coral-fringed motus in the eastern part of the bay are difficult to identify when approaching from the west and should be given safe clearance. Anchorage can be taken in 6 - 8 fathoms, good holding sand, in the center of the bay or you may also anchor closer to the eastern shore where the effect of the swell may be less noticeable. Landing may be made at the concrete wharf in the southeast corner of the bay where a road leads to town. The swell combined with slippery steps can make landing on the wharf quite difficult and extreme care must be taken. The bay is exposed to the north and with fresh breezes from northeast to north-northwest, the anchorage becomes untenable as the current enters the bay and a strong northwesterly set develops. Because of its exposure, the bay is always affected by swell making it a very rolly anchorage.

For those who are interested in archeological sites, Puamau must be near the top of the list since this is the location of one of the most extensive archeological sites on the island. It is a half-hour walk through the town to Iipona where Takaii, the largest tiki in the world, standing at 8 feet, can be admired. In addition, massive terraces, petroglyphs and various statues on the site make it truly a spectacular place to visit. A road links the Puamau to Atuona.

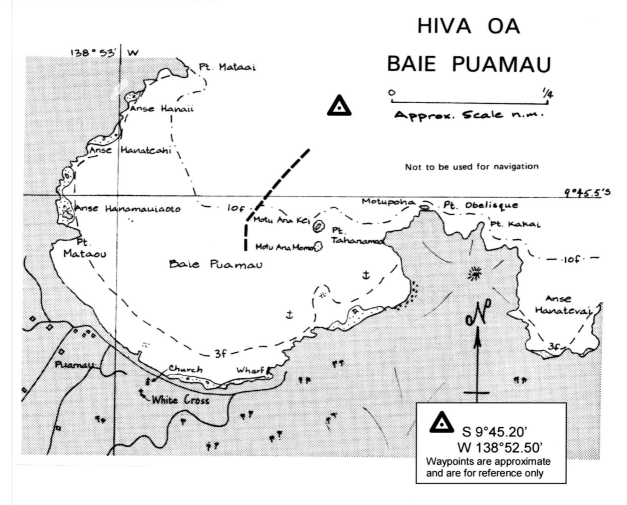

HIVA OA

BAIE PUAMAU

0 ———————— ¼
Approx. Scale n.m.

Not to be used for navigation

S 9°45.20'
W 138°52.50'
Waypoints are approximate
and are for reference only

UA HUKA (pronounced wa-huka)

The smallest of the inhabited islands in the northern group, Ua Huka lies about 24 miles east of Nuku Hiva. This crescent-shaped island is topped by a high ridge which splits at its western end to form two valleys. A curved line of peaks form the spine of the island, the highest of which is Mount Hitikau at 1,800 feet. Near its base is a vast plateau with arid, desert-like topography and scrub brush that resembles California's Big Sur country or Ireland's rural landscape. Few yachts visit this beautiful island, which has much of interest to enjoy.

The island is overpopulated with more than 1,500 wild horses and 3,000 goats, which have almost deforested the landscape. With less than 600 people living on the island, the combined population of horses, goats and cattle outnumber the people by about ten to one. Plans are underway to reduce the number of horses and goats to a level that the island's vegetation can support.

The island gives good radar returns for up to 30 miles distant. All available anchorages are on the southern side and include Baie de Vaipaee, Baie d'Hane and Baie Haavei.

Baie de Vaipaee (Invisible Bay)

About a mile east of Pointe Tekeho, the southwestern point of the island is the narrow slot of Baie de Vaipaee. It is aptly named, for it is very difficult to identify until directly opposite the entrance when the beach at its head is visible. The steep, black walls at the entrance appear forbidding and a rough sea always seems present, but once inside, the water is calm.

The head is shoal and anchorage in about 3 fathoms is found about two-thirds of the way in. As swinging room is limited, use bow and stern anchors to hold your vessel into the swell. In northerly or easterly winds the bay is a satisfactory anchorage. However, if the wind sets southeasterly, the swell sets into the bay. This can make it a very dangerous anchorage and departure can be difficult.

Landing can be made at the concrete boat launching ramp and jetty, or on the beach at the head of the bay, where the village of Vaipaee is located. The best museum in the Marquesas is located in the Mayor's office, and is well worth a visit. One of the special features you'll find there is a 300-year-old canoe. Two small stores, an attractive church and very friendly people are in this village. The villagers are excellent wood carvers and numerous craft shops attest to the skill of their handiwork.

About a mile west of the entrance to the bay is the steep, cliffy southern tip of the island at Cap Tekeho. The huge sea caves in the cliffs are ancient burial sites and seabirds now use them as nesting sites.

Two small islands, Ilots Hemeni and Teuaua, .5 miles west of Cap Tekeho and .25 miles offshore are known as Bird Islands. Hundreds of petrels, terns, tropicbirds, boobies and frigate birds can be seen soaring above the islands and the cacophony of their calls is unimaginable. A rope hanging down the cliff on Ilot Teuaua aids in the collection of tern eggs, and with their red yolks and distinctive fishy flavor, these are considered a local delicacy

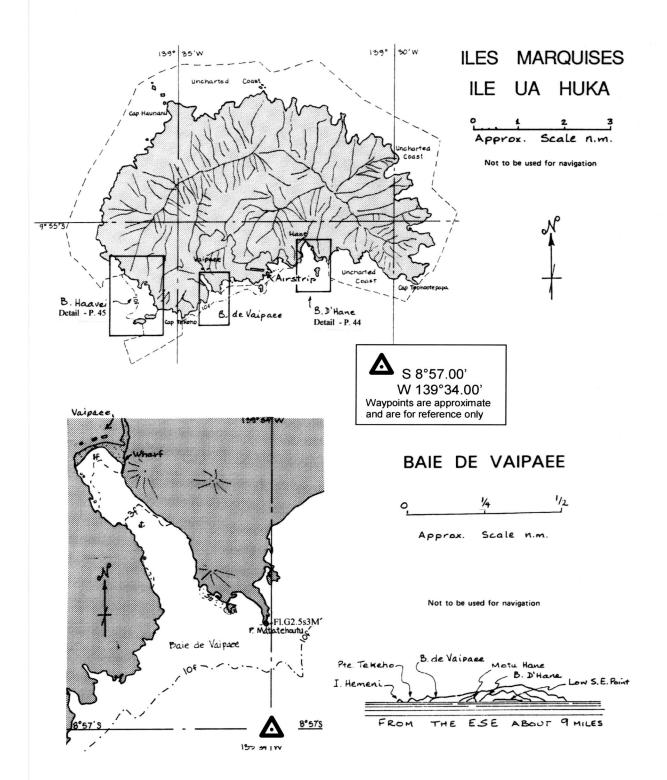

ILES MARQUISES
ILE UA HUKA

0   1   2   3
Approx. Scale n.m.

Not to be used for navigation

139° 35'W

139° 30'W

Uncharted   Coast

Cap Haunanu

Uncharted Coast

9° 55'3'

Hane

Vaipaee

Airstrip

Uncharted Coast

B. Haavei
Detail - P. 45

Cap Tekeho

B. de Vaipaee

B. D'Hane
Detail - P. 44

Cap Teohootepopa

S 8°57.00'
W 139°34.00'
Waypoints are approximate
and are for reference only

BAIE DE VAIPAEE

0   ¼   ½
Approx.   Scale n.m.

Not to be used for navigation

Vaipaee

139° 34'W

Wharf

3f

Baie de Vaipaee

Fl.G2.5s3M
P. Matatchautu

10f

8°57'S

8°57'S

139° 34'W

Pte. Tekeho   B. de Vaipaee

I. Hemeni   Motu Hane
                      B. D'Hane
                              Low S.E. Point

FROM   THE   ESE   ABOUT   9 MILES

44

Baie d'Hane

Two miles to the east of Baie de Vaipaee is Baie d'Hane, recognizable by the 508 foot reddish-purple rocks of Motu Hane lying to the east of the entrance. The bay is a little wider than Baie de Vaipaee and good anchorage can be taken in 8 to 10 fathoms about midway into the bay. Strong gusts sometimes blow off the hillside and some swell enters the bay. Landing on the beach through the surf can be challenging; the best place for going ashore is in the northwest corner.

Near the stream at the head of the bay is the village of Hane, where you can find stores and a bakery. In the annex of the city hall is an arts and crafts center and next door is a small maritime museum. The archeological site of Meaiaute is well worth the somewhat strenuous walk up the valley beyond the village. Of particular interest are several interesting tiki, one of which is headless and another with a tattoo on its face. Be prepared for abundant mosquitoes in the area.

A scenic, winding road links Hane to the town of Vaipaee. Along the route is a massive botanical garden featuring hundreds of plants found in Polynesia. In addition to the wide variety of flora, many birds can be seen in the arboretum such as the beautiful and rare ultramarine lorikeet, Marquesan reed-warblers, iphis monarchs and fruit doves. Beyond the airfield is an area of reefs and rocks marking the location of an abandoned archeological site boasting a spectacular setting.

The coastal road continues eastward to the small village of Hokatu. The selection and quality of wood carvings of everything from bowls to walking sticks as well as replicas of javelins and axes is by far the best to be found in Polynesia and the prices are most reasonable.

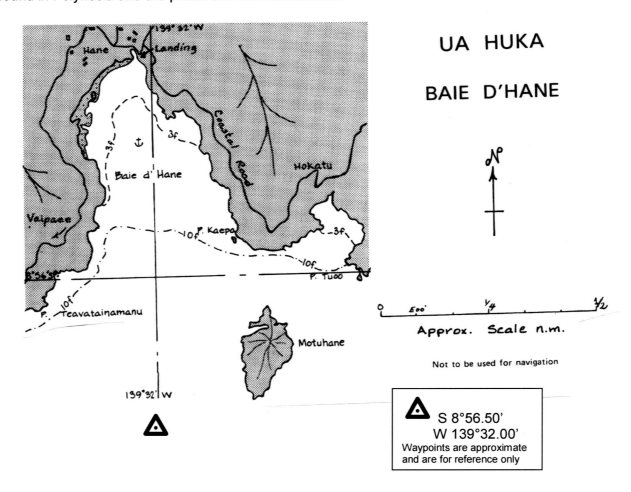

UA HUKA

BAIE D'HANE

Approx. Scale n.m.

Not to be used for navigation

S 8°56.50'
W 139°32.00'
Waypoints are approximate
and are for reference only

Baie Haavei (Baie Chavei, Baie Blanche, Shaveb Bay and Shavay Bay)

This open bay near the southwestern part of the island is about a mile northwest of Cap Tekeho. Two islets, Hemeni and Teuaua help to protect it from wind and swell. Anchorage is off a beautiful sandy beach, with Ilot Hemeni lying a little east of south from the vessel.

The bay is owned by the influential Lichtle family, founders of the Community Museum of Ua Huka in Vaipaee and the arboretum on the Vaipaee-Hane road. The valley is like a tropical garden park, and since it is private land, permission is needed before walking around. Landing on the sandy beach may be difficult because of the surf.

There are two archeological sites in the vicinity that can only be reached by sea. In Hatuana Bay, west of Haavei there are petroglyphs depicting tiki faces and geometric designs carved into the lava flow. At low tide, footprints may be seen in the floor of the cave known as the Ghost Cave of Anavenihae.

The coast of Ua Huka is pock-marked with sea caves and is the perfect habitat for spiny rock lobsters. These often appear in the menus of local restaurants as langouste. Because of the prolific goat population on the island, the islanders have developed a tasty variety of recipes which include barbecued goat, stewed goat and curried goat served in coconut milk. By the way, when helping yourself to coconut milk, be aware of the fact that generous servings act as a laxative. However, by eating several guavas the results of over-indulgence in coconut milk can be overcome.

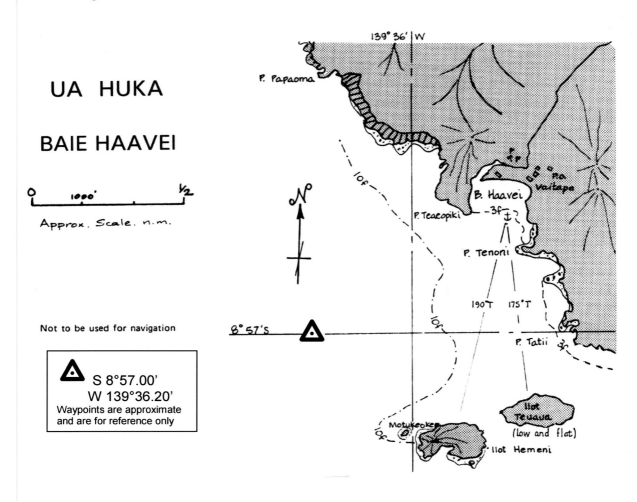

UA HUKA

BAIE HAAVEI

0   1000'   ½

Approx. Scale. n.m.

Not to be used for navigation

⚠ S 8°57.00'
W 139°36.20'
Waypoints are approximate
and are for reference only

UA POU (Ua Pu or Hua Pou, pronounced as wapoo)

This diamond-shaped island lies about 25 miles south of Taiohae Bay on Nuku Hiva. It is about 10 miles long and 7 miles wide and has a spectacularly serrated skyline. It has countless soaring mountain spires and towers, the highest being Mt. Oave, a volcanic plug reaching 4,040 feet high. Often shrouded in cloud, it is a commanding and unforgettable sight when visible. Many bays indent the coastline, but only those most useable by small craft are described. A dirt road circles the central part of the island and has spectacular views. Good radar returns are received for distances up to 26 miles.

Baie d'Hakahau

This bay lies midway on the northeast coast and is thus exposed to northeast winds. A large white cross is prominent on top of a hill to the east of the harbor. The village of Hakahau is the main settlement and its 1,000 residents are half the island's population. A breakwater/wharf combination extending out from the east side of the bay affords yachts considerable protection from the swell. Landing on the surf-free, sandy beach is easy, making this a convenient place to visit. Boats visiting Ua Pou should check in with the gendarmerie before visiting other anchorages on the island.

This is the third most populated village in the Marquesas (following Taiohae and Atuona) and has a post office, gendarmerie, stores, bakery and an infirmary. Hakahau is noted for the beautiful wood, stone and coconut shell carvings done by local craftsmen. The spectacular use of stone and local woods in the construction of Eglise Saint-Etienne is amazing. The pulpit is a massive block of tou meticulously carved in the shape of a boat's prow, on a huge base with many detailed symbolic carvings. Nearby is *Rosalie's Restaurant*, featuring Marquesan foods such as poisson cru (fish marinated in lime juice and soaked in coconut milk), breadfruit, curried goat, barbecued rock lobster, taro, octopus, green mango, tapioca and sweet red bananas.

Beyond the school is a restored paepae where a replica of a typical Marquesan house has been built. Sometimes wood and coconut shell carvings are sold here and occasionally local dancers perform traditional dances.

A hiking trail has been built leading to the spires. It is recommended that you hire a guide—Pasqual is known to be a good and reliable one.

On the ridge to the east is a large, white cross overlooking the bay. An easy trail leads up the hill, giving a nice view of the bay. The last part of the trail is overgrown with shrubs but with some scrambling the cross can be reached. Part way down the hill the road branches to the east, leading to a beautiful sandy beach at the head of Anaho Bay. Except in June and July when jellyfish sometimes invade the bay, the waves are great for surfing once you have run the gauntlet of swarms of nonos.

A road further to the east leads to what was once a thriving and vibrant community at Hakamoui. Known as "The Valley of the Kings" when it was inhabited over a hundred years ago, only a few people now live in the area and the archeological remains are neglected.

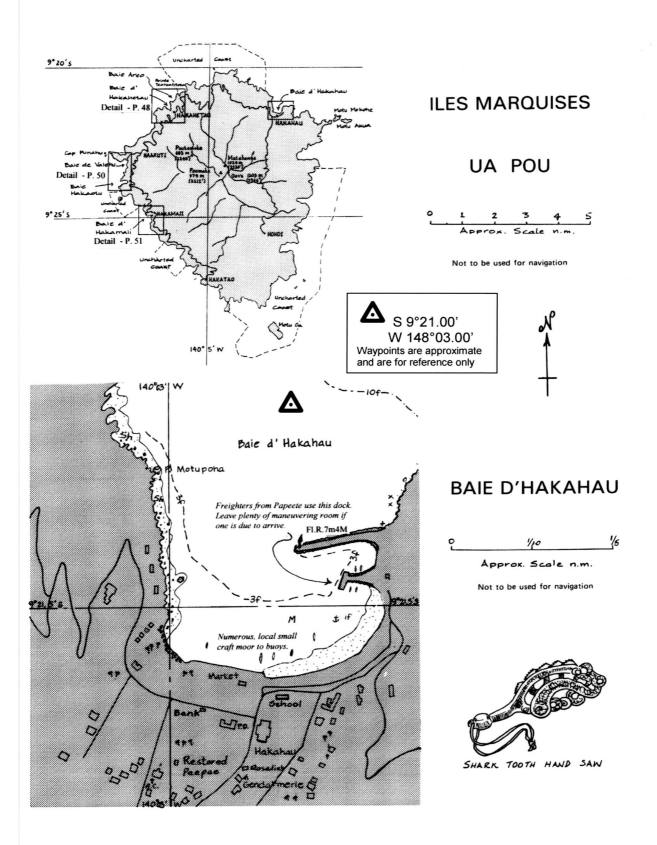

ILES MARQUISES

UA POU

0   1   2   3   4   5
Approx. Scale n.m.

Not to be used for navigation

▲ S 9°21.00'
W 148°03.00'
Waypoints are approximate
and are for reference only

Baie d' Hakahau

Freighters from Papeete use this dock.
Leave plenty of maneuvering room if
one is due to arrive.
Fl.R.7m4M

Numerous, local small
craft moor to buoys.

BAIE D'HAKAHAU

0   1/10   1/5
Approx. Scale n.m.

Not to be used for navigation

SHARK TOOTH HAND SAW

Baie D'Hakahetau

This bay lies about midway along the northwest coast of the island and has several identifying features. A whitish patch can be seen on the spectacular volcanic cliffs on the eastern shore. Below the cliffs is an islet, Motu Koio and farther out, Rochers Rouges. At the center of the head of the bay is a conspicuous rock, Rocher Anapuai, with an island, Motu Kivi, in front. Coral reefs line the eastern shore and extend past Rochers Rouges. The western point, Pointe Tehena, has a coral patch before it. The red roof of the church and a long, aluminum-clad open market stand out from the luxuriant, green vegetation. A broad valley opens up beyond the town, overseen at the far end by a sharp, pyramid-shaped spire.

Anchoring can be taken in about 6 fathoms, sand, about 1,000 feet off Motu Koio. Though this is a rolly anchorage, it is the best spot available. During summer months locals prefer to anchor in Baie D'Hakamaii since it is less affected by swell. The swell is never completely absent; though landing is possible at the cement dock, east of a reddish islet at the head of the bay. The steps are quite slippery and the swell can make going ashore difficult. The village of Hakahetau welcomes cruisers and has made an effort to provide services. Located behind the beach and palm trees, the town has a church, store with fax service and school. Fresh water is available on the pier and arrangements can be made for laundry service. Cruisers may purchase fresh produce from the operator of a large vegetable garden in the village.

The interior of the island can be explored by renting a 4 wheel drive vehicle, taking a guided tour or by renting horses. The horses are small and the wooden saddles are hard. This part of the island has a luxuriant variety of flora and a wealth of bird life.

Etienne Hokaupoko, the Marquesan mayor/school teacher is very knowledgeable about the history of the Marquesas and is involved in establishing a museum on Ua Pou. Fluent in English, French and Marquesan, he enjoys visiting with cruisers and extends a warm invitation to visit the village.

DISTANT VIEW UA POU FROM ENE.

Baie Aneo

This bay lies about 1.5 miles northeast of Baie d'Hakahetau. It has a wide entrance split in two by a reddish rock, Rocher Tauna, which is surrounded by coral. Though you may enter on either side, the western entrance is easier and deeper. When using the eastern entrance stay about 300 feet from the eastern shore to avoid the coral patch near the island, and watch the current setting at the entrance.

Anchorage can be taken in 6 fathoms southwest of Rocher Tauna, where there is sufficient swinging room. Landing can be made ashore, but the swell can make this anchorage somewhat uncomfortable.

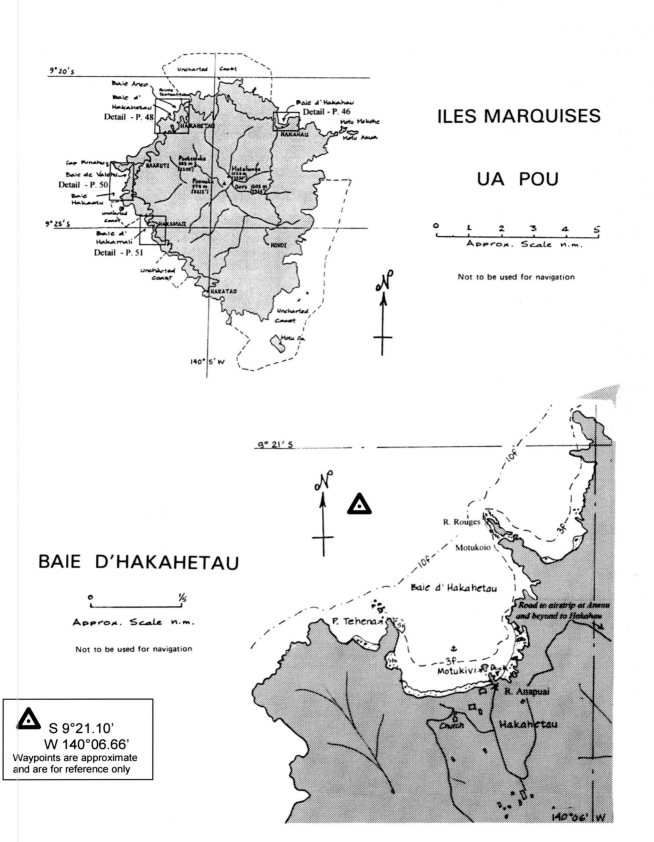

ILES MARQUISES

UA POU

0   1   2   3   4   5
Approx. Scale n.m.

Not to be used for navigation

BAIE D'HAKAHETAU

0   1/5
Approx. Scale n.m.

Not to be used for navigation

S 9°21.10'
W 140°06.66'
Waypoints are approximate
and are for reference only

Baie de Vaiehu (Vaieo Bay)

This is a large, open bay at the westernmost part of the island, between Cap Punahu on the north and Pointe Motukoio, with a prominent obelisk, on the south. Anchorage can be taken in the northern part of the bay close to shore in about 8 fathoms, where there is good protection from easterly winds. Landing is easiest in the northeast corner of the bay. Swell is a factor and thus the other bays are generally preferred. Baie de Vaiehu is uninhabited, but a short hike over the ridge to the north leads to the village of Haakuti and further along to Hakahetau. The coastal road to the south leads to the village of d'Hakamaii.

Baie Hakaotu

A small indentation between Pointe Motukoio and the peninsula where the prominent landmark of Pain de Sucre (Sugarloaf) is located is Baie Hakaotu. Snug, protected anchorage can be taken with limited swinging room, necessitating bow and stern anchors. Landing is easiest in the northeast corner of the bay.

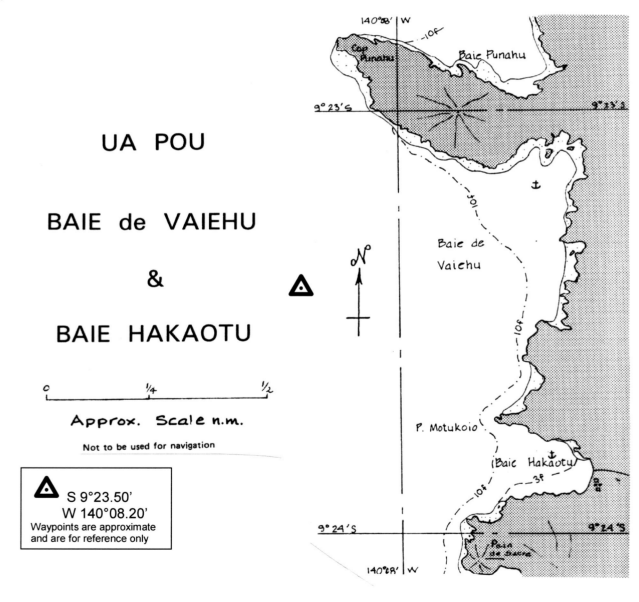

UA POU

BAIE de VAIEHU

&

BAIE HAKAOTU

0   ¼   ½

Approx. Scale n.m.

Not to be used for navigation

△ S 9°23.50'
W 140°08.20'
Waypoints are approximate
and are for reference only

51

Baie Hakamaii (Baie Haka Maii)

This small bight lies 2 miles SSE of Baie Vaiehu (1.5 miles SE of Sugarloaf) and has traditionally given cruisers a warm welcome. The yellow, blue and red painted panels on the front of the stone church resemble large stained glass windows when viewed from the sea. Good holding anchorage may be found about 200 yards from the head of the bay, midway between the southern shore and a large, low, black rock near the northern side of the entrance. It may be necessary to set a stern anchor to keep the yacht perpendicular to the swell at night when the wind changes direction. Landing on the beach at the head of the bay must be well timed, depending on sea conditions.

The tiny village is quite isolated and the people use traditional canoes for fishing. The sale of wood and stone carvings and copra support the local population. A trail inland from the village of Hakamaii follows the river, where mosquitoes are a pest.

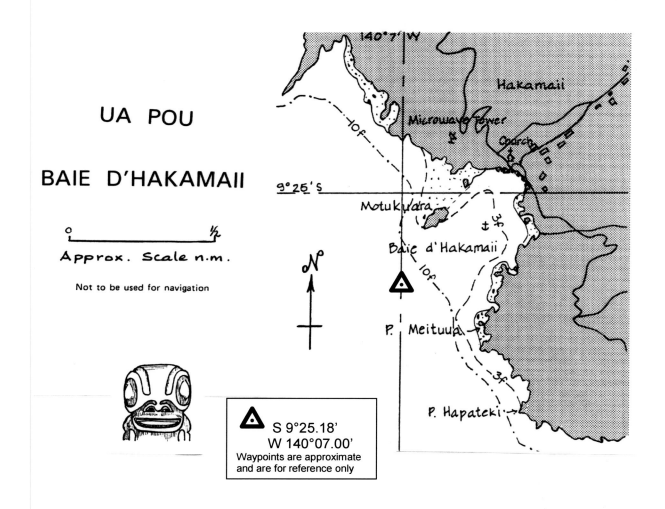

UA POU

BAIE D'HAKAMAII

Approx. Scale n.m.

Not to be used for navigation

S 9°25.18'
W 140°07.00'
Waypoints are approximate
and are for reference only

ILE NUKU HIVA

This is the principal island of the Marquesas and Taiohae is a **Port of Entry** where cruisers must report to the gendarmerie. Bonds can be purchased using a credit card only on Tuesdays and Wednesdays. Nuku Hiva is precipitously high, with Takao the highest point, at 3,888 feet. Other heights along the northern coast give rise to many beautiful waterfalls. Toovii Plateau is in the center of the island. Several bays are on the northern and southern coasts, many of which can be used as anchorages, depending on the direction of the wind and swell. Baie de Taiohae is the principal bay and a popular stop-over for cruisers.

Baie de Taiohae (Hakapehi)

Located about 3.5 miles east-northeast of Baie Tai Oa, this is the safest and most important anchorage in the Marquesas. At the entrance are two rocky islets (the Sentinels / Les Sentinelles) and a large white cross of crystalline rocks rises above the cliffs to the east. Rocky cliffs line each side of the bay; on the western side a steep-sided lava plug rises above the slopes. Within the bay, Pointe Arquee is a curved, bare, rocky spur that projects from the eastern shore. The remaining shores are covered with green growth except for a few black volcanic outcrops. The bay holds a fascinating place in history for it was here that 23-year old Herman Melville jumped a whaling ship in 1842.

In the northeastern part of the bay a light on the hill near the ruins of Fort Collet defines the anchorage for large ships, in the green sector. The best area for cruisers is on the west side of the head of the bay in 6 fathoms, sand. There is a restricted zone covering the area about 300 yards westward from the east side of the harbor where supply ships and barges maneuver. Since swell often makes the bay uncomfortable, a stern anchor should be set to keep the yacht perpendicular to the shore and swell.

Taiohae is the administrative capital and the largest town in the Marquesas. It lies in the open remains of a volcanic crater with the caldera walls surrounding the town. The red roofs of village buildings stand out on the eastern side at the head of the bay. Here, the ruins of Fort Collet are beyond a small, green hill that protrudes from the shore. Landing can be made either at the concrete wharf below the Fort (which is not visible on first approach) or at the concrete boat ramp inshore of the wharf. The town has a radio station, hospital, post office, satellite telephones, a few stores, a gendarmerie and other administrative offices. An airstrip at the northwest corner of the island can be reached in about 2.5 hours by boat or costs about $60 by helicopter. Points of interest include the Roman Catholic cathedral "Notre Dame des Iles Marquesas," the Herman Melville memorial and two archeological sites. Moana Nui, approximately in the center of the north of the harbor on the main road, is reported to be a great place to eat.

Water may be taken on but it is often contaminated and should be boiled or purified before drinking. Taiohae is the only place in the Marquesas where polluted water is a problem; it is caused by the many goats and pigs which live in the catchment area. Hakatea, 5 miles to the west, is a much better place to fill your water tanks providing the town has enough to spare.

Fuel is available from the Total fuel dock on the east side of the bay. Drop a bow anchor and take a stern line ashore when taking on fuel. Propane tanks may be filled at the fuel dock or at Magasin Bigot. Butane burns satisfactorily but the gas in the tank is at a much lower pressure than propane. Close to the concrete landing ramp and Dive Center is a Yacht Service that provides boat care at US$100 per month for cruisers who wish to leave their vessels for a while to hike the island or fly home. They charge US$90 to complete paperwork for the purchase of duty-free diesel. This is a bargain if a vessel takes on more than 100 gallons of fuel.

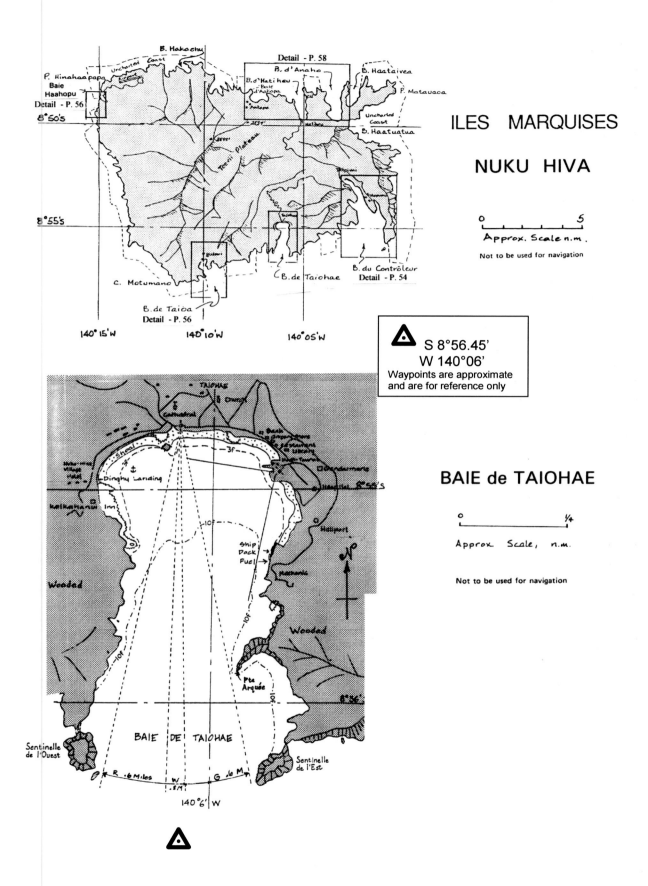

ILES MARQUISES

NUKU HIVA

0 _____ 5
Approx. Scale n.m.

Not to be used for navigation

⚠ S 8°56.45'
W 140°06'
Waypoints are approximate
and are for reference only

BAIE de TAIOHAE

0 _____ ¼
Approx. Scale, n.m.

Not to be used for navigation

54

Baie de Controleur (Controller Bay)

This large bay is immediately west of the long, narrow projecting point of Cap Tikapo. Within the bay, two rocky points (one shorter than the other) divide the head of the bay into three narrow coves. Anchorage may be taken in good holding sand and mud near the head of each cove in 7 to 10 fathoms. Some swell may disturb the anchorages, though there is good protection from the prevailing winds. The westernmost cove, L'Anse Haka Paa, is the least affected by swell. It is advisable to set a stern anchor to keep the vessel perpendicular to the shore and swell.

The village of Taipivai is located a short distance up the river at the head of Anse Hakahaa, the middle and largest cove. A concrete loading dock in the village provides easy shore access and several excellent hikes can be taken from the village. A fifteen-minute walk north of the village, past a vanilla plantation, leads to a path which zigzags up the hill. Located here are the ruins of an important archeological site, Paeke, which has several large tikis and a huge marae (ceremonial platform made from huge basalt blocks which was used only by priests and chieftains for worship, burials and sometimes human sacrifices). This marae measures 557 feet by 82 feet. A hike along the west bank of the river up the valley leads to two waterfalls. The dirt road linking Taipivai to Taiohae has many scenic viewpoints. Abandoned paepaes (ancient stone platforms that acted as house foundations) are beside the road from Anse Hanga Haa to Anse Hooumi. Insect repellant is necessary to guard against nonos.

Whaleboats (lighters) from the passenger-carrying freighter, *Aranui*, arrive every three weeks from Papeete. Its arrival gives an excuse for the local people to congregate at the dock and visit, while their wide-eyed children gaze quietly at the tourists. Freight is off-loaded and, similar to many villages in the Marquesas, sacks of copra (dried nutmeat from which coconut oil is extracted), barrels of fermented noni*, limes and bananas are taken on for delivery to Papeete.

It is interesting to note that this area is the setting for Herman Melville's well-known book, *Typee*. To get an appreciation for the rugged terrain on the island and the way of life prior to the influence of western civilization, this descriptive book is a "must read."

* * * * *

*Noni (Morinda citrifolia) produces a green, pear-sized fruit with round, whitish markings. In contrast to coconut-producing palm trees, it grows quickly, does not need special care and is easy to harvest. The fruit is loaded into barrels and shipped to Papeete in a fermented state. The pulp is then shipped to the Morinda juice factory in Salt Lake City, Utah where it is processed and mixed with various fruit juices. The final product is promoted as an elixir for various ailments. Since 1996 the sale of noni has added an economic boost to the Marquesas. It is amazing to see the proliferation of 4 x 4s and other late-model vehicles on islands which have only a few miles of roads.

One of the problems of producing coconuts are the rats living on the islands. A band of metal around the trunk of coconut palms prevents them from climbing up to the coconuts and destroying the fruit.

ILES MARQUISES
ILE NUKU HIVA

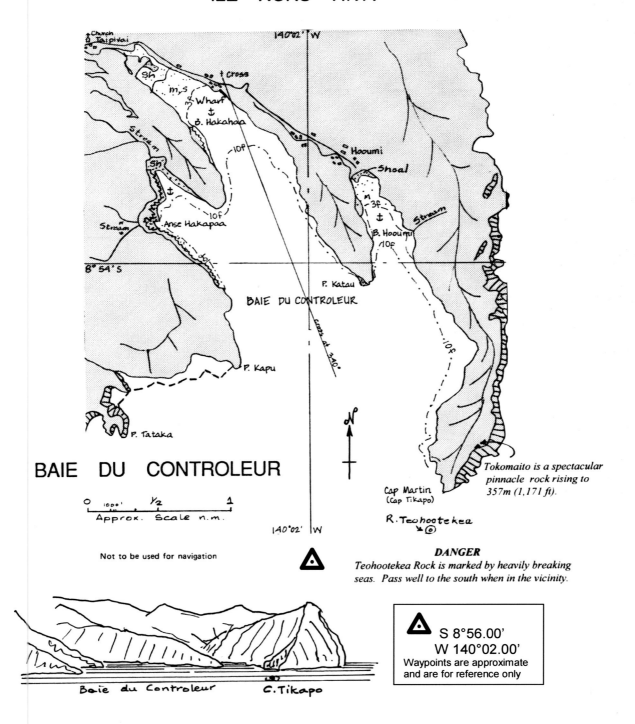

BAIE DU CONTROLEUR

0   1000'   ½   1
Approx. Scale n.m.

Not to be used for navigation

Baie du Controleur   C. Tikapo

Tokomaito is a spectacular
pinnacle rock rising to
357m (1,171 ft).

DANGER
*Teohootekea Rock is marked by heavily breaking
seas. Pass well to the south when in the vicinity.*

S 8°56.00'
W 140°02.00'
Waypoints are approximate
and are for reference only

Baie de Taioa (Tai 'oa or Hakatea)

The southernmost point of Nuku Hiiva is Pointe Motumano. One and a half miles east-northeast is the small bay of Baie Taioa. It provides good anchorage and is less affected by swell than is Baie de Taiohae, 5 miles to the east. On some charts it is called Baie Hakatea, though this name is more correctly applied to the eastern lobe of the bay. It is also known as Daniel and Antoinette's Bay, after the friendly Marquesan couple who have lived here for over 60 years. Daniel still lives at the northeast corner of Anse Hakaui. A river exits from the Hakaui valley, a spectacular and precipitous area often viewed by tourists via sight-seeing helicopters flying from Taiohae.

The opening to the bay is difficult to identify from seaward since the entrance points overlap. The west side is a steep, 1,600-foot mountain; the east side is a lower, black cliff with a flat-topped point. A rough sea is often at the entrance and surf breaks on the eastern point, but you can find a calm anchorage at its head off the beautiful white sand beaches. The western cove, L'Anse Hakaui is shallow, and the better anchorage is in the eastern cove, L'Anse Hakatea, in about 6 fathoms, midway into the bay. Swinging space is restricted if there are several boats in the anchorage. Though the bay is calm, strong squalls sometimes blow down the two valleys. Landing can be made on the rocky shore east of the beach. Pesky nonos infest the beaches and sometimes can affect the anchorage.

Potable water is no longer available here.

Boats can land near the river at the eastern head of L'Anse Hakaui. Close behind the beach are the ruins of the old village and a church with some ancient statues. A walk through the coconut palms and up the slope leads through the valley to Vaipo waterfall, a breathtakingly high and narrow waterfall cascading from the 2,000-foot plateau to the valley floor below. The hike takes 2.5 hours but it is well worth the effort as this is the third highest waterfall in the world. There are also many tikis and ruined paepae in the valley.

Baie d'Haahopu

This bay is 1.7 miles south of Point Hinahaapapa, the northwestern extremity of the island. Anchorage in good holding sand can be taken inside the entrance of the bay, where there is protection from easterly winds.

A boat dock is at the terminus of a road linking the bay to the Nuku-Ataha airport, the only airport on Nuku Hiva. *Le Truck* shuttle service operates between the airport and the boat dock where passengers board a boat for the one-hour trip to Taiohae. Air Tahiti operates three regular flights per week between Tahiti and Nuku Hiva.

Hebrew Cone *(Conus ebraeus Linne)*
Strigate Auger *(Terebra strigilata Sowerby)*

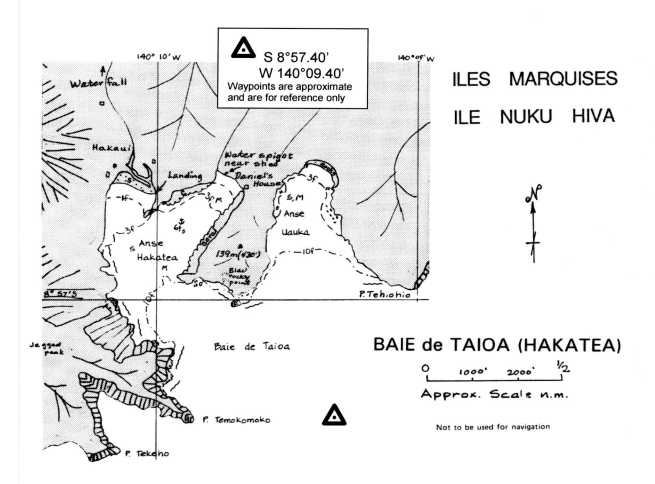

ILES MARQUISES

ILE NUKU HIVA

S 8°57.40'
W 140°09.40'
Waypoints are approximate
and are for reference only

BAIE de TAIOA (HAKATEA)

0   1000'   2000'   ½

Approx. Scale n.m.

Not to be used for navigation

BAIE HAAHOPU

0   100   200   300

Approx. Scale yds.

Not to be used for navigation

S 8°49.30'
W 140°15.12'
Waypoints are approximate
and are for reference only

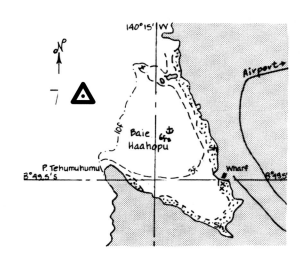

Baie D'Anaho

This large bay on the north coast near the eastern end of the island is one of the calmest anchorages in the Marquesas. On one side is a long, narrow peninsula and on the other is a steep mountain about 1,000 feet high. The bay indents the coast by about 1.5 miles and provides a sheltered anchorage from the prevailing trade winds and swell. But during periods of the year when the wind moves northerly, the swell can enter the bay and be bothersome. The low pass on the east side near the head of the bay lets easterly squalls through in bad weather.

The entrance to the bay is clear and open. Pointe Tekea and Pointe Mataohotu project from the western side about a mile into the bay, narrowing it slightly. Some coral reefs are on the western side and at the head of the bay; the eastern side is clear and steep-to. Small vessels may anchor in the shelter given by Pointe Mataohotu on the western side in about 10 fathoms, fine sand bottom, and in a position keeping the entrance open and avoiding the coral.

Landing can be made through a gap in the coral near the huts on the western side. A dirt road with a view of Baie D'Anaho traverses Teavaimaoaoa Pass (650feet) and leads to Baie D'Hatiheu. A short hike along the beach to the east, passing rocks at the point then crossing sand dunes, leads to Haatuatua, one of the oldest archeological sites in the Marquesas. A road over the saddle leads to the village of Taipivai, at the head of Baie du Controleur.

Baie D'Hatiheu

Two miles west of Baie D'Anaho is Baie D'Hatiheu where good anchorage may be taken in 5 fathoms with easy landing on a wharf to the east. Bordering the waterfront is a collection of tikis and intricately carved arches that add a special ambience. A craft center and museum are in the village. High up on one of the spires over-looking the village, is the *Madonna of Hatiheu*, a white statue built in 1872 by Frere Blanc. The unique crown on the *Madonna* is made of branch coral. The village of Hatiheu was a favorite spot of Robert Louis Stevenson's.

One of the best restaurants in the islands, *Chez Yvonne*, (owned by the town's mayor) is famous for cooking pork in an earthen oven (imu). The pig and bananas are wrapped in ti leaves and placed on hot rocks, covered with banana leaves, burlap, and earth and left to cook for six hours. The reward for the wait is a feast that is tender and delicious!

Three archeological sites are within easy walking distance. The most important one is the tohua (public plaza) Hikoku'a, a large, well-restored ceremonial center consisting of stone platforms. A local dance group periodically performs dances in this exotic setting. Two other significant sites are just up the hill at the marae (temple) to the goddess Tevanaua'ua'a, where a huge sacred banyan tree is located. Further up the hill is tohua Kamuihei with petroglyphs of turtles, human figures and fish tiki faces. Mosquitoes and nonos abound so be sure to bring along your insect repellant

Baie Hakaehu

Baie Hakaehu, six miles west of Baie D'Hatiheu, provides good anchorage in 6 fathoms, sand bottom. Fresh water is available from the inhabitants of Pua, who warmly welcome cruisers.

Caution: Since this part of the coast has not been hydrographically surveyed, cruisers must give the coast a safe clearance and maintain a sharp lookout for unmarked reefs or other dangers.

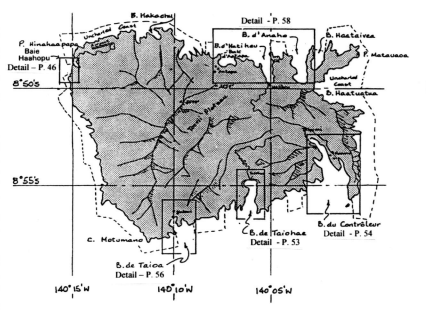

ILES MARQUISES

NUKU HIVA

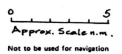

0 — 5
Approx. Scale n.m.
Not to be used for navigation

S 8°48.80'
W 140°05.00'
Waypoints are approximate
and are for reference only

BAIE D'ANAHO & BAIE D'HATIHEU

0 1000' ½ 1
Approx. Scale n.m.

S 8°48.00'
W 140°03.60'
Waypoints are approximate
and are for reference only

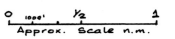

Not to be used for navigation

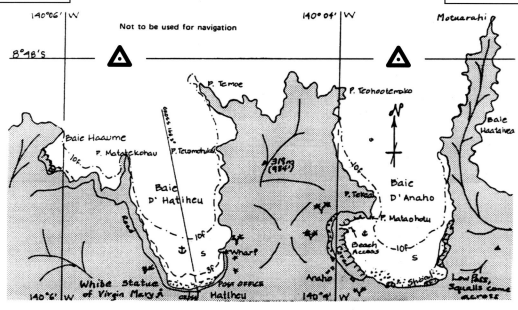

APPROACHING NUKU HIVA FROM THE N

NORTHERN ISLETS

Two groups of small, uninhabited islands are located west and north of Nuku Hiva. One group is Motu Iti; the second group is comprised of Eiao, Hatutaa, and Motu One. This group is about 52 miles northwest of Nuku Hiva.

WARNING: Fish poisoning is reported to be prevalent around the islands; trolling well offshore from the area does not seem to present the same hazard.

Motu Iti

Motu Iti is a cluster of three rocky islets. The largest islet is a sheer 722' rock, 23 miles WNW of Nuku Hiva. Deposits of guano on the smaller rocks present a whitish appearance from a distance.

Eiao

Eiao is about 7 miles long and rises to about 1,900 feet at its northwestern end. The south coast is steep and inaccessible; the north coast has several small bays. About midway up the island is Baie Vaituha, the largest bay, where vessels can anchor near its head, in 12-13 fathoms. Landing is possible on the sand and stone beach but the swell can make going ashore troublesome and the stay uncomfortable. At one time the island was inhabited but now only sheep and goats live here and are gradually destroying the vegetation.

Hatutaa

Hatutaa is an uninhabited island, smaller than and about 3 miles ENE of Eiao and rising to 1,400 feet. The channel between these two islands should not be used.

Motu One (Ile de Sable or Sand Island)

Motu One consists of two small islands 11 miles ENE of Hatutaa. The sea breaks heavily on the banks surrounding the islands.

SOUTHERN ISLANDS

MOTANE (San Pedro Island)

This small island, 1,700 feet high, lies about 12 miles east of Tahuata and is south of Hiva Oa. Hunters from Hiva Oa and Fatu Hiva visit the island, seeking the wild goats and mouton sheep which roam the island and have almost denuded it of its vegetation. There is little incentive to visit Motane for it has no harbors or anchorages, though landing is possible in the lee of the NW side.

FATU HUKA

This cliff-edged islet, reaching 1,184 feet, is 20 miles north of Hiva Oa and 65 miles east of Ua Pou. Breakers mark two rocky heads 2 miles NNW and 1.25 miles NE of it.

ROCHER THOMASSET

This dangerous, solitary rock lies 14 miles ENE of the northern extremity of Fatu Hiva.

TATTOOS

The ancient art of tattooing has been practiced for centuries in many parts of the world, including the Pacific islands. Marquesan tattoo artistry is considered to be the ultimate because of the intricacy and quality of the designs.

In the South Pacific, distinctive patterns are unique to each area and are clearly recognizable. At one time, even newborn infants were given a small tattoo and as the child matured, more were added. In some cases the entire body was completely covered. Tattoos were considered elegant and were believed to give the bearer additional power and status. The use of geometric patterns in Marquesan tattoos is supplemented by stylized motifs such as these:

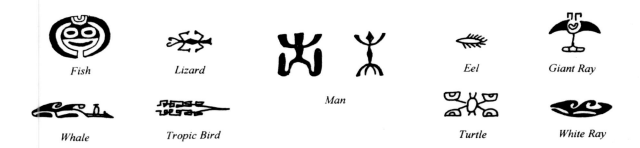

Fish   *Lizard*   *Eel*   *Giant Ray*

Man

Whale   *Tropic Bird*   *Turtle*   *White Ray*

TAPA CLOTH ARTISTRY

This example of a tapa cloth from Fatu Hiva illustrates the intricate and beautifully designed use of patterns similar to those used by tattoo artists. The actual size of the tapa shown here is 16" x 13". It was done on the dark brown bark from a banyan tree; some of the texture of the tapa shows through.

ARCHIPEL DES TUAMOTU (TUAMOTU ARCHIPELAGO)

This group of 78 islands, all but two being coral atolls, is spread across 150° of longitude and extends almost 1,000 miles in a NW-SE direction. In contrast to the lush vegetation of the Marquesas, the atolls have little greenery except for palm trees and short grass. Together with the Marquesas and Society Islands they form French Polynesia, and are administered from Tahiti.

These islands have justifiably been called the "Low or Dangerous Archipelago" because their low-lying character makes them visible only when the vessel is within 8 miles. Typically, the motus (islets) on the reefs are clustered to a greater degree on the northern and western sides while the southern sides are often bare, awash coral reefs. This is very dangerous, since even in daylight the reef cannot be seen until close-to and the sound of the wind and sea often masks the sound of the breakers.

Not so long ago, most cruising plans aimed at only sighting and passing the Tuamotu safely. Today, a few atolls are regularly visited and are included in cruising itineraries. But do not underestimate the dangers of traveling in these waters; the increased number of yachts lost and stranded on reefs attests to the hazards.

The atolls most often visited are Manihi, Ahe, Takaroa and Rangiroa, since they are close to the usual route to Tahiti. Occasional visits are made to Arutua, Apataki, Aratika and Fakarava; sketches of these and other atolls follow, but this does not imply that they are easy to visit, or that the Tuamotu may be cruised with greater safety than previously.

Routes Through the Archipelago

The Tuamotu may be avoided by steering well to westward of Mataiva, the westernmost atoll, before reaching down to Tahiti. The most direct, and most used, route through the archipelago makes a landfall at Takaroa and then passes through the 20-mile gap between Rangiroa and Arutua. An alternate route through the Chenal de Fakarava provides the most direct route to Tahiti from the Panama Canal. Alternatively, one may stop at Raroia or Makemo and leave the Tuamotu for Tahiti from Tahanea.

Current Variations

In the northwestern Tuamotu (Tikehau, Ahe, Manihi and Rangiroa) it has been reported that the current in the passes changes 30 minutes after high or low water as indicated by the tide tables. But in the passes of Toau, Fakarava or Faaite the prevailing conditions (spring tides, surf and air pressure) dominate and even the Admiralty Methods, *Pacific Island Pilot* do not always work.

French Nuclear Tests

The testing of nuclear weapons in the southeastern part of the Tuamotu Archipelago ended in January, 1996 and the islands of Mururoa and Fangatauta remain off limits to cruisers. Mururoa is peppered with monitoring sensors for seismic, radiation and environmental surveys and vessels could disturb the area causing false readings for the surveys. In addition, there is concern regarding the slight possibility of a partial collapse of the reef as was experienced in Bikini following US tests.

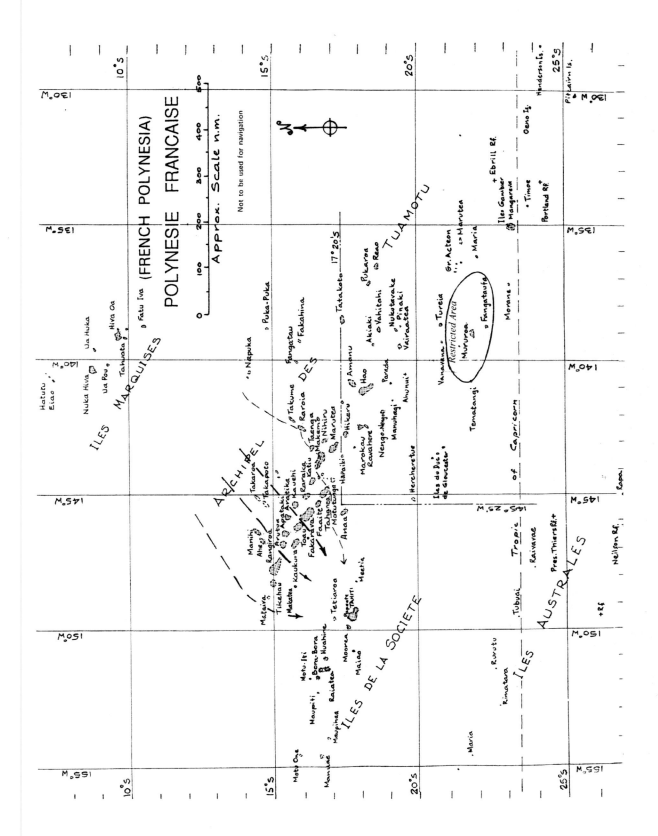

POLYNESIE FRANCAISE
(FRENCH POLYNESIA)

64

ATOLL MANIHI (Wilsons Island)

This atoll and its companion, Ahe, together with the other pair of Takaroa and Takapoto, are the northernmost of the Tuamotu. As a result, they are close to the usual route followed by the majority of cruisers and are likely to be visited. For this reason they are described in more detail than other locations. Manihi and Ahe lie close together and about 40 miles WNW of Takapoto.

Passe Tairapa is an easily identified, well-defined pass on the southwest side of Manihi. The village of Manihi, on the eastern side of the pass, is visible from offshore and is a good landmark for identifying the pass. On its western side is a long, curving island where an airstrip is about 2.5 miles northwest of the village. Two sandy patches on either side of the entrance offer temporary anchorage if you are waiting for improved conditions before entering the pass. The coral reef is close to shore on the ocean side, but on the lagoon side the reef awash extends inward for some distance.

The pass is about 250 ft. wide, decreasing at the inner end to 130 ft. The noticeable V made by incoming and outgoing tidal currents indicates the deepest part of the channel. Within the pass is a straight concrete wharf on the village side. Two large trees are in the little square behind the wharf; casuarina bushes are on the other side of the pass. Though a strong current runs out of the pass, it is usually possible to enter and proceed to the lagoon. Continue in a straight line through the pass until just past the end of the coral reef to starboard.

Once clear of the coral reef beyond the entrance, the best anchorage is in a bight about 0.5 miles ESE of the village, where it is sheltered from the chop of prevailing southeast trade winds and has only modest coral to foul the anchor rode. A good spot is reported to be at 14°27.83'S, 146° 02.20'W. Vessels with very shallow draft can moor at the small boat basin at the village, but check water depths before entering.

Other anchorages can be found in the lagoon, but a route must be threaded through numerous coral heads, a nasty chop is common and there is little swinging room due to coral patches. Such an anchorage is in the curved bight with a white sand beach about 0.5 miles west of the pass. Do not anchor in front of the hotel as the area is foul with telephone cables, tanks and piping associated with desalination operations.

Most of the lagoon can be explored but there are shallow spots and many coral heads to be avoided. The underwater visibility is excellent and diving is superb. There is good shelling on the outer side of the motu. A pearl culture station for black-lipped oysters operates on the atoll.

WARNING: Fish poisoning has been reported here.

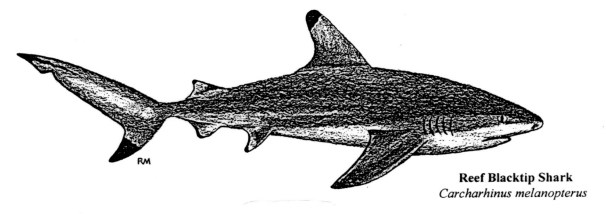

Reef Blacktip Shark
Carcharhinus melanopterus

ARCHIPEL DES TUAMOTU
AHE & MANIHI

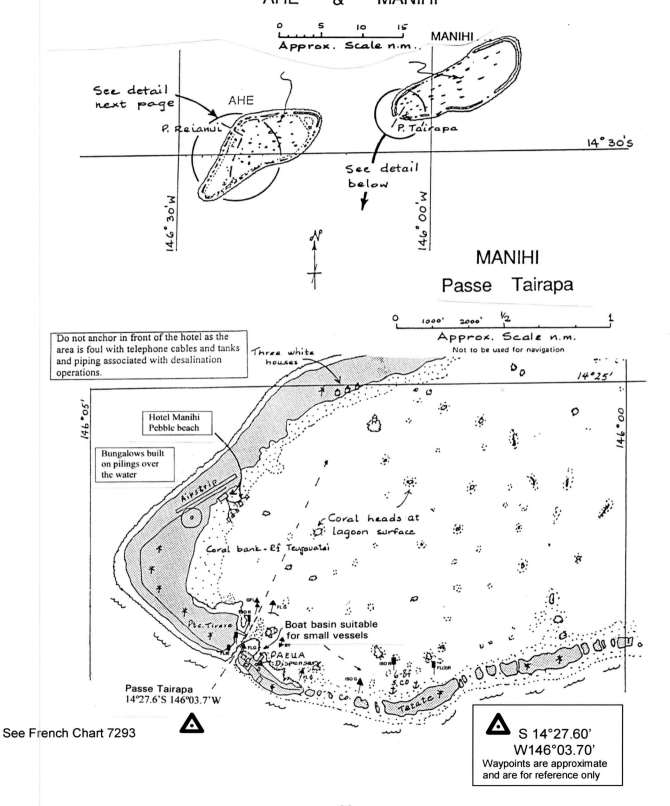

0 5 10 15
Approx. Scale n.m.

MANIHI

See detail next page

AHE

P. Reianui

P. Tairapa

See detail below

14° 30'S

146° 30'W

146° 00'W

N

MANIHI
Passe Tairapa

0 1000' 2000' ½ 1
Approx. Scale n.m.
Not to be used for navigation

Do not anchor in front of the hotel as the area is foul with telephone cables and tanks and piping associated with desalination operations.

Three white houses

14°25'

146°05'

146°00

Hotel Manihi
Pebble beach

Bungalows built on pilings over the water

Airstrip

Coral heads at lagoon surface

Coral bank - Rf Teugauatai

Boat basin suitable for small vessels

Pte. Tirara

PAEUA
Dispensary

Talata

Passe Tairapa
14°27.6'S 146°03.7'W

See French Chart 7293

S 14°27.60'
W146°03.70'
Waypoints are approximate and are for reference only

ATOLL AHE (Peacock Island)

This wooded atoll, 13 miles long and 5 miles wide, is about 8 miles west of Manihi. There are less than 200 inhabitants in the village, which is located on the southwestern part of the atoll. Good radar readings can be received for distances up to 19 miles. The water within the lagoon is clear and the diving is magnificent; the area has been the site of pearl farming.

Passe Reianui is the only pass into the lagoon and is located about 2 miles southwest of the northwestern point of the atoll. It is about 450 feet wide at the entrance but is reduced to a navigable width of approximately 85 feet at the inner end, where the bar limits use to vessels having a draft of less than 12 feet. Entry should be made during slack water since strong tidal currents affect the pass. It is important to have someone aloft to identify the deeper water over the bar and spot coral heads. With the sun overhead, conning is made easier by the exceptionally clear water.

Inside the lagoon are many coral heads exposed and awash between which a route can be threaded to an anchorage. South of the pass is a series of beacons set on coral heads which mark a route to the village of Tenukupara. Anchorage can be taken either outside a coral bar in 12 fathoms, sand and coral bottom, or with care, a boat can pass between the heads to Med-moor to the concrete wharf. Many yachts have visited Ahe and the village's hospitality is well known. Unfortunately, the great increase in traffic in recent years has placed a heavy load on the resources of the atoll and as a result, the once exuberant welcome has been toned down. Being mindful of this and leaving as small a footprint as possible will help ensure the viability of this small, friendly village as a stop for future cruisers.

Anchorage can also be found off the motus near the entrance in about 15 fathoms. In addition, there is good, but isolated, anchorage at the partially shoaling northeastern end of the atoll.

EVEN THE MORAY EEL AVOIDS THE POISONOUS LION FISH.

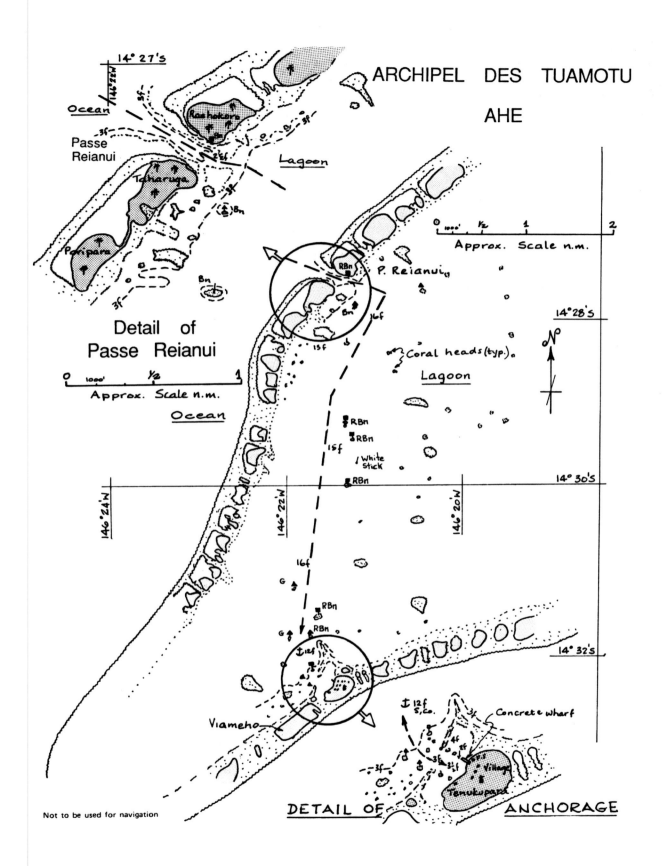

ARCHIPEL DES TUAMOTU

AHE

14° 27'S

Ocean

Passe
Reianui

Toharuga

Ponipara

Detail of
Passe Reianui

0   1000'   ½   1
Approx. Scale n.m.

Ocean

Lagoon

RBn

P. Reianui

0   1000'   ½   1   2
Approx. Scale n.m.

14°28'S

Bn

15f

16f

Coral heads (typ.)

Lagoon

N

146°24'W

146°22'W

146°20'W

RBn
RBn
White
Stick

15f

RBn

14° 30'S

16f

G

RBn
RBn

G

12f

Viameho

12f
S. Co.

Concrete wharf

14° 32'S

Tenukupara

Village

DETAIL OF   ANCHORAGE

Not to be used for navigation

68

ILES DU ROI GEORGES (Takaroa, Takapoto and Tikei)

TAKAROA

This is the northernmost atoll of the group and is often used as a landfall for the Tuamotu. It is easily identified from the north by the large skeletal wreck of the iron sailing ship *County of Roxburgh* rusting on the beach about 4 miles northeast of the pass. At least three other smaller wrecks lie around the island, two on the same beach as the *Roxburgh* and another on the other side of the atoll. Takaroa is lined with palm trees on all sides.

Passe Teavaroa is on the southwest side about 4 miles from the south point of the atoll. Three pairs of beacons, red on the north, black on the south, delineate the pass. It is about 250 feet wide, rimmed with coral on both sides and a strong current can set out from the pass. The village of Teavaroa and the red-roofed Mormon Church on the north side of the pass help to confirm the location. A 200 foot stone wharf projects from the end of Teavaroa motu into and along the pass. Moorage at the wharf requires large fenders and 75 feet of mooring lines or temporary anchorage can be taken off the reef on the north side of the pass, out of the current, in about 10 fathoms.

A large sign has been erected prohibiting entry to the lagoon due to pearl farming. Occasionally cruisers tied to the dock are invited to visit the pearl farms within the lagoon. After obtaining permission, the vessel is guided across the lagoon, taking care to avoid coral patches and the numerous ropes and buoys of the pearl farms. Entry into the lagoon involves a turn to port followed by a sharp turn to starboard to avoid the bar at the inner (lagoon) end of the pass. This should be done only at slack water or on the early ebb for ebb currents in the pass can reach up to 9 knots. The sharp bend and strong currents limit vessels entering to 60 feet in length, 9 foot draft maximum. Most set an anchor in the channel and stern-tie to the wharf, and leave the wharf with assistance from the current. During heavy winds vessels have been pinned to the wharf by the current for as many as three days.

TAKAPOTO

This coral atoll lies about 5 miles southwest of the south end of Takaroa. It is about 10 miles long and well rimmed with islets and palm trees. Although it has no entry pass, there are villages ashore. The population of the island is about 800 and it has an airport and telephone service. At one time it was one of the richest pearl oyster atolls of the archipelago and pearl farming is still a major occupation. The lack of a pass causes a higher level of calcium to accumulate in the lagoon, an advantage for pearl farming.

In calm conditions landing can be made at the wharf off the village of Fakatopatere which is easily identified by the red clock tower of the church. It is situated about 0.5 miles northwest of the south point of the atoll. Two miles to the north is the village of Okukina where a vessel can anchor off the reef and tie up to it. The south point of the reef is marked by a pyramid. The *Aranui* drops off cargo monthly and tourists are ferried to the island for a few hours.

TIKEI

Located about 140 miles ESE of Takapoto is the two-mile long treed, coral island of Tikei. The island has a small village where landing at the small wharf is reputed to be difficult.

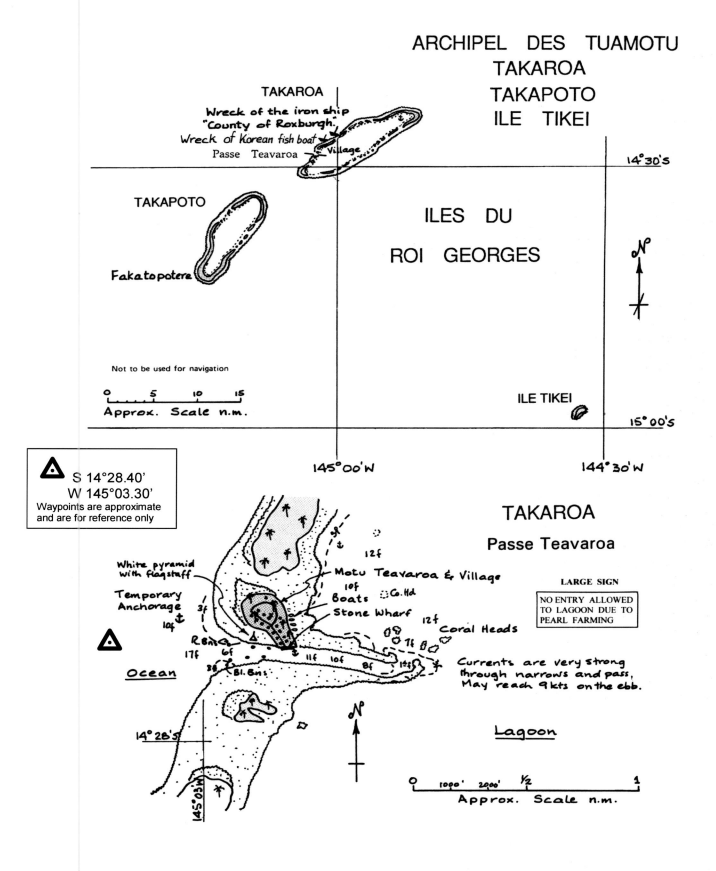

ARCHIPEL DES TUAMOTU
TAKAROA
TAKAPOTO
ILE TIKEI

TAKAROA
Wreck of the iron ship
"County of Roxburgh."
Wreck of Korean fish boat
Passe Teavaroa
Village

14°30'S

TAKAPOTO

Fakatopotere

ILES DU
ROI GEORGES

N

ILE TIKEI

15°00'S

Not to be used for navigation

0   5   10   15
Approx. Scale n.m.

145°00'W   144°30'W

S 14°28.40'
W 145°03.30'
Waypoints are approximate
and are for reference only

TAKAROA

Passe Teavaroa

White pyramid
with flagstaff
Temporary
Anchorage
3f
10f

12f

Motu Teavaroa & Village
10f   Co.Hd
Boats
Stone Wharf
12f
Coral Heads

LARGE SIGN
NO ENTRY ALLOWED
TO LAGOON DUE TO
PEARL FARMING

R.Bn
17f   6f
8f   Bl.Bns
Ocean

11f   10f   8f   14f

Currents are very strong
through narrows and pass,
May reach 9 kts on the ebb.

14°28'S

145°03'W

N

Lagoon

0   1000'   2000'   ½   1
Approx. Scale n.m.

70

MATAHIVA

This is the westernmost atoll of the Tuamotu Archipelago. Located 22 miles WNW of Tikehau, a deep channel separates the two atolls. It measures about 5 miles from east to west and 3 miles from north to south and has a dense covering of coconut palms. At its northwestern end is a small boat passage, marked by a little obelisk on the south side. Southwest of the boat passage is the village of Pahua with a population of about 200. Nearby the village is an airport. Anchorage is not possible off this atoll.

TIKEHAU

This populated, oval atoll is often used as a passage check-point to by-pass the Tuamotu chain. The many palm-covered islands and motus around its perimeter make it clearly visible; a sand bar occupies the center of the lagoon. Sharks abound in the lagoon which is a bird sanctuary. Little Eden is a religious center located on an atoll on the eastern side of the lagoon.

Passe de Tuheiava is at the western end of the atoll. A draft of up to 19 feet can be carried over the bar, but the tidal stream can be very strong and can make entry difficult. Two red and white columnar range markers aligned at 127° mark the pass. The first two red (port) and one green (starboard) buoys are lit with ISO lights as is the lower pylon of the range (ISO white). A few small coral heads are scattered along the sandy bottom of the anchorage indicated on the north side of the inner entrance to the channel. The "village" is a working camp for fishermen and copra workers. When waiting for improved conditions in the pass, anchor on a bank about 450 feet north of the entrance in about 8 to 10 fathoms, provided the weather is suitable. When the tide permits, the pass can be traversed easily, the southwestern side of the channel having slightly deeper water.

The closest anchorage is off the small village on the north side of the entrance in depths of about 3 to 4 fathoms. It is somewhat confined by the patches of coral that limit swinging space but can accommodate 4 or 5 vessels. Buoys mark the channel leading to a second anchorage off the main village of Tuherahera at the southwestern extremity of the atoll. The passage is well marked but careful conning is necessary to avoid coral heads scattered along the way. In calm weather it may be possible to tie alongside the concrete wharf. This friendly village of 400 inhabitants has three stores, a bakery and several small pensions. A well-marked channel branches off the main entrance channel and leads eastward about 3 miles to Motu Aua where the luxurious Pearl Beach Resort is located. Daily air service links the atoll to Papeete.

ILE MAKATEA

This small, 360 feet high coral island is about 44 miles south of Tikehau. The coast is composed mainly of coral cliffs, known as makatea, and rising above sea level. The island was once mined for phosphate, but mining activity has ceased and port facilities are not maintained. There are mooring buoys at the west end of the island, but no protected anchorage. Since landing can be very difficult this island is often bypassed.

ARCHIPEL DES TUAMOTU
TIKEHAU
MATAHIVA

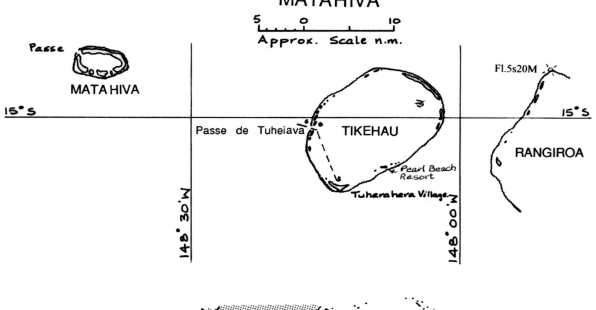

5　0　10
Approx. Scale n.m.

Passe

MATAHIVA

15°S

Fl.5s20M

15°S

148° 30'W

Passe de Tuheiava　TIKEHAU

Pearl Beach
Resort

Tuherahera Village

RANGIROA

148° 00'W

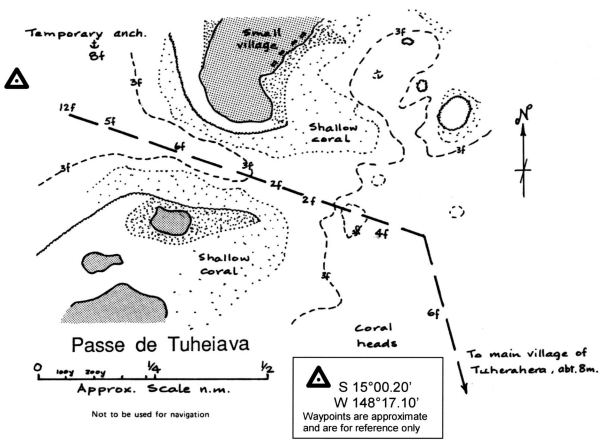

Temporary anch.
⚓
8f

Small
village

3f

12f

5f

3f

6f

3f

2f

2f

Shallow
coral

3f

8f　4f

Shallow
coral

3f

6f

Coral
heads

To main village of
Tuherahera, abt. 8m.

Passe de Tuheiava

0　100y 200y　¼　½
Approx. Scale n.m.

Not to be used for navigation

▲ S 15°00.20'
W 148°17.10'
Waypoints are approximate
and are for reference only

72

RANGIROA

This is an important landfall for vessels making a transit of the Tuamotu and is the largest atoll, having a circumference of about 100 miles. Located about 8 miles east of Tikehau, it is 40 miles long and 17 miles wide at its widest point, making it the second largest atoll in the world. The ring is formed by some 240 motus or islets separated by about 130 channels called "hoas," most being very shallow. The only deep water passes, Passe Avatoru and Passe Tiputa, are on the north side, and a village of the same name is near each pass. Cruisers are expected to check in at the gendarmerie, which is located south of Kia Ora Village Hotel. The total population is almost 2,000. Black pearl farming is a major operation in the lagoon so care must be taken to avoid underwater lines associated with pearl farming.

When a strong outgoing current meets an easterly wind and ocean current at either of the two passes, steep, short seas and swells occur. These seas favor the western side of the passes and sometimes roll through the entrance and into the lagoon and are dangerous to a small vessel attempting to enter. In addition, a slick may sometimes extend beyond the breaking seas, giving a false sense of security. The tidal currents are so strong that eddies and rips can be found on the inside when the flood is in force. It is best to enter at or near slack water or during quiet sea conditions with a favorable current (provided rips are small). If it is necessary to await slack water, an emergency anchorage (difficult to find and usable only in easterly winds), is on a sand patch outside the reef about 1 mile south of the SW end of Rangiroa, in the lee of a small motu.

Passe Avatoru is about 8 miles east of the northwestern point of the atoll. Good landmarks are the large village on the eastern side and the conspicuous spire and red roof of a white church. The control tower and other buildings at the airport are visible from offshore. A small, wooded motu, Motu Kaveo, lies in the center of the channel at the inner end of the pass, dividing it in two. Two white range markers lead into the pass. Swells and rips can be seen on the west side where the bar reduces depths to 10 feet and an A-frame hut is visible among the palms and casuarina trees. The east side is the normal route, passing a red post beacon on a spit. Once past this red beacon, follow the deep blue water around the point to anchorage within the lagoon. Avoid the pale blue water with brown coral ribs along the shore.

Before reaching the anchorage, you will pass a small boat basin that is too shallow for yachts. A concrete wharf, intended for use by trading schooners, is at the lagoon end of the pass. Yachts cannot tie to the wharf for long. When strong trade winds are blowing across the lagoon, fore and aft anchors may be set ahead of the wharf at the side of the pass. However, the anchorages in the lagoon are both safe and attractive. The most popular anchorage is off Kia Ora Village Hotel which affords protection in east to southeast winds. A bank, post office, gas station and several grocery stores are located in the village of Avatoru. An interesting tour of the pearl farm can be arranged at the Hotel and black pearls can be purchased directly from the pearl farm showroom.

The lagoon is safe to cross, as it is deep in most areas and the coral heads are generally visible. Trading vessels and yachts travel from Avatoru across to the anchorage at Tiputa and often leave by that pass. In good conditions you can sail across the lagoon to visit motus on the other side. The Isle of Birds (Ile des Oiseaux), in the middle of the lagoon, is a nesting ground for fairy and sooty terns and frigate birds. At the southwestern corner is the "Blue Lagoon," a small, beautiful atoll within the larger one and often visited by tourists from the hotel.

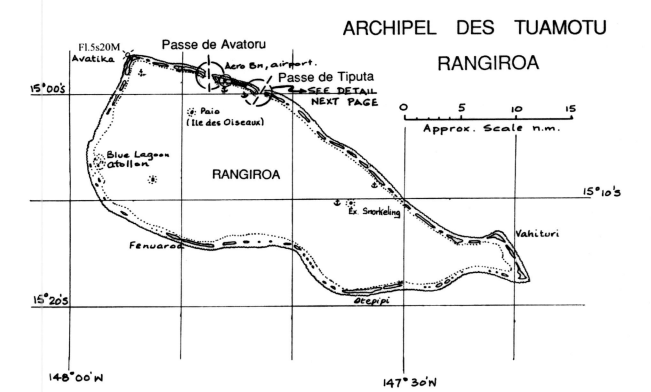

ARCHIPEL DES TUAMOTU
RANGIROA

Fl.5s20M
Avatika

Passe de Avatoru

Aero Bn, airport.

Passe de Tiputa

SEE DETAIL
NEXT PAGE

15°00'S

Paio
(Ile des Oiseaux)

0   5   10   15
Approx. Scale n.m.

Blue Lagoon
atollon

RANGIROA

15°10'S

Ex. Snorkeling

Vahituri

Fenuaroa

15°20'S

Otepipi

148°00'W

147°30'N

Not to be used for navigation

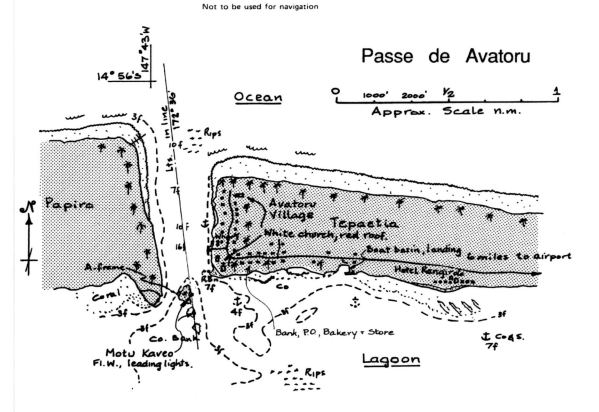

Passe de Avatoru

147°43'W

14°56'S

Ocean

0   1000' 2000'   ½   1
Approx. Scale n.m.

Rips

3f

10f

Lts. in line 172°36'

7f

N

Papiro

10 F

16f

Avatoru
Village

Tepaetia

White church, red roof.

Boat basin, landing 6 miles to airport

A.frame

Hotel Rangi

Co

Dixon

Coral

3f

Co

3f

7f

Bank, P.O., Bakery + Store

I Co 4 s.
7f

3f

Co. Bank

4f

3f

Motu Kaveo
Fl. W., leading lights.

Lagoon

Rips

74

RANGIROA Continued....

Passe Tiputa is a wide, clear pass and is the main entrance to the lagoon. A good landmark on the corner of the reef on the eastern side of the entrance is a tall, white concrete tower that is readily visible. About 0.25 of a mile to the southeast is a resort on the outer coast with a prominent tower. The inner end of the pass is divided into two channels by Motu Fara, a sandy coral cay with a light structure. Behind this is a taller post with a green flashing light which provides a leading line through the pass. Buoys on each side of the channel and one on the southeastern side of Motu Fara define the entrance. The deep blue of safe water is clearly seen as the vessel passes around Motu Fara. A buoy on the east side of the anchorage marks the shoals. Cruisers are welcome to pick up an unoccupied mooring buoy in the anchorage, though a quick dive to check on security is advisable. Before departure, you may tie to the wharf while waiting for slack water in the pass.

At the tip of the land on the western side of the pass is a concrete wharf and behind it is a concrete block warehouse with a green roof. A good anchorage is off the old village in the bight west of the pass, level with the warehouse. Keep clear of any light blue water and brown coral patches. Provisions are available at the magazin, where there is a very friendly operator. The footpath leads inshore about 30 yard to a business that is marked by a red oil drum and sells everything from produce to outboard oil, an amazing variety of fishing gear, pareus and fresh baguettes delivered from the village. For fresh baguettes you have to shop early, 7 a.m. or at 3 p.m. for the second delivery. By prepaying, the order will be held for you. Baguettes are not available on Sundays.

Further to the east, a crude ramp in the coral beach leads to a workshop owned by Jerome. Jerome, the owner, is skilled at making repairs on any brand of outboard motor and spare parts can be delivered from Papeete in two days. The shop also does welding and brazing jobs and in an emergency, arrangements can be made for haul-outs for fiberglass repair jobs. He also sells gasoline.

The Gendarmerie and luxury hotel, the Kia Ora Village, are less than a mile from the entrance. The hotel is a great place for a drink or a superb, but expensive dinner. Nearby are three scuba dive operators and for a modest fee you can join one of their dives in the pass, complete with dive master and chase boat. Bicycles can be rented at the hotel; a pleasant way to visit the village of Avatoru, about 6 miles distant.

An interesting snorkeling experience is to drift snorkel down straight passes such as those found here. The safest time to do this is at incoming tide, near slack water when the water is relatively smooth, and easy pick-ups can be made. Using an inflatable or a dinghy that can be boarded by a swimmer without tipping, snorkelers enter the water about one-third of the way up the pass and drift down with the current. They should keep together and watch that the current does not take them close to coral motus, where collisions are best avoided. Be sure to agree on a location for pick-up.

The eastern side of Passe Tiputa is prettier for drift snorkeling, as it has coral and many fish along the side of Motu Fara. The west side has coral in addition to a deeper, darker zone where sharks can be seen. A variety of coral can be seen, as well as a myriad of tropical fish such as parrot, yellow butterflies, Napoleon and majestic angelfish. The sharks are so accustomed to being fed by crew on the glass-bottom boats from the hotel that they congregate where the boats anchor and wait patiently for the fish handout to begin. In Passe Avatoru, the eastern channel is prettier than the western one for snorkeling.

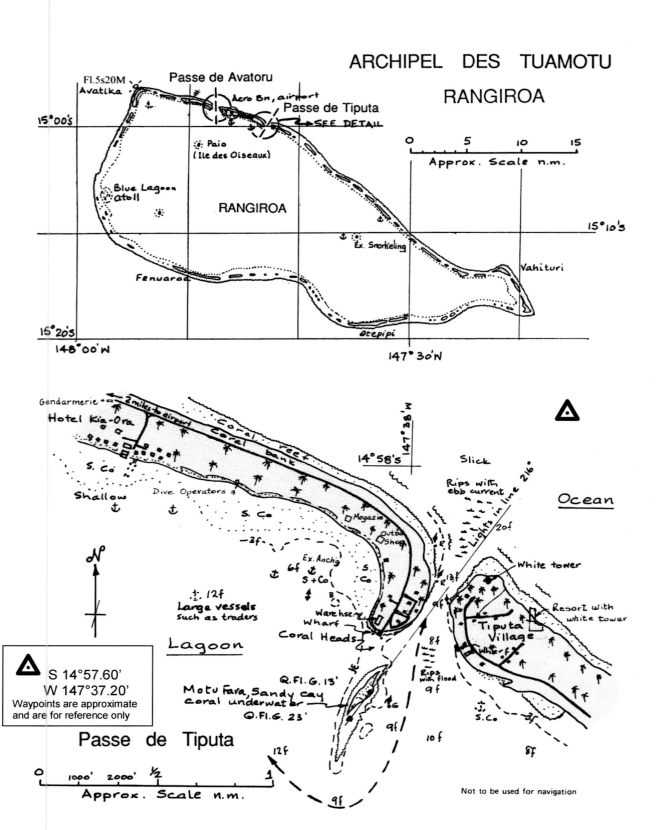

ARCHIPEL DES TUAMOTU

RANGIROA

Fl.5s20M
Avatika

Passe de Avatoru

Aero Bn, airport

Passe de Tiputa

SEE DETAIL

15°00'S

Paio
(Ile des Oiseaux)

Blue Lagoon atoll

RANGIROA

15°10'S

Ex. Snorkeling

Vahituri

Fenuaroa

Otepipi

15°20'S

148°00'W

147°30'W

Approx. Scale n.m.

Gendarmerie

2 miles to airport

Hotel Kia-Ora

Coral reef

Coral bank

147°38'W

14°58's

Slick

Rips with ebb current

Ocean

Lights in line 216°

S. Co

Shallow

Dive Operators

S. Co

Magazin

Outig Shop

20f

White tower

Resort with white tower

-3f-

Ex. Anch'g

6f

S+Co

S. Co

13f

N

9f

12f
Large vessels
such as traders

B

Warehse.

Wharf

Coral Heads

8f

Tiputa Village

white f.

Lagoon

Rips with flood
9f

S 14°57.60'
W 147°37.20'
Waypoints are approximate
and are for reference only

Q.Fl.G. 13'

Motu Fara, Sandy cay
coral underwater

Q.Fl.G. 23'

8f

S. Co

3f

1c

9f

8f

Passe de Tiputa

12f

10f

0   1000' 2000' ½   1

Approx. Scale n.m.

9f

Not to be used for navigation

76

GROUPE DES ILES PALLISER

This group is made up of three atolls, Arutua, Kaukura, and Apataki. They are east and southeast of Rangiroa and southwest of the northernmost islands of Manihi, Ahe, Takaroa, and Takapoto.

ARUTUA

Arutua is located about 20 miles east of the southern part of Rangiroa. This wide channel forms one of the preferred routes for passage through the Tuamotu, especially if the vessel has made a landfall on Takaroa and is heading for Tahiti. An airport is northeast of the village.

When approached from the northeast, enroute from the Marquesas, the palm-treed islets along the north and east sides help to make the atoll visible. But if your approach is from the south, the atoll is extremely dangerous since its southern sides are mostly bare, with the reef awash. Consequently, the reef is hidden by waves and spray until critically near and thus passage in the vicinity is particularly hazardous at night.

Passe Porofai, the only pass into the lagoon, is near the south end of the eastern side. The village of Rautini is on the northern side of the pass and can be recognized from offshore by its flagstaff. This is a difficult pass to traverse and is only used by small vessels. The inner end of the pass is partially blocked by coral heads, forming three channels. Entry may be made by using either the center or southern channel. Anchorage may be taken off the village of Rautini within the pass as shown on the sketch. Entry to the lagoon is possible, but should be done only at slack water when the shallow bar is quiet and a route can be threaded between the coral heads.

KAUKURA

South of Arutua is a 25 mile long, oval atoll, Kaukura. Similar to Arutua, it has many islets on the northern and eastern sides and few on the southern side, making it dangerous to approach from this direction. However, during a hurricane many years ago, large coral blocks, some as much as 30 feet high, were thrown onto the reef and they help to give it some visibility.

A pass into the lagoon is near the middle of the northern side near Motu Ura, which is recognizable by large clumps of palm trees. Tidal streams in the pass are very strong, setting eastward on the flood and westward on the ebb. The lagoon is shallow and filled with coral heads and shoals.

The village of Raitahiti is on the largest islet at the northwestern end of the atoll, making it the only permanently inhabited atoll in the area. The shallow boat passage north of the village near Motu Panao should not be transited. An airport is located on the northwestern part of the atoll.

ILE NIAU (Located in the general vicinity, but not one of the Groupe des Iles Palliser)

Located about 17 miles southwest of Toau, this well wooded atoll has a village on the northeast side that is conspicuous from seaward. Strong currents in the vicinity set both east and west at various times.

15°00'S   15°00S

ARUTUA, APATAKI, KAUKURA, & ILE NIAU

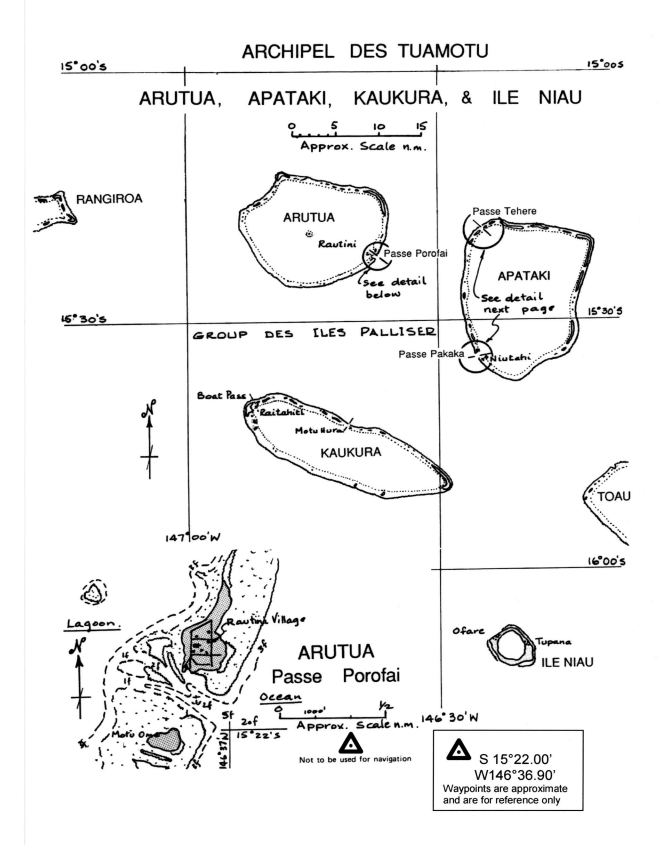

0   5   10   15
Approx. Scale n.m.

RANGIROA

ARUTUA

Rautini

Passe Tehere

Passe Porofai

See detail below

APATAKI

See detail next page   15°30'S

15°30'S

GROUP DES ILES PALLISER

Passe Pakaka   *Niutahi*

Boat Pass

Raitahiti

Motu Hura

KAUKURA

TOAU

147°00'W

16°00'S

Lagoon.

Rautini Village

ARUTUA
Passe Porofai

Ofare   *Tupana*
ILE NIAU

Motu Oma

Ocean

0   1000'   ½
Approx. Scale n.m.   146°30'W

5f   2of
15°22'S

Not to be used for navigation

S 15°22.00'
W146°36.90'
Waypoints are approximate
and are for reference only

APATAKI

This square-shaped atoll lies 10 miles east of Arutua and is 15 miles northwest of Toau. It is fairly well rimmed with wooded motus except for the southern side where the barrier reef is submerged. Strong currents on the southern side make travel along this coast dangerous. On the western side are two passes which give access to the lagoon. **WARNING**: Fish poisoning has been known to occur here.

Passe Haniuru (Passe Pakaka) is the southernmost pass, about 5 miles north of the southern end of the atoll. Two pilings (one with a light that usually doesn't work) mark the entrance to the small anchorage that is usually occupied with numerous pangas. The 2.5 to 3 knot current changes direction in accord with high/low water in Ahe. Standing waves develop when SE winds oppose a flooding current. A range leading through the pass consists of two white pylons with the inner (higher) one situated on a coral reef west of Banc Toavete. The bearing of the two red flashing lights in line is 70.5°T. Numerous local boats occupy the niche in the western side of the reef close to the village. Their permanent moorings prevent its use as a vessel anchorage as swinging room has been eliminated.

The wharf is in disrepair so use numerous fenders and be prepared to move when the supply ship arrives. Vessels may tie to the wharf but the village's diesel generator building on the main wharf makes an unpleasant noise 24 hours a day, every day. The anchorage between the village and Banc Teanoa is filled with buoys associated with pearl oyster farming and anchoring is discouraged. The best anchorage in prevailing conditions (E to SE 15 – 20 knot winds) is 4 miles ESE of the village, close to Motu Rua Vahine where protection is obtained by the motu and reef. The bakery (boulangerie) is open in the afternoon every other day.

Entrance to the lagoon should be made only at slack water and in sunny conditions for good visibility to identify coral heads. Only limited provisions can be obtained at the village of Niutahi. Beyond Ile Niutahi, the pass is divided by a reef and a bank forming three channels. When proceeding into the lagoon, steer down the center of the pass and take the middle channel. There are two current streams in the pass and they both change direction with the tide. The north side sets with the tide at about 4 knots, while the south side is a counter-current. The current increases in intensity to 5 or 6 knots in the narrow channels at the inner end of the pass. A few beacons mark some coral heads but don't expect them all to be marked.

Passe Tehere is at the northwestern tip of the atoll. When entering, line up the pass from at least 0.5 mile offshore to avoid the shoals located on both sides of the outer entrance. Shoals continue through the pass, reducing its width to about 400 feet. The pass is straight, short, fairly deep and clear. Currents of up to 4 knots run out of the pass. A black and white beacon marks a coral reef, covered 2 feet located 1.5 miles ENE of the pass. Once inside the lagoon, anchorage can be found off the village of Rotoava following the route shown. It provides protection from north to easterly winds but is exposed to south/southeasterly winds.

ARCHIPEL DES TUAMOTU
APATAKI

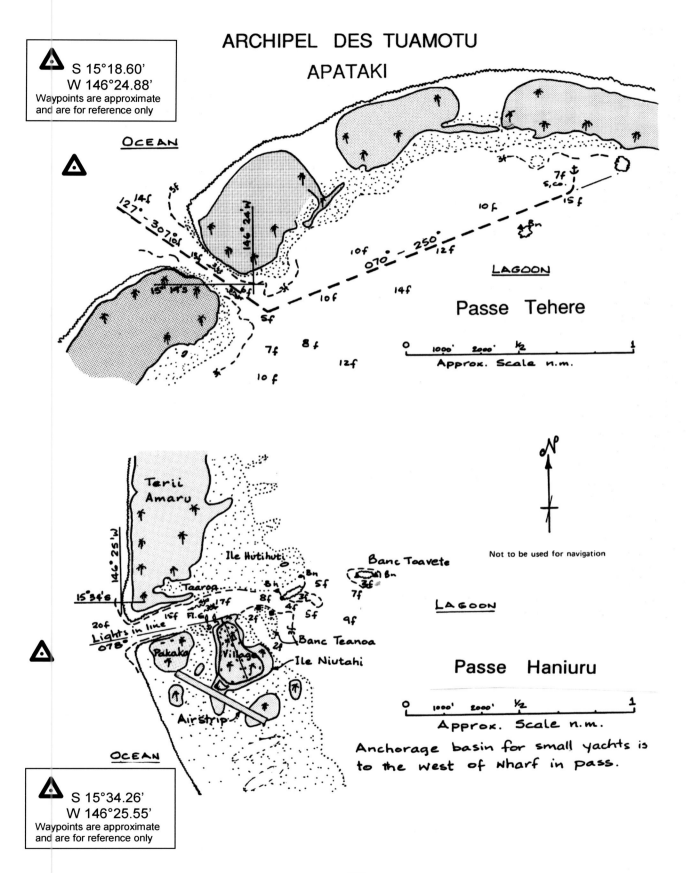

S 15°18.60'
W 146°24.88'
Waypoints are approximate
and are for reference only

Ocean

Ocean

Lagoon

Lagoon

Passe Tehere

Passe Haniuru

Approx. Scale n.m.

Approx. Scale n.m.

Terii Amaru

Ile Hutihuti

Banc Toavete

Taaroa

Lights in line
078°

Pakaka

Village

Banc Teanoa

Ile Niutahi

Airstrip

Anchorage basin for small yachts is
to the west of wharf in pass.

S 15°34.26'
W 146°25.55'
Waypoints are approximate
and are for reference only

ARATIKA

A roughly triangular atoll, Aratika lies about 22 miles northeast of Toau on the northwestern side of Chenal de Fakarava. The north side is virtually one long island, low but well covered with palm trees. Smaller islets lie along the sides, but the entire southwestern side is bare and dangerous and the reefs are submerged. Many coral heads, visible and awash, are scattered throughout the lagoon. About 60 inhabitants live on the atoll. An airstrip located near the southern end of the atoll provides a means of travel for guests from Tahiti, who can find accommodation in the small native hotel. **WARNING**: Fish poisoning has been known to occur here.

Both passes into the lagoon are challenging, even for an experienced cruiser, and may be considered hazardous for a first-time sailor to the Tuamotus. Experience in other easier passes such as those at Manihi and Ahe give confidence and an understanding that prepares a skipper for the more demanding passes such as these. In addition, a less definitive means of identification makes passage via Chenal de Fakarava not as suitable as the route past Rangiroa when traversing the Tuamotus.

Passe Tamaketa is about 3 miles SSW of Pointe Turepuku, the northern extremity of the atoll. The pass is between two small islets on the reef, though the northern side is more reef than land. The opening is narrow, broadening out at the inner end where an inner reef splits the pass into two passages. The northern passage is the better one, but be aware a bar of coral reduces depths to a scant 7 feet. The other passage however is even shallower. Not only may very strong currents be encountered in the pass but there are also several large coral heads in the lagoon just within the entrance.

Passe Fainukea is about 1 mile southwest of the northeastern corner of the atoll. It is harder to spot than Passe Tamaketa since it is bordered by reefs on both sides and only treeless islands are near the pass. On the northern side is a partially exposed portion of the coral reef extending southwest from the island and continuing underwater. It is visible in the sunlight and care should be taken to identify it. Currents in the pass run at 5 to 6 knots and easterly winds create dangerous rollers, making it impassable. The pass has a least depth of 16 feet but as it curves slightly and is bordered by underwater coral reefs, it should be traversed only in good conning conditions, preferably with the aid of a local guide.

Anchorage may be taken in an area roughly south of the thatched-roof hotel in the village of Paparara, which is visible on the inside shore of the northern island. A spot clear of coral heads can be found that is large enough to allow swinging room.

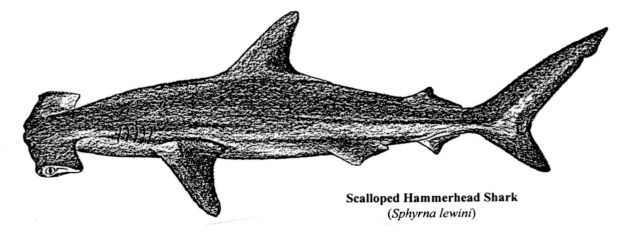

Scalloped Hammerhead Shark
(*Sphyrna lewini*)

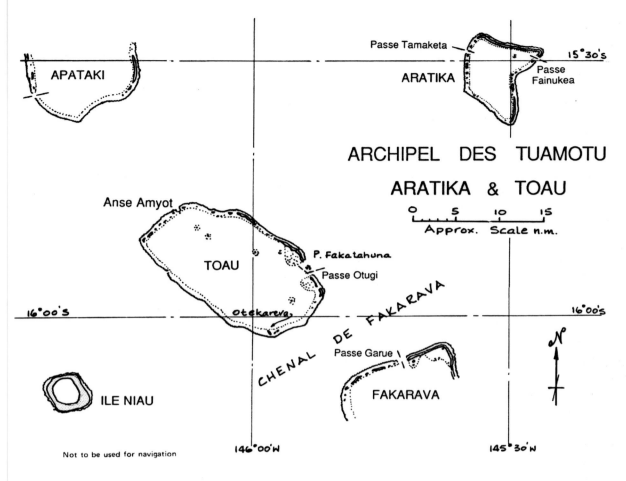

APATAKI

Passe Tamaketa

ARATIKA

Passe Fainukea

15°30'S

ARCHIPEL DES TUAMOTU

ARATIKA & TOAU

Anse Amyot

TOAU

P. Fakatahuna

Passe Otugi

Otekareva

16°00'S

0   5   10   15
Approx. Scale n.m.

CHENAL DE FAKARAVA

Passe Garue

FAKARAVA

ILE NIAU

Not to be used for navigation

146°00'W

145°30'W

16°00'S

N

ARATIKA
Passes Tamaketa & Fainukea

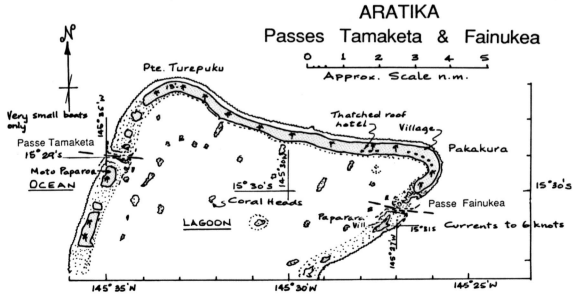

0   1   2   3   4   5
Approx. Scale n.m.

N

Pte. Turepuku

Thatched roof hotel

Village

Pakakura

Very small boats only

Passe Tamaketa

15°29'S

145°36'W

Moto Paparoa

OCEAN

15°30'S

145°30'W

15°30'S

Coral Heads

LAGOON

Paparara Vill.

Passe Fainukea

15°31S

Currents to 6 knots

145°27'W

15°30'S

145°35'W

145°30'W

145°25'W

82

TOAU

This rectangular atoll lies between Apataki (15 miles to the NW) and Fakarava (8 miles to the SE). The atoll has many wooded islands along the NW and NE sides and dangerous submerged reefs are on the southern sides. Two passes are close together on the NE side and a small niche in the reef that can be used as an anchorage is on the northwest side. The village of Maragai no longer exists. A large, permanent work camp belonging to the Wang Pearl Imperium of Tahiti conducts pearl farming and landing ashore by cruisers is discouraged. A large workforce from China mans the pearl farm though a few villagers from Anse Amyot also work here. Pearls are not sold from the camp. **WARNING:** Fish poisoning has been reported in the area.

Passe Otugi is about 3.5 miles NNW of the eastern tip of the atoll. The pass has a lighted range, white pylons flashing red, bearing 240°T. The entrance is wide and clear of danger with depths of at least 4 fathoms. ISO red range lights in line (242.8°T) are on a coral head in the lagoon about 2 miles southwest of the pass; characteristics are: 4s 10m 6M and 4s 6m 6M. Vessels should keep a little south of the range line to avoid the strongest part of an out-going current, which at times are so strong eddies have been felt up to 2 miles outside the pass.

Two anchorages are within the lagoon. The most convenient is about 0.5 mile south of the inner end of the pass in about 7 fathoms. This anchorage is some distance from the large area of coral heads and submerged coral reef within the lagoon. A masonry cistern, partially hidden by trees, is east of the anchorage. Alternatively, a route to the northwest for anchorage off the seasonally occupied settlement of Maragai can be taken through an area of coral heads by following the buoyed channel.

Passe Fakatahuna is less than a mile northwest of Passe Otugi and is separated from it by an island and section of reef. It is narrower than Passe Otugi and effects of the current are felt to a greater degree. Small boats with local knowledge use this pass. A quick flashing light is on the southern tip of an exposed coral bank about 0.5 miles west of the entrance and several other flashing green and red lights mark the route to an anchorage used by local vessels. See French Chart 7456 for details.

Anse Amyot is about 3 miles from the northern extremity of Toau, on the northwestern side. It is a slot in the reef which appears to be a pass, but which is really a cul-de-sac blocked by a coral bank across the inner side. Reefs and banks on each side reduce the entrance to less than 200 feet. Vessels with drafts up to 15 feet can anchor here. Range lights in line with100.8°T have been established on the coral bank at the inner end of Anse Amyot off the southern tip of Motu Matarina. Characteristics of the inner (eastern) range light are Fl.G.4s 8m 5M, while the outer (western) range light shows Fl.G 4s 6m 5M. A red marker on the northern side of the basin lies about 140 yards east of the northern end of the coral bank at the entrance to the pass. About 220 yards south of the red marker, a green marker indicates the northern edge of the shoal area on the southwestern side of clear water.

A shallow bank within the cove and extensions from the southwestern side reduce the useable part of the cove to anchorage in the northern part. Though the current is very strong, a yacht can lie here comfortably, as the spot is well sheltered from wind and swell. Safe anchorage during SE winds can be taken in the SE corner at 15°56.7S, 145°52.7W. Local families have been known to prepare meals for cruisers given a day's notice. Patrons of the restaurant may moor to the buoys.

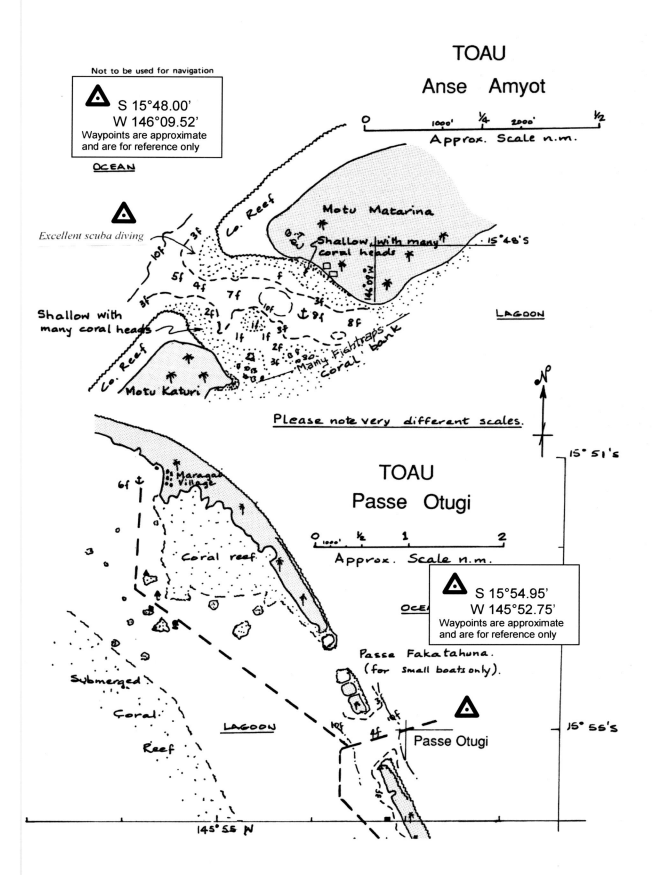

S 15°48.00'
W 146°09.52'
Waypoints are approximate
and are for reference only

OCEAN

TOAU
Anse Amyot

0   1000'   ¼   2000   ½
Approx. Scale n.m.

Lo. Reef

Motu Matarina

Shallow with many
coral heads

15°48'S

146°09'W

Excellent scuba diving

10f

3f

5f   4f

7f

3f

3f

2f

10f

⚓ 9f   8f

LAGOON

Shallow with
many coral heads

Lo. Reef

1f   1f   3f

2f

3f   030

Many Fishtraps
Coral bank

Motu Katuri

Please note very different scales.

N

TOAU
Passe Otugi

0 1000'   ½   1   2
Approx. Scale n.m.

15°51'S

Maragau Village

6f

Coral reef

OCEAN

Passe Fakatahuna.
(for small boats only).

S 15°54.95'
W 145°52.75'
Waypoints are approximate
and are for reference only

Submerged

Coral

Reef

LAGOON

10f

1f

Passe Otugi

15°55'S

145°55 N

84

FAKARAVA

This is the second largest Tuamotu atoll and is a 32-mile long by 15-mile wide rectangular shape lying roughly NW - SE. Fakarava is located 8 miles southeast of Toau and 10 miles northwest of Faaite. Chenal de Fakarava, which separates Fakarava from Toau, is a passage through the archipelago that is the most direct route from the Panama Canal to Tahiti. Currents are irregular and strong in the channel, usually setting westward.

Three sides of the atoll: northern, northeastern, and southeastern, have many islands and palm trees, particularly on the northeastern side. The southwestern side is low-lying and the few small islets along it are a mile or so in from the edge of the reef give little warning of its presence. The tower in the northeastern part of the atoll, hidden by coconut palms from some directions, is 1.5 miles WNW of the village of Rotoava. Prominent landmarks in the town include a red-roofed residence and two churches. Three passes lead into the lagoon, the most important being Passe Garue, a wide pass on the northern side. The atoll is visible by radar from a distance of about 15 miles. **WARNING**: Fish poisoning has been known to occur on this atoll.

Passe Garue (Garuae/Ngarue) A green flashing light is on the islet on the south side of the channel. The channel often appears forbidding because the outgoing stream, when strong, creates breakers across the entire entrance. Flood currents average 3 knots and ebb, 6 knots. Small vessels must wait for slack water or enter with a favorable flow. The width of the pass allows vessels with speeds of more than 8 knots to enter at any time.

After clearing the entrance, give a safe berth to Pufana Reef that lies about 0.75 of a mile east of the inner end of the pass. Its southern extremity is indicated by a red marker, which is also a navigational aid for the waterway leading 40 miles south to Passe Tumakohua and described on the following page. After clearing this reef, two other drying coral reefs (Togamaitu-i-tai and Togamaitu-i-uta) marked by beacons, are about 2.5 miles along the route shown on the sketch. When approaching the anchorage they should be left to starboard and the vessel aimed for the flagstaff at the village. Anchorage is generally taken off the pier, with the church bearing 72°T, in about 6 to 10 fathoms, sand and coral. Although it is still deep closer in, the bottom has more coral and does not provide comparable holding. The anchorage is well sheltered except from southerly winds that may raise a sea across this large lagoon.

Safe anchorage during southeast winds can be found in the southeast corner at 16°23.2S, 145°22.25W. Lighted beacons mark channels within the lagoon: Green triangular markers denote reef-side dangers; red square markers denote lagoon-side hazards. Caution is necessary as numerous pearl floats and unmarked coral heads are near the channel

A cement dock at the village can be used as a landing. This is the largest village on Fakarava and has a store, post office, some tourist bungalows and a very old cemetery. The store has a variety of packaged food and miscellaneous items. There is an airport, with weekly flights to Papeete.

Another anchorage is southwest of the entrance at Passe Garue. It is on the lagoon side of Point Teheko (the northwestern extremity of the atoll), off a small island with a hut and palm trees. To reach this anchorage, good light and conning are needed to avoid shoals and to find the clear area that is located within a small group of reefs. This anchorage is lovely, though more exposed to wind and surge.

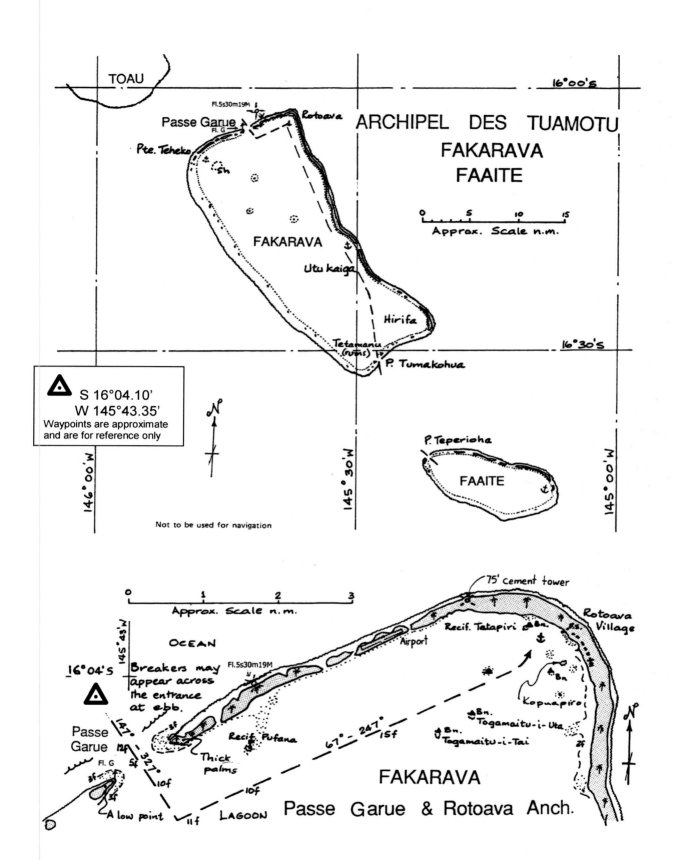

TOAU

FI.5s30m19M

Passe Garue
FI. G

Rotoava

ARCHIPEL DES TUAMOTU
FAKARAVA
FAAITE

Pte. Teheko

Sn

0   5   10   15
Approx. Scale n.m.

FAKARAVA

Utu kaiga

Hirifa

Tetamanu
(ruins)

P. Tumakohua

16°00'S

16°30'S

S 16°04.10'
W 145°43.35'
Waypoints are approximate
and are for reference only

N

146° 00' W

145° 30'W

P. Teperioha

FAAITE

145° 00' W

Not to be used for navigation

75' cement tower

0   1   2   3
Approx. Scale n.m.

OCEAN

FI.5s30m19M

Airport

Recif. Tatapiri

Rotoava
Village

145° 43' W

16°04'S

Breakers may
appear across
the entrance
at ebb.

Kopuapiro

Bn.

Passe
Garue

147°
327°
FI. G

3f

5f
10f

3f

Recif. Pufana

67° - 247°

15f

Bn.
Togamaitu-i-Uta

Bn.
Togamaitu-i-Tai

N

2f

Thick
palms

A low point

10f

11f

LAGOON

FAKARAVA

Passe Garue & Rotoava Anch.

86

FAKARAVA Continued...

Passe Tumakohua (South Pass) is about 2 miles northeast of the southern end of Fakarava. The entrance is marked by a lighted range (red and white pylons) flashing red (155°T). It is advisable to enter at or near slack water, which lasts 30 to 45 minutes. Vessels having drafts of up to 12 feet can be carried through the entrance. Two green markers indicate the western edge of Recif Tohea and a black/yellow marker is on the northwest side of this reef. This marker also indicates a change of fairway direction for vessels following the channel across the lagoon from Passe Garue.

The inner end of the pass is divided into two channels by a dark coral patch. The eastern channel is narrow, but feasible for shallow draft vessels. The western channel is broader, and though it appears blocked by dark coral which makes it appear shallow, it is deep enough for large vessels to use. Two families live in the village of Tetamanu, which is now mostly in ruins. Anchorage may be taken close to the shore in 6 to 8 fathoms, sand and coral bottom. Approach the anchorage by passing north of the two banks which are almost awash. Another anchorage is north of Utu kaiga as shown, near the gap in the trees almost midway up the eastern side of the atoll.

A marked channel crosses the lagoon from Passe Garue to Passe Tumakohua. The red marker on Pufana Reef is also the first left-hand marker for the channel crossing the lagoon from north to south. Within the lagoon, keep green markers to starboard until reaching the black and yellow marker of Recif Tohea. Keep green to port when leaving the lagoon at Passe Tumakohua.

FAAITE

Lying about 10 miles southeast of Fakarava, this atoll is only thinly covered with palms on its northern side. It is bare and low on its southern side, making it a dangerous atoll to approach, especially at night. A prominent wreck of a large fishing vessel lies on the outer reef at 16°48.85'S, 145°09.74'W and gives a good radar echo from 14 miles distant.

Passe Teperioha, the only pass on the atoll, is about 0.5 mile north of the western end of the atoll. The approach is indicated by a range (119°T) on red and white pylons flashing red. Two red/green markers show the entrance to the lagoon. A series of small islets lie on each side of the entrance, with the village of Hitiamaa on the south side. The town meeting hall, the largest building in the village, is conspicuous from off the entrance.

The deep section of the entrance to the pass is about 400 feet wide with a depth of about 15 feet. At its inner end it is divided into two by a coral patch which forms a cul-de-sac on the northeastern side of the opening and a channel on the south, which has a depth of about 12 feet. Since the southern channel is only 45 feet wide, the ebb current reaches velocities of 6 knots or more. The southern channel leads past the village wharf into the lagoon. Vessels can tie to the 60 foot wharf, which has depths to 9 feet alongside, but the strong current and height of the wharf can make this difficult.

The best anchorage is found by threading a route through a few coral heads to the eastern end of the lagoon, where there is an area that is quite comfortable when winds are from north to SSE. A good spot is reported to be at 16°44.9'S, 145°07.3'W. However, access to the village is difficult because of the current. A passable anchorage can be found about 0.25 miles south of the village in about 5 fathoms, sand and coral. This anchorage is not protected from prevailing winds, although it is close to the village.

ARCHIPEL DES TUAMOTU

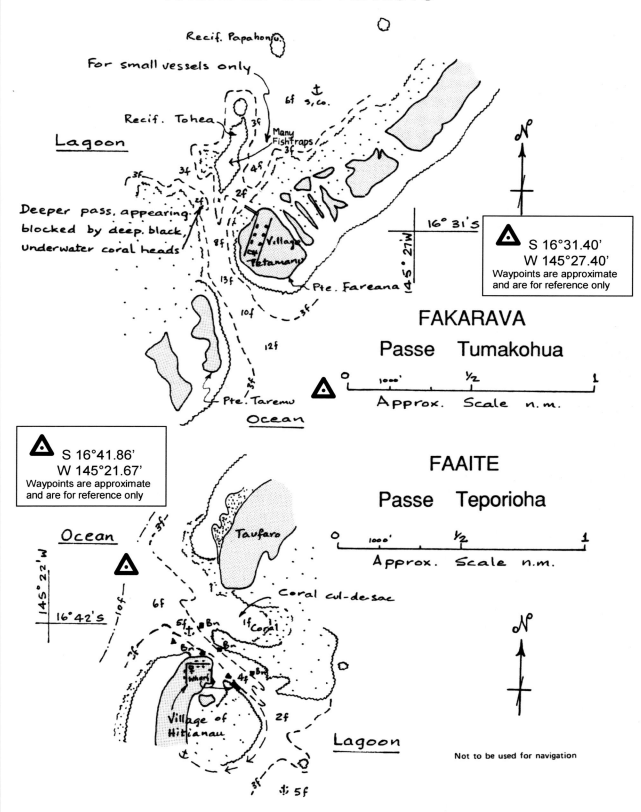

Recif. Papahonu

For small vessels only

Recif. Tohea

Lagoon

6f 3, co.

3f

Many Fishtraps 3f

3f 3f

4f

2f

Deeper pass. appearing blocked by deep. black underwater coral heads

2f

1f

8f

Village Tetamanu

13f

Pte. Fareana

10f

3f

12f

3f

Pte. Taremu

Ocean

16° 31'S

145° 27'W

S 16°31.40'
W 145°27.40'
Waypoints are approximate
and are for reference only

FAKARAVA

Passe Tumakohua

0   1000'   ½   1

Approx. Scale n.m.

S 16°41.86'
W 145°21.67'
Waypoints are approximate
and are for reference only

FAAITE

Passe Teporioha

0   1000'   ½   1

Approx. Scale n.m.

Ocean

3f

Taufaro

Coral cul-de-sac

145° 22' W

16° 42'S

10f

6f

5f

5f Bn

1f Coral

Bn

Bn

Wharf

4f Bn

2f

Village of Hitianau

Lagoon

Not to be used for navigation

3f

5f

88

KAUEHI (Vincennes Island)

This green, low atoll is 18 miles southeast of Aratika and 24 miles northeast of Fakarava. It is well wooded except on the southwestern side, which is bare and dangerous to approach. A prominent tower on the northern extremity of the atoll is a good landmark and the eastern edge is conspicuous.

Passe Arikitamiro is a deep, clear channel on the southwestern side of the atoll. Though the pass is about 500 yards wide, the channel is about 300 yards across. A flashing red light indicates the port side of the pass. Entry should be made slightly south of the centerline. A course of 24°T leading to the village is free of coral heads and the three reefs on either side are marked by green and red flashing markers. The current is slack 1.5 hours after low water in Tahanea, the closest tidal reference point.

Coral heads are scattered in the lagoon, necessitating careful conning when looking for a spot to anchor. The small village of <u>Tearavero</u> lies across the lagoon on the northeastern side. Anchorage in sand and coral may be taken about 0.5 miles southwest of the wharf off the village. As swinging space may be restricted it may be necessary to set two anchors. By weaving your way between coral heads north of the village you can find another spot to anchor in 4 – 5 fathoms, sand and coral. A small infirmary is in the village but no post office.

Shelter from south to southwest winds may be taken in the bay behind the town. It requires a wide swing to enter. The water shoals quickly inside the two fathom line.

RARAKA

This circular atoll is about 11 miles southeast of Kauehi and 23 miles northwest of Katiu. The lagoon is surrounded by islands except on the southern side which is low, bare, and dangerous.

Passe Manureva provides a tricky entrance to the lagoon and can only be entered by small vessels using caution. Outgoing currents reach 6.5 knots. An islet and coral patch at the inner side of the entrance combined with strong currents demand careful seamanship. A buoyed channel marks the route to anchorage off the village of <u>Motutapu</u>. Landing can be made by passing through a gap in the reef, in front of the lodge with a mast.

TAIARO (King's Island)

This high, circular atoll, only 3 miles in diameter, lies slightly outside the main group and is about 24 miles northeast of Raraka. The lagoon is completely encircled by an island that is well covered with palm trees. The island is visible on radar from a distance of 15 miles.

There is no entry to the lagoon, but landing can be accomplished off a group of huts on the western side. Here, small vessels can make fast to the reef when the winds are east to southeasterly. Another landing is near the village on the southeastern corner, but this area is affected by the swell.

W. A. Robinson of *Svaap* and *Varua* fame leased the island and it was his home during his efforts to investigate elephantiasis, which was once prevalent in the South Pacific. His book, *Deep Water and Shoal* remains a classic in the annals of early circumnavigation on a small yacht.

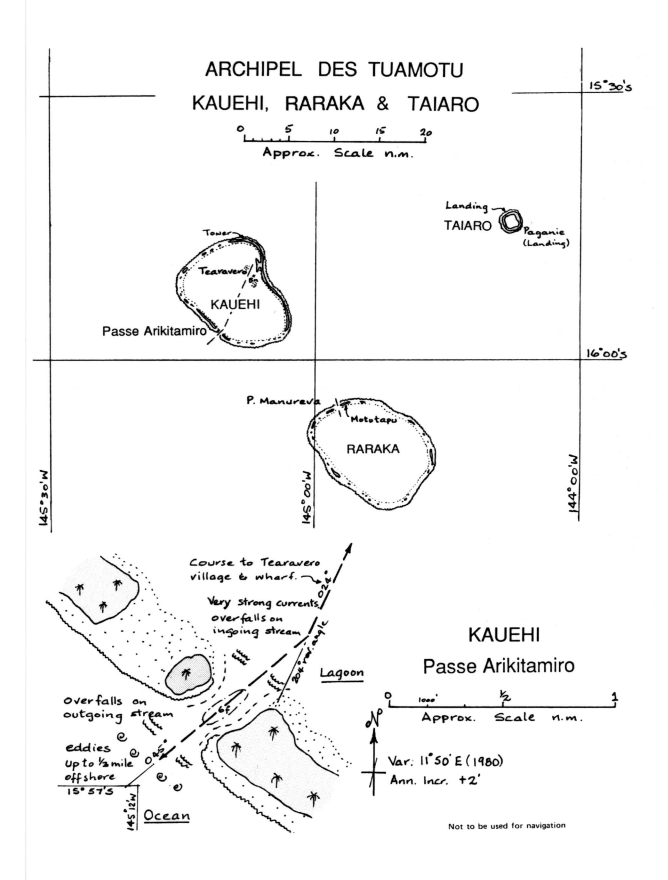

ARCHIPEL DES TUAMOTU
KAUEHI, RARAKA & TAIARO

0   5   10   15   20
Approx. Scale n.m.

15°30's

Landing
TAIARO
Paganie
(Landing)

Tower
Tearavero
KAUEHI
Passe Arikitamiro

16°00's

P. Manureva
Mototapu
RARAKA

145°30'W

145°00'W

144°00'W

Course to Tearavero
village & wharf.

Very strong currents,
overfalls on
ingoing stream

Lagoon

Overfalls on
outgoing stream

eddies
Up to ½ mile
offshore

15°57'S

145°12'W

Ocean

KAUEHI
Passe Arikitamiro

0   1000'   ½   1
Approx. Scale n.m.

N

Var: 11°50' E (1980)
Ann. Incr. +2'

Not to be used for navigation

90

ANAA (Chain Island)

This atoll is the southern outpost of the northern group of Tuamotu atolls and is about 35 miles SSW of Faaite. The 19-mile long atoll is partially rimmed by islands within the encircling reef. About 425 people reside in the five villages located here. The atoll is linked to Papeete through weekly air service. Several guesthouses have accommodations for tourists. Fishing and copra production provide a livelihood for the inhabitants.

There is no pass into the lagoon but anchorage may be taken on the northeastern side of the island, abreast of the village of <u>Tukuhora.</u> The village cannot be seen from offshore, but two sheds and a road lead to it. A current sets toward the reef, making it advisable to have an anchor watch aboard. Poultry, fish and lobster are sometimes available in the village. A radio station and airstrip are located on the island and it is a regular stop for inter-island freighters from Papeete.

The island has several unique claims to fame. In 1906 a tidal wave devastated the atoll, leaving 100 people dead. Cyclones have devastated the villages on numerous occasions, and this may have been the basis for Nordoff and Hall's book, *Hurricane.* The men of the island have a well-known and highly respected reputation as sailors and make excellent crew when they can be persuaded to sign on with a vessel. A unique feature of Anaa is that it creates a curious mirage effect whereby the atoll projects on the clouds a beautiful greenish reflection, often visible from a great distance.

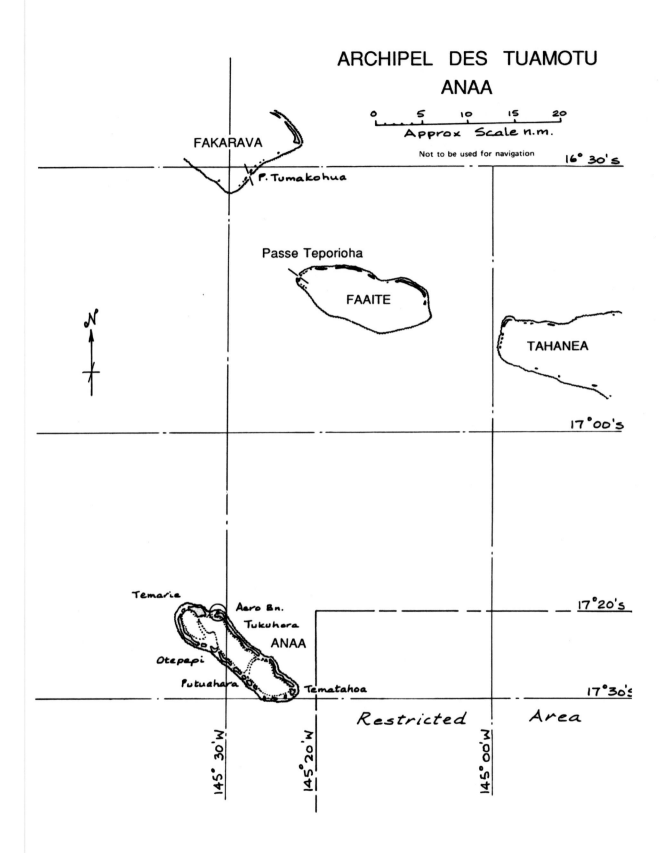

ARCHIPEL DES TUAMOTU
ANAA

0   5   10   15   20
Approx Scale n.m.

Not to be used for navigation

16° 30's

FAKARAVA

P. Tumakohua

Passe Teporioha

FAAITE

TAHANEA

N

17° 00's

Temaria

Aero Bn.

Tukuhora

ANAA

17°20's

Otepapi

Putuahara

Tematahoa

17°30's

Restricted   Area

145° 30'W

145° 20'W

145° 00'W

92

KATIU (Saken Island) The atolls forming a group that includes Katiu are not well known since they lie far from the routes normally taken through the archipelago. Other atolls, Makemo and Hao, are east of this group near an old sailing ship route through the Tuamotus.

Katiu is a low atoll, covered with brushwood, located about 23 miles ESE of Raraka and 16 miles west of Makemo. Similar to most atolls, the northern sides are well rimmed with islets and palm trees, while the southern sides are poorly defined and consequently are dangerous to approach. There are about 250 inhabitants on the atoll, many of which are occupied with pearl farms.

Passe Pakata is on the northeastern side, about 4 miles southeast of the northern extremity. It is identifiable by the clear gap between the palm trees, and as the distance closes, by the flagstaff at the village of <u>Hitianau,</u> on the northwestern side of the entrance. Two red spar beacons mark the edge of the reef on the eastern side of the entrance. This is a narrow pass which demands careful and precise attention to the vessel's position. Two black and white striped range markers/beacons are within the lagoon, south of the flagstaff. Best depths in the entrance are found by keeping these beacons in line, bearing 193°T. Because of the difficulty of entering the lagoon, most vessels anchor within the pass, off the wharf in about 7 fathoms, near the western side. Currents through the pass can attain a velocity of 6 knots.

Coral reefs and underwater heads block much of the inner part of the pass except for a narrow navigable passage that follows a southeasterly direction. This narrow route is between the coral bank on the inner side of the main reef and a small, isolated reef marked by a white spar beacon. After traversing the 100-foot wide opening, vessels entering the lagoon must then avoid the inner banks of coral heads. Pass clear of the 3 fathom line before turning west toward an anchorage which is southwest of the village of Hitianau

Passe Okarare is near the westernmost extremity of the atoll. It is used only by small local vessels.

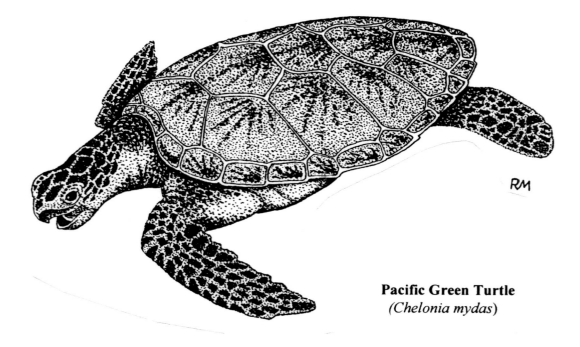

Pacific Green Turtle
(Chelonia mydas)

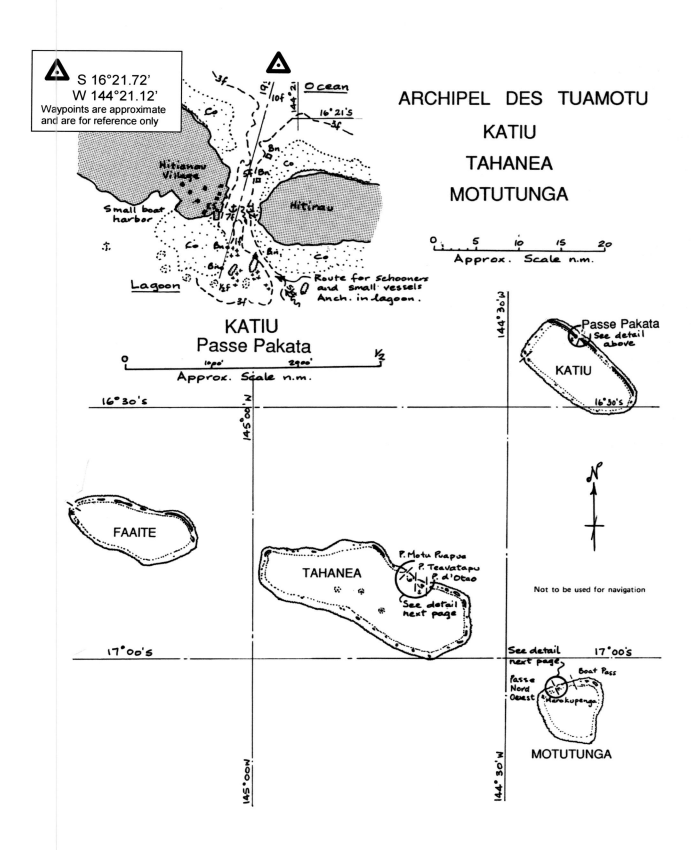

Ocean

ARCHIPEL DES TUAMOTU

KATIU

TAHANEA

MOTUTUNGA

Hitianau Village

Hitirau

Small boat harbor

Route for schooners and small vessels Anch. in lagoon.

Lagoon

0   5   10   15   20
Approx. Scale n.m.

KATIU
Passe Pakata

0   1000'   2000'   ½
Approx. Scale n.m.

Passe Pakata
See detail above

KATIU

16°30'S

16°30'S

FAAITE

N

TAHANEA

P. Motu Puapua
P. Teavatapu
P. d'Otao

See detail next page

Not to be used for navigation

17°00'S

17°00'S

See detail next page

Passe Nord Ouest

Boat Pass

Harokupenga

MOTUTUNGA

145°00'N

144°30'W

TAHANEA (Tchitschagoff Island)

This rectangular atoll is 7 miles southeast of Faaite. It is roughly 25 miles long and has islands distributed fairly well around its perimeter; those on the north side are large and well covered with palms. Three adjacent passes on the northeast side lead into the lagoon. Many coral reefs, visible and awash, are scattered in the lagoon, but in good visibility a vessel can find deep water routes between them. Anchorage here is exposed to southwesterly winds. An atoll within the lagoon is one of the few places where the endangered Tuamotu sandpiper survives as it is one of the only atolls where there are no rats. Their nests consist of small hollows in the lagoon coral or shell debris, lined with grass or other similar matter. As it is estimated that there are less than 100 of these rare birds in existence on this island, use extreme caution not to disturb one if found.

Passe d'Otao (Otaho Pass) is about 5 miles from the eastern end of the atoll. It is the narrowest of the passes and is generally preferred for leaving the lagoon rather than for entry. The village of d'Otao is on the eastern side of the pass, but two large coral heads block this side except for a narrow passage used only by local boats. The straighter, western passage has a least depth of 3 fathoms and can be used by larger vessels. Although there are several houses, a church, and a cistern in the village of d'Otao, the island is uninhabited except during copra harvesting.

Passe Teavatapu (Passe Manino) is a deep 6-fathoms and wide 328 yard entrance to the lagoon and is the normal passage of choice. It lies about 2 miles northwest of Passe d'Otao. The width and depth of the pass permit the swell to come well past the opening and this has given it a poor name. However there should be no difficulty in using it if care is taken and transit is made when seas are not high. A course down the center of the pass gives a vessel plenty of room for maneuvering. There is a westerly drift during ebb tide that must be considered by the helmsman.

Good anchorage can be taken to the east or west of this pass. The western anchorage is in the bight formed by Teuakiri Islet and a coral reef. The eastern anchorage, off the village of Kari Karina, is reached by passing between the island and Mauru Nahi Nahi reef. Keep a good watch for coral patches.

Passe Motu Puapua, the westernmost pass, is one mile north of Passe Teavatapu. It is 4.5 fathoms deep and about 650 feet wide. A reef on the west side of the pass, Motu Taunoa, is covered by only 1.5 fathoms and must be avoided.

MOTUTUNGA (Motu Tuga)

This almost circular atoll lies 10 miles ESE of Tahanea and 34 miles south of Katiu. It is very low and has several treed islets on its northern side. One mile east of the northwestern end is Passe Nord-Ouest (Passe Motu Tuga), which is actually a cul-de-sac since an underwater reef blocks off the inner end of the opening. On the island to the east of the opening is a village with a wooden wharf in disrepair where vessels may tie, gaining good protection and surprisingly little effect from the current. A cistern is located on each side of the pass.

A small boat passage into the lagoon is about 2 miles ENE of Passe Nord-Ouest, but it is not useable by vessels though local boats use it when the village is occupied during the copra collecting season.

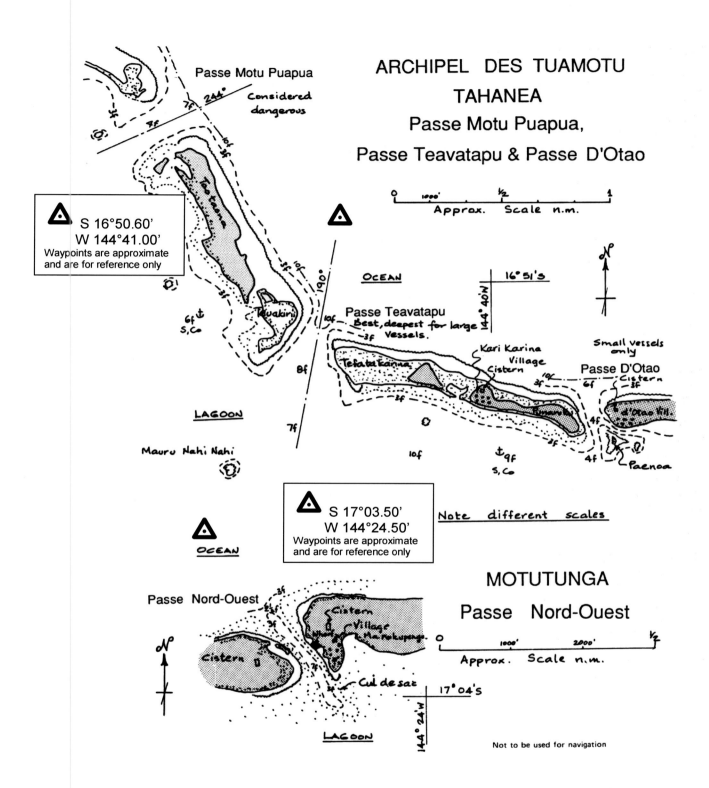

ARCHIPEL DES TUAMOTU

TAHANEA

Passe Motu Puapua,

Passe Teavatapu & Passe D'Otao

Passe Motu Puapua

Considered dangerous

S 16°50.60'
W 144°41.00'
Waypoints are approximate
and are for reference only

OCEAN

Passe Teavatapu
Best, deepest for large
vessels.

Kari Karina
Village
Cistern

Small vessels
only

Passe D'Otao
Cistern

Paenoa

LAGOON

Mauru Nahi Nahi

S 17°03.50'
W 144°24.50'
Waypoints are approximate
and are for reference only

Note different scales

OCEAN

MOTUTUNGA

Passe Nord-Ouest

Passe Nord-Ouest

Cistern
Village

Cistern

Cul de sac

LAGOON

Not to be used for navigation

96

GROUPE RAEVSKI

This group is made up of three small, uninhabited atolls: Hiti, Tepoto, and Tuanake. They lie to the southeast of Katiu, with about 9 miles of channel separating Tuanake from Katiu. All three of the atolls are bare on the south side and heavily wooded on the north side.

HITI

This atoll is three miles in diameter and does not have a pass into the lagoon.

TUANAKE

This atoll is four miles in diameter. Though not practicable for cruising vessels, a pass on the south side of the atoll is used by small local boats.

TEPOTO

This is the smallest and southernmost atoll of the group and a cairn is situated near its eastern extremity. A pass, subject to strong tidal currents, is located on the northeastern side of the atoll. It is used only by small, local boats that tie to the small, wooden wharf in the pass.

TAENGA (Holt Island)

This atoll is about 19 miles northeast of Makemo and is less than half its size. Similar to other atolls, it is mostly bare on the southern side where the reef is submerged. Few vessels visit this atoll because of the consistently high speed of the permanently outflowing current from the lagoon. It has a population of fewer than 50 people.

Passe Tiritepakau is the only pass into the lagoon and it lies about 3 miles WNW of the southwest end of the atoll. It is about 50 yards wide and 600 yards long before it opens into the lagoon and is divided by a drying coral bank. The pass is about 8 fathoms deep until near Tarioi, where it shoals to less than 3 fathoms. The shoal continues as far as the village of Fenuaparea, which is on the south side of the bank. Sufficient swell comes over the submerged south side of the atoll to create an almost continuous outflowing stream in the pass, often reaching 10 knots. The village wharf is out of the strongest current and it is possible to moor here by setting a bow anchor toward the lagoon, while tied to the wharf.

Spider Conch
(Lambis lambis Linne)

ARCHIPEL DES TUAMOTU
MAKEMO
GROUPE RAEVSKI

0   5   10   15
Approx. Scale n.m.

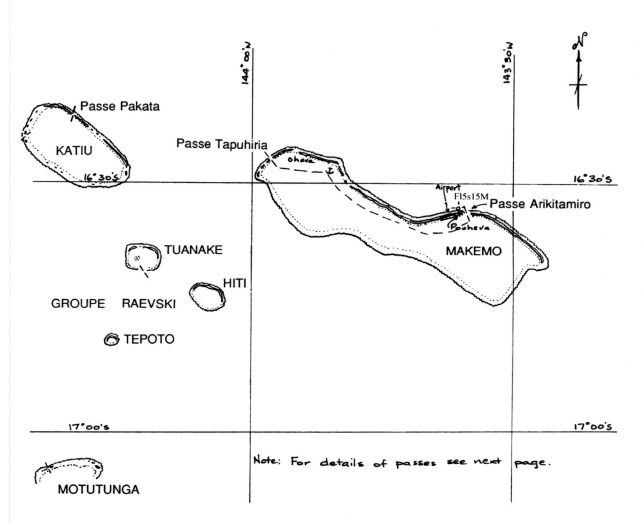

Passe Pakata

KATIU

Passe Tapuhiria

ohava

16°30'S

Airport
Fl5s15M
Passe Arikitamiro

Pooheva

MAKEMO

16°30'S

TUANAKE

HITI

GROUPE RAEVSKI

TEPOTO

17°00'S

17°00'S

Note: For details of passes see next page.

MOTUTUNGA

Not to be used for navigation

98

MAKEMO (Philipps Island)

This elongated atoll, lying 16 miles west of Katiu, is about 40 miles long and 10 miles wide at its widest point. The northern side of the atoll has several long islands that are well treed with palms, but the southern side is bare and low, making approach from the south very dangerous. Two passes lead into the lagoon, Passe Arikitamiro and Passe Tapuhira. The lagoon accumulates enough water from swells over the southern reef to cause very strong outgoing currents in both passes. Many shoals and coral heads, both visible and awash, are in the lagoon, but in good sunlight they can be easily seen.

Passe Arikitamiro is on the northeastern side of Makemo, about 10 miles from the eastern end. It is about 80 yards wide and has a least depth of 6 fathoms. It is easily recognized by a lighthouse north of the village, a break in the wooded reef and by the flagstaff at the village of Pouheva on the western side of the pass. At the inner end of the pass a coral reef, Rikiriki and a coral shoal, Ekoedo, divide the channel into three.

The seaward side of the pass is about 100 yards wide and 10 fathoms deep, decreasing to 7 fathoms at the lagoon side. Enter at slack tide, aligning the range lights at 147°T. The seaward range marker is at the north end of Ekoeko Nord Reef and the westernmost on Ekoeko Sud Reef. When the bearing of the light at Pouheva reads 270°T, steer 157°T to pass between Ekoeko reef on the east and Rikiriki reef to the west. This reef is marked by three buoys, two of which are lit. In this passage beware of strong currents that can cause the vessel to swerve from the course. When transiting the pass, large vessels use the center channel before turning toward the anchorage. Small vessels can use any of the passages, though the side channels are narrower and need more care to negotiate. Entry is best at or near slack water since the outgoing current can reach 8 or 9 knots. It is possible to sail between the two passes inside the lagoon in good light. A careful lookout is needed to identify the few scattered coral patches.

The village of Pouheva (Puheva) is located on the western side of the pass. The population is less than 300 and the harvest of copra is their only source of income. There is an airport which has weekly air service to Papeete. The village has a huge cathedral as well as a dispensary and several small stores. Fresh produce and fuel are not available.

Passe Tapuhiria (Vahinatika Pass), at the northwestern end of the atoll, is 85 yards wide and a least depth of 10 fathoms. Within the pass there are two detached reefs, dividing it into three channels. Beacons mark the passage between Rikiriki Ruga Reef on the east and Rikiriki Raro Reef on the west. A visible shoal lies to the east of the entrance and vessels waiting for slack water or improved conditions for entry can anchor on this shoal. Similar to Passe Arikitamiro, the outgoing stream can reach a velocity of 8 or 9 knots.

Transit of the pass is straightforward and well-marked. The closest anchorage to the pass is south of Turuki in about 7 fathoms. Another excellent anchorage is about 8 miles from the pass inside the curve of the northeast coast, in 2.5 fathoms, sand. The village of d'Ohava, at the northwestern end of the atoll, is inhabited only during the harvesting season for copra. Conning is needed when traveling the lagoon to avoid the coral heads scattered about.

ARCHIPEL DES TUAMOTU
MAKEMO

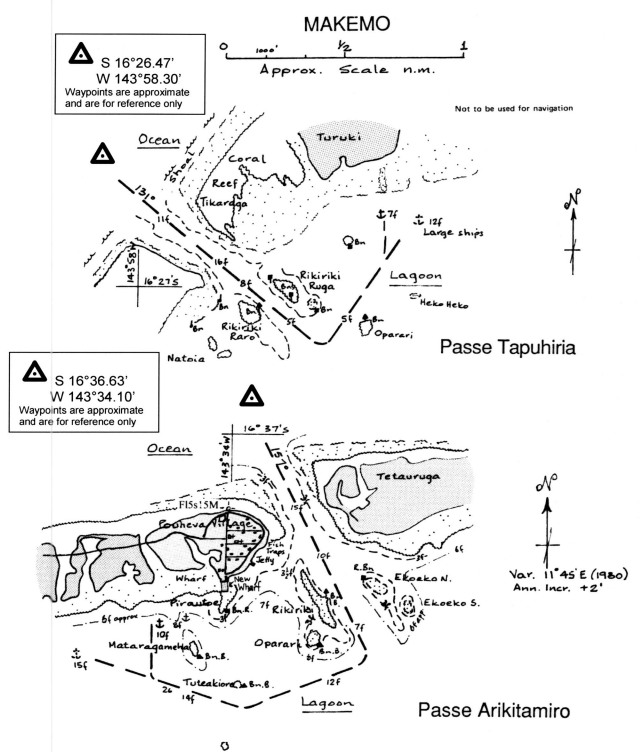

S 16°26.47'
W 143°58.30'
Waypoints are approximate
and are for reference only

0   1000'   ½   1
Approx. Scale n.m.

Not to be used for navigation

Ocean

Turuki

Coral

Reef

Tikaraga

Shoal 6f

131°

11f

16f

8f

↧7f

↥12f
Large ships

Bn

Lagoon

Heko Heko

Rikiriki Ruga

Bn

143°58'W

16°27'S

Bn

Bn

5f

5f

Bn

Oparari

Bn

Rikiriki Raro

Bn

Natoia

Passe Tapuhiria

S 16°36.63'
W 143°34.10'
Waypoints are approximate
and are for reference only

16°37'S

Ocean

151°

143°34'W

Tetauruga

Fl5s!5M

Pouheva Village

15f

6f

8f

Fish Traps

Jetty

10f

3f

R.Bn

Ekoeko N.

Wharf

New Wharf

3½f
2f

f.s.

Ekoeko S.

Pirautoe

Bn.B

7f

Rikiriki

6f approx

8f

Matarağameha

Bn.B

10f

Oparari

Bn.B

6f

7f

15f

26

14f

Tuteakiore

Bn.B.

12f

Lagoon

Passe Arikitamiro

Var. 11°45'E (1980)
Ann. Incr. +2'

100

RAROIA and TAKUME

RAROIA (Barclay de Tolley Island)

This island lies about 49 miles northeast of Makemo and 5 miles southwest of Takume. With its partner atoll, Takume, it is the northeasterly spur to the line of the Tuamotu chain, in a very similar manner to the Manihi-Ahe and Takaroa-Takapoto groups. Further to the northeast are Napuka, Pukapuka, Fangatau and Fakahina, which are not included in this guide, as they are not generally visited by cruisers.

The northern and western sides of Raroia have much vegetation and the southwestern point is covered with brushwood. The westerly running current sets on to the eastern side of the atoll which is sparsely wooded and very dangerous to approach. Thor Heyerdahl's craft, Kon-Tiki, grounded on the eastern side of Raroia, thus ending his adventurous voyage.

Passe Garue/Ngarue (North Pass) is the only pass into the lagoon and it lies about midway down the western side. It is wide and clearly indicated by the open water between two heavily treed parts of the atoll. The pass is deep, except as described below, and fair sized vessels can use it safely. Tidal streams and currents can reach 8 knots and slack water is usually of short duration.

The route through the pass favors the northern side where a channel about 130 yards wide has a least depth of 4 to 5 fathoms. A sand bank extends from the south side of the opening for about for 350 yards and a lesser bank reaches southwest from the north side. Once through the pass, there are many coral heads visible and awash, several with beacons marking the passage to the village. Anchorage may be taken off the village jetty at Ngarumoava in 4 to 5 fathoms, sand and coral bottom. Use caution, as the jetty has depths of only about 2 feet alongside. A small boat harbor lies beyond the old coral jetty, but the depths may not accommodate vessels of average draft.

The village of Ngarumoava is not easily seen from offshore as it is almost hidden behind a mass of coconut palms on the long island southwest of the pass. The population is less than 50 and supplies are not available.

TAKUME (Wolkonsky Island)

This atoll lies 5 miles northeast of Raroia and the channel separating them has a strong westerly current that is often turbulent. The atoll is wooded except in the southeastern part where the broken reef is partially submerged.

There isn't a pass into the lagoon available for yachts or larger vessels. A boat pass used by the islanders is near the north end of the atoll. The village of Temania is at the southwest end of the atoll where a flagstaff and an obelisk can be seen from offshore. Landing can be done here, but the current and trade winds cause heavy seas and swell that run through the gap between the atolls, making landing difficult. It is unsafe for a vessel to remain near this reef.

HAO Island

Thisatoll is about 30 miles long and 9 miles wide and the only pass leading to the lagoon is at the northern end. The channel has a depth of about 2 fathoms and normally has an outgoing current. Currents in the pass can be up to 15 knots during or after strong southerly winds. Local people welcome yachts and cruisers who are able to use, free of charge, an abandoned marina with GPS coordinates of 18°05.95' S, 140°54.77' W. The town has several shops, a Post Office, doctor, dentist and fuel. There are four weekly flights to Tahiti.

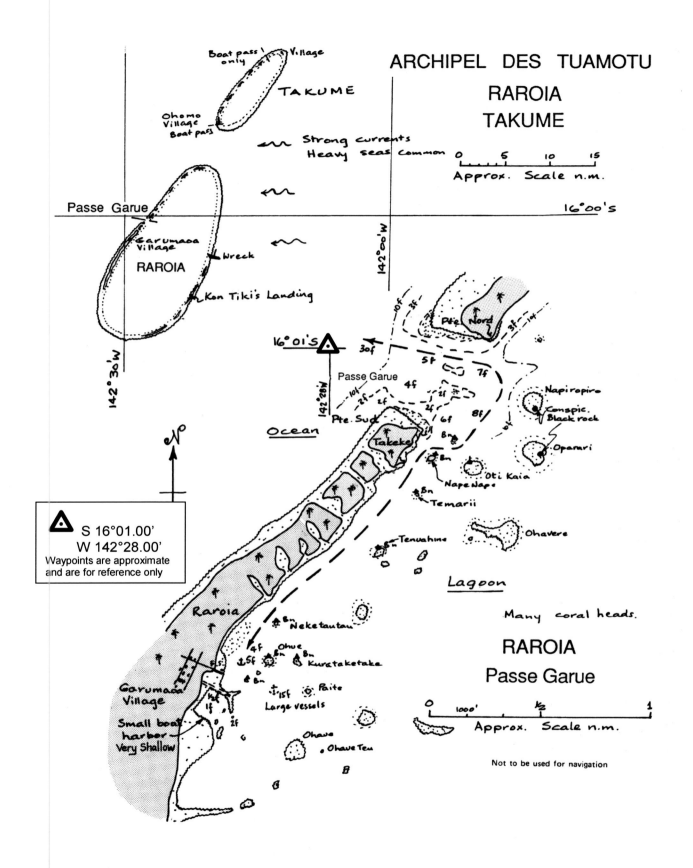

ARCHIPEL DES TUAMOTU
RAROIA
TAKUME

Boat pass only — Village
TAKUME
Ohomo Village
Boat pass

Strong currents
Heavy seas Common

0   5   10   15
Approx. Scale n.m.

16°00'S

Passe Garue

Garumaoa Village
RAROIA
Wreck

Kon Tiki's Landing

142°30'W
142°00'W

16°01'S

Passe Garue

10f 8f
Pte. Nord
3f 15f
30f
5f 7f
4f 2f 7f
2f 2f
Pte. Sud
6f 8f
Bn
Takeke
Bn
Bn
Napiropiro
Conspic. Black rock
Oparari

Ocean

Oti Kaia
Nape Nape
Temarii

Ohavere

Lagoon

Many coral heads.

S 16°01.00'
W 142°28.00'
Waypoints are approximate and are for reference only

Raroia

Neketautau
Ohue Bn Bn
Bn 4f Kurataketake
1.5f Bn
Paite
Large vessels 15f
Garumaoa Village
1f
Small boat harbor — Very Shallow
2f

Tenuahine

Ohave
Ohave Teu

RAROIA
Passe Garue

0   1000'   ½   1
Approx. Scale n.m.

Not to be used for navigation

ILES GAMBIER

Located at the southeastern end of the Tuamotu is a group of about ten volcanically formed islands and numerous small islets within a barrier reef. The large islands of Mangareva, Taravai, Aukena and Akamaru are of volcanic origin, the reef and motus are of coral. The surrounding reef is roughly a square set on its diagonal in a north-south direction. The northern end is partially visible and partly awash, but it is submerged on the southern sides. Three passes lead over sunken portions of the reef into the lagoon. On approach, especially from the north, the pointed peaks of Mont Duff, 1,447 feet high and Mont Mokoto, 1,394 feet high are good landmarks. The total population is about 700. The channels and dangers are well marked with navigational aids. Use French charts 6418, 6463 and 6464.

ILE MANGAREVA

Passe de l'Ouest is on the northwestern side about 2.75 miles southwest of Motu Tenoko. It is easily identified by the gap between Iles Mangareva and Taravai, at the reef by Motu Tenoko, and the surf breaking over Banc de Tokorua. The sketch shows the proper line leading through the pass and the successive ranges as a vessel turns past Pointe Teonekura into the Rade de Tikitea on the eastern side of Mangareva. The bar between the two islands has shallow spots, limiting entry to vessels with a maximum draft of 13 feet. Another shallow spot is at Seuil d'Aukena where the route crosses a submerged reef between two buoys. When the village of Rikitea is clearly visible and the beacons near the wharf bear 298°T, the vessel can be taken through the coral heads into a well-protected anchorage with good holding in 11 fathoms, gray mud.

The village of Rikitea is the largest on the island and the local administrator and gendarme reside here. Entry formalities should be followed as this is a **Port of Entry.** The attractive village is neat and tidy with much lush greenery giving it a garden-like ambience. Water and some fresh produce can be obtained and bread is available twice every day except Sunday afternoon unless they run out of flour. Juicy pamplemousse (grapefruit) can be found growing wild. The islanders have numerous pearl farms in the lagoon, many of which are marked by floats.

There are two passes, safe and deep enough for any cruising boat. The buoyage follows IALA 'A' and all lights are usually working. The main anchorage is abreast of the village of Rikitea on the SE side of the Island of Mangareva, in 7 to 8 fathoms, good holding coral mud where excellent shelter is provided by an inner reef. The approach through the inner reef is well marked and has a minimum depth of 3.5 fathoms.

The town has several shops, a post office and an infirmary staffed by a doctor who speaks some English. Potable water can be obtained at the Trans Ocean Base, operated by Fritz Didier Schmack, a very helpful man. He also operates the wireless LAN station of the ioranet and has one of the few hot water washing machines in the South Pacific. For large amounts of water (100 gal. or more) the municipal works will make arrangements for a container to be placed on their service dock and water pumped aboard a cruising vessel moored stern-to.

Twice weekly air service to Papeete is operated by Air Tahiti, which has an agency in the village. The villagers are very friendly and welcome cruisers, especially Lady Major Monique who speaks some English. The mairie has an information leaflet featuring the history and sights of the Gambier Islands. Connections to Tahiti by air have eliminated any sense of isolation and food from France and New Zealand is common.

Diesel must be ferried in jerry cans during the bi-weekly visit of the supply ships *Nukuhau* and *Tiare Taporo*. Gasoline can be purchased at Magazin Edmond near the main wharf.

Passe du Sud-Ouest is an easy, straightforward pass to transit. It joins the northwest route near the island.

Passe du Sud-Est is another easy entrance, well suited to sailing vessels because of the prevailing wind. The islet of Makapu acts as a milestone along the route, and when passed, a direct course can be laid for the range leading across Seuil d'Aukena to Rikitea. Travel across the lagoon should be done with care since coral heads are in the vicinity of all routes.

The record of Honore Laval, a Jesuit priest who came here in 1834 is shameful and unfortunately, typical of the track record of missionaries in Polynesia. After converting and dominating Maputeoa, the last king, Laval ruled the island as a despot. He set stringent rules, and forced the people to erect stone churches, convents and other buildings. In the process, he caused the death of over 5,000 people, eliminated the will of the people to survive and destroyed an entire culture.

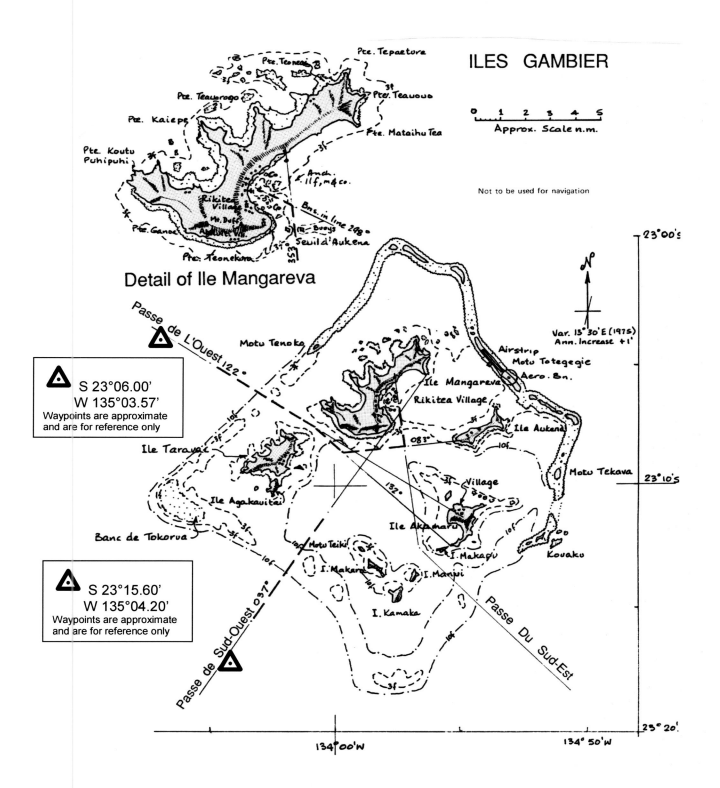

ILES GAMBIER

0 1 2 3 4 5
Approx. Scale n.m.

Not to be used for navigation

Detail of Ile Mangareva

S 23°06.00'
W 135°03.57'
Waypoints are approximate
and are for reference only

S 23°15.60'
W 135°04.20'
Waypoints are approximate
and are for reference only

Passe de L'Ouest 122°

Motu Tenoko

Ile Taravai

Ile Agakauitai

Banc de Tokorua

Passe de Sud-Ouest 037°

Motu Teiki

I. Makaro

I. Kamaka

Ile Mangareva

Rikitea Village

Airstrip
Motu Totegegie
Aero. Bn.

Var. 13° 30' E (1975)
Ann. Increase +1'

Ile Aukena

Motu Tekava

Village

Ile Akamaru

I. Manui

I. Makapu

Kouaku

Passe Du Sud-Est

23°00'S

23°10'S

23°20'

134°00'W   134°50'W

104

PITCAIRN ISLAND

Pitcairn Island lies about 330 miles southeast of Iles Gambier and about 860 miles west of Ile Rapa. In the general area is a group of small, widely scattered, uninhabited islands that includes Ducie, Henderson and Oeno. Of volcanic origin, Pitcairn is high, rising to about 1,000 feet and most of the coast is composed of steep cliffs. The soil is fertile and luxuriant vegetation covers the island.

Pitcairn is a British dependency. The inhabitants are mostly descendants of mutineers of the *Bounty* and Tahitians who accompanied them into exile. The remains of the *Bounty* lie in 25 feet of water in Bounty Bay where she was driven ashore and set afire by Fletcher Christian. The main settlement of Adamstown was named after John Adams, the last mutineer to die.

Bounty Bay is an open bay on the northeastern coast, about 0.5 miles northwest of St. Paul's Point, the easternmost point. From offshore, the roof of a boathouse near the water and one or two bright tin roofs of the houses above, help to identify the anchorage and main landing place. Large vessels anchor about 0.5 mile offshore with St. Paul's Point visible past Adams Rock. Smaller vessels can anchor a little closer, in about 6 to 8 fathoms, sand bottom with rocky patches. Holding is good in the sandy areas, but an anchor watch aboard is advisable because of possible wind shifts. For extra security, two anchors are advised. If the wind shifts to northerly quadrants neither Tedside nor Bounty Bay are safe anchorages and vessels may have to heave to for several days while waiting for better weather.

During easterly or southerly winds anchorage may be taken on the northwestern coast at Tedside. The anchorage is deep, 7 to 10 fathoms, sand and coral and landing ashore is possible. A trail leads to Adamstown. As stated above, neither Tedside nor Bounty Bay can be used if the wind shifts to the northern quadrants. Another anchorage is in Down Rope Bight on the southeastern coast, but this is seldom used as landing ashore is impossible.

Landing ashore may be very difficult and should not be attempted in rough conditions. When visiting Bounty Bay it is best to contact the islanders who maintain a radio watch on VHF Ch 16 and have them take you ashore in their own surf boat, trips cost about NZ$10. Landing here can be a spectacular feat for at the last minute as the boat rushes in it must be swung hard to port around a stone wall and run up a concrete ramp built out from the boathouse. An inflatable tender is satisfactory for landing in moderate conditions. A steep pathway leads to the plateau above.

The islanders are exceedingly hospitable and will often sell their surplus fruit and vegetables to visitors. A small co-op store has a limited selection of canned, frozen and dried foods. Except during periods of drought, drinking water may be available from a tap at the boat shed in Bounty Bay. Diesel and gasoline are not available to cruisers as the island's supplies are purchased with difficulty and considerable expense from passing ships. Visas are not required for brief visits, but those wishing to stay ashore for an extended period must obtain permission from the Island Council and pay a $150 landing fee. Entry fees are approximately US$11 per person.

Letters mailed from Pitcairn Island may take up to five months to reach their destination. The beautiful Pitcairn stamps with hand-canceled postmarks are rare and become valuable with time. Wood carvings, finely crafted baskets and printed T-shirts make good souvenirs.

PITCAIRN ISLAND

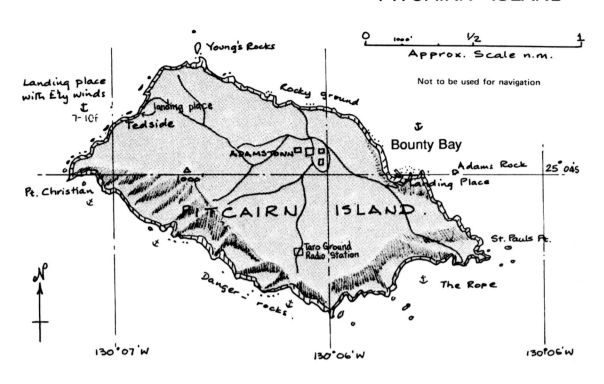

Young's Rocks

Landing place with E'ly winds
7-10f

Tedside

landing place

Rocky ground

Bounty Bay

ARAMSTONN

Adams Rock   25°04S

Landing Place

Pt. Christian

PITCAIRN   ISLAND

St. Pauls Pt.

Taro Ground Radio Station

The Rope

Danger rocks

N

130°07'W   130°06'W   130°05'W

0   1000'   1/2   1
Approx. Scale n.m.

Not to be used for navigation

FROM THE SSE, DISTANT ABOUT 7 MILES

Not to be used for navigation

8 to 10f
s with r.

S 25°04.00'
W 130°05.70'
Waypoints are approximate and are for reference only

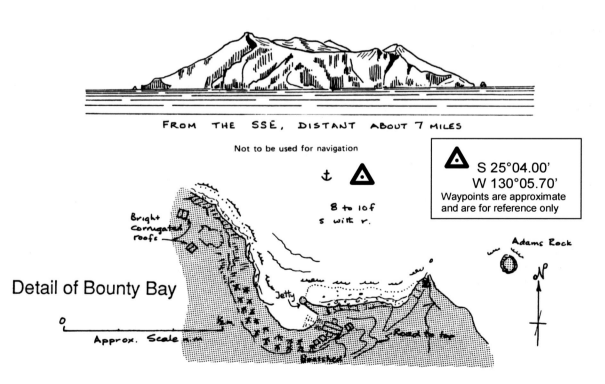

Detail of Bounty Bay

Bright Corrugated roofs

Jetty

Adams Rock

N

0
Approx. Scale n.m.

ISLA de PASCUA (EASTER ISLAND)

Famous for its huge stone statues known as moai, this is the easternmost outpost of Polynesia. Truly isolated, it is 1117 miles east of Pitcairn Island, 1,400 miles east of the Gambiers and over 1,900 miles from Valparaiso, Chile. Easter Island is a Chilean possession though the governor is a Rapanui (locally-born Polynesian). Seventy percent of the population is of Polynesian descent and speak Pascuan (a Polynesian dialect) when conversing among themselves. Weekly flights connect the island to Papeete and Santiago, Chile.

It is a volcanically formed island having several extinct volcanoes as high points. Cerro Terevaka at 1,400 feet is the highest and nearby is the crater of Volcan Rano Aroi; when seen from a distance they appear to be two islands. The shores are predominantly rocky and steep-to with no sheltered anchorages. The main village and **Port of Entry** is **Rada Hanga Roa**, which is visible from offshore. The roadstead is encumbered with rocky patches and foul ground. Approach should be made on the ranges as indicated. It is best to anchor outside the 6 fathom line to be clear of the rocky ground, although it is possible with extreme care to move slightly closer to the pier.

The Port Captain, an officer of the Chilean Navy, monitors VHF Ch 16 and may attempt to contact entering vessels. He and the officers from Health, Agriculture and Immigration, board arriving yachts that anchor off Hanga Roa. A call on VHF Ch 16 to "Pascua Radio" will contact the Port Captain and the launch will come out. Several boats have been damaged by the over enthusiastic islanders who give officials a ride to the yachts in their large, rough and unwieldy fishing skiffs, so have fenders and fender boards ready. The officials process tourist cards and clearances on board. At present, entry and exit fees and visas are not required for brief visits.

In the summer months (October to April) when the southeast trades blow, Hanga Roa is a reasonable anchorage. During northerly gales the vessel should move to Rada Vinapu on the south coast. During the winter months or when westerly winds are blowing, reasonable anchorage may be taken on the north coast at Anakena Cove which is identified by a white sand beach at its head. It is protected from all but northerly winds and landing through the surf is usually possible on the beach where a dinghy dock is located. **La Perouse Bay** offers more protection from swell during westerly winds than tying to the Armada mooring buoy.

Hanga Piko is used by motorized barges unloading supply ships from Chile every six months. It is sheltered in all but westerly winds, when it becomes an extremely dangerous trap. Vessels drawing less than 6 feet may obtain permission from the Port Captain to tie up inside Hanga Piko Harbor, where the yacht will be placed in the middle of the harbor with lines ashore in four directions. This is at the discretion of the Port Captain, who often allows only one yacht at a time in the harbor. Weather forecasts are available from the Armada on VHF Ch 16. At the first forecast of a westerly wind, yachts inside Hanga Piko should either put to sea or shift to another anchorage after obtaining permission from the Port Captain. Water is sold at the Hanga Roa landing or inside Hanga Piko harbor; diesel and kerosene are available at a service station near the airport.

The Armada may direct yachts to anchor next to the Armada buoy that is nearly in line with the day mark beacons. Do not anchor if you feel conditions are too rough in Hanga Roa, regardless of what the Armada says. **Vinapu** may be safer, but landing can be difficult at the broken down oil tanker wharf. Conditions frequently exist in which none of the "anchorages" of Easter Island are tenable, e.g. a moderate to strong Norther or Northwester, combined with a heavy swell from the south. Pilot charts indicate that N and NW winds are more common than S and SE winds in April. It is compulsory to engage the services of a navy-approved pilot to enter and exit from Hanga Piko. A popular choice is Carlos, a local yachtsman who charges a fee of US$100. Landing at Hanga Roa is difficult in the best of times. At least a 10 hp outboard is needed and there is almost always a surf line (sometimes two) to be crossed. A good selection of fresh produce is normally available in the two or three small supermarkets in Hanga Roa village at prices only a little higher than on the Chilean mainland. US currency is widely accepted. There are several Internet cafes in Hanga Roa.

Hana Hotu Iti is a spectacular location with a row of 15 moai at the head of the anchorage and the famous moai "nursery" only a half hour walk away. Anchor in at least 15 meters (any closer and you will be in the surf line if a heavy swell comes in), favoring the NE side of the bay. Be careful to choose a spot with sand bottom (visibility is usually good).

SSB/Ham-equipped vessels proceeding from Easter Island to Chile may wish to check in with the Patagonian Cruisers' Net; 8164 kHz at 0900 Chilean local time (all year; UTC timing shifts by one hour in Chilean summer/winter time.)

Mary Ho

Easter Island 'Moai' Welcoming Committee

Mary Ho

The landing at Hanga Roa, Easter Island

A "Bommie" - Lovely to look at but you don't want to run into one of these

EASTER ISLAND
(ISLA DE PASCUA)

Hana Hotu Iti is a spectacular location with a row of 15 moai at the head of the anchorage with the famous moai "nursery" only a half hour walk away. Anchor in at least 15 meters (any closer and you will be in the surf line if a heavy swell comes in), favoring the NE side of the bay. Choose a spot with sand bottom. Visibility is good.

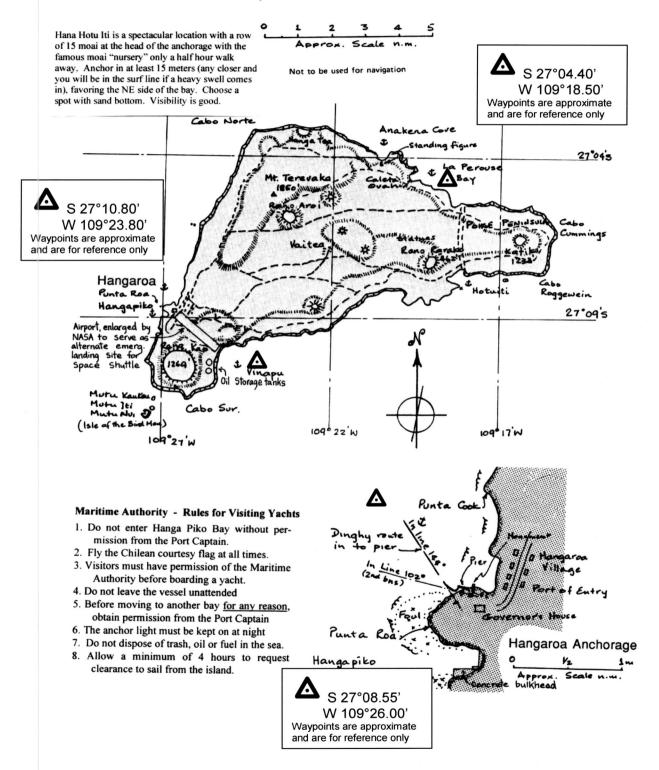

S 27°04.40'
W 109°18.50'
Waypoints are approximate
and are for reference only

S 27°10.80'
W 109°23.80'
Waypoints are approximate
and are for reference only

S 27°08.55'
W 109°26.00'
Waypoints are approximate
and are for reference only

Maritime Authority - Rules for Visiting Yachts

1. Do not enter Hanga Piko Bay without permission from the Port Captain.
2. Fly the Chilean courtesy flag at all times.
3. Visitors must have permission of the Maritime Authority before boarding a yacht.
4. Do not leave the vessel unattended
5. Before moving to another bay for any reason, obtain permission from the Port Captain
6. The anchor light must be kept on at night
7. Do not dispose of trash, oil or fuel in the sea.
8. Allow a minimum of 4 hours to request clearance to sail from the island.

110

ILES DE LA SOCIETE - SOCIETY ISLANDS

These islands extend over 400 miles in a WNW direction and are divided into two sections for administrative purposes. The Iles du Vent (Windward Isles) are the southeastern group and include Meetia, Tahiti, Moorea, Tetiaroa, and Maiao (Tubuai Manu). The Iles Sous le Vent (Leeward Isles) are the northwestern group and include Huahine, Raiatea, Tahaa, Bora-Bora, Maupiti, Tupai, Maupihaa, Manuae and Moto One.

With the exception of Tetiaroa and the smaller western islands, all of the islands are high, volcanically formed and surrounded by coral reefs. Coral formations that are detached from the island leaving a passage with sufficient water for a vessel to travel are known as fringing reefs. The islands are the worn remnants of once tall volcanoes that are now jagged, rocky towers and rugged, grass and shrub-covered mountainous terrain. The largest of the South Seas islands, they enjoy an ideal climate. This has made them the favored base for all the major explorers of the Pacific, beginning with the Polynesians.

Though probably seen by Quiros in 1606, it was not until the late 1700's that Tahiti became important on the evolving charts of the Pacific. In 1767, Captain Samuel Wallis in the frigate *Dolphin*, anchored in Matavai Bay during the first recorded visit by Europeans. In 1768, Louis Antoine de Bougainville visited the islands briefly and stayed at Hitiaa. But it was Captain James Cook's many weeks in Tahiti, observing the transit of the planet Venus in 1769, that brought the island to the full notice of the Western world. Though Cook was an ideal observer and one unusually concerned with the effects of his visits, it was the many less scrupulous people who came after him, including the missionaries, who radically changed this culture. In 1880 these islands were taken under French protection, and by 1888 were made part of the French nation. Discussions are ongoing regarding independence, and in 1977 the territory was granted Interne Autonomie, or self-government.

The islands lie within the southeast tradewind belt, with winds from the southeast to east predominating. The trades are strongest in the winter months of July to September. Gales are infrequent, though at times an off-season cyclone can be experienced such as in January of 2004 when Cyclone Heta struck a devastating blow to Niue. Except during showers, visibility is very good. In the vicinity of high islands the winds are altered and affected in various ways; land and sea breezes have greater force and in the lee of the islands there may be calms and variable winds. The currents follow the direction of the wind, except near the coasts. With the dominating easterly wind driving it, the current runs west at about 10 to 15 miles per day.

In some 14 locations in the Societies (including Marina Taina) Wi-Fi internet access is available to cruisers at prices marginally lower than those offered by land-based internet cafes. The service's home page provides free access to the latest regional weather forecast.

http://www.ioaranet.pf/index.php?changelg=en

ILES DE LA SOCIETE

Not to be used for navigation

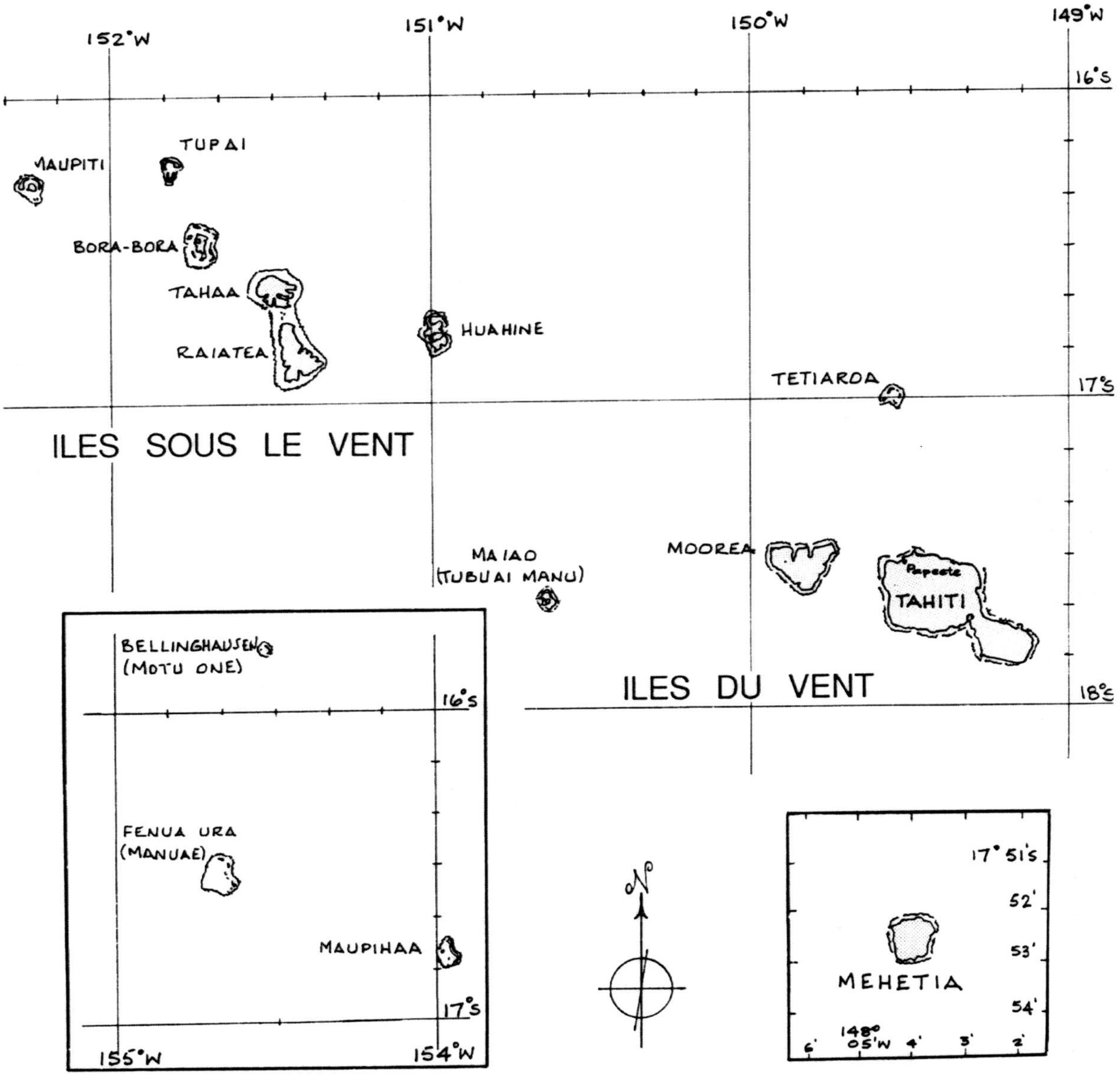

152°W 151°W 150°W 149°W

16°S

MAUPITI

TUPAI

BORA-BORA

TAHAA

RAIATEA

HUAHINE

TETIAROA 17°S

ILES SOUS LE VENT

MAIAO
(TUBUAI MANU)

MOOREA

Papeete
TAHITI

ILES DU VENT 18°S

BELLINGHAUSEN
(MOTU ONE)

16°S

FENUA URA
(MANUAE)

MAUPIHAA

17°S

155°W 154°W

N

MEHETIA

17°51'S
52'
53'
54'

148°
05'W
6' 4' 3' 2'

ILE TAHITI

Tahiti is the largest island and easternmost of the group, with the exception of little Meetia, which lies some 60 miles further east. The hourglass shape is due to a double volcano that once formed the island. The larger, almost circular section in the northwestern part is called Tahiti Nui; the oval-shaped smaller section is Tahiti Iti or the Taiarapu Peninsula. The short neck of land joining them is the Isthmus of Taravao. Both parts of the island are broken into high, spectacular, sharp peaks, those on Tahiti Nui rising to Orohena at 7,340 feet, on Tairapu to Pic Ronia at 4,340 feet.

A strip of coastal plain surrounds the peaks. It is larger on the western side, which is where most of the people live. The mountain peaks are often obscured by clouds or mist but when visibility is good they can be seen from a great distance. The valleys between them are striking because of their depth and size, and together with the peaks are used as guides to the passes through the coral barrier reefs. Since most skippers using this guide will be making their landfall enroute from the Tuamotus or the Marquesas', the key feature is Pointe Venus, which should be identified before closing the coast. The second paragraph on page 124 has a description of Pointe Venus.

The entire island is surrounded by a coral barrier reef varying from 0.5 miles to 2 miles off the coast, and in two areas it is a submerged shoal. There are many passes allowing entry or exit through the reef. Several good anchorages are behind the reef, Papeete on the northwestern side and Port du Phaeton on the south. Passage behind the reef and between the passes is possible at many places, and in a detailed section that follows, information on these passes and anchorages is given.

The main port and administrative center for French Polynesia is <u>Papeete</u>. It is the largest city in French Polynesia and a steady population drift to it from the other islands has been continuous for a long time. It has been a gathering place for yachts cruising the South Pacific for many years, however, there is much more to Tahiti than Papeete that shouldn't be missed. Details of entry to the harbor and yacht facilities are given on the following page.

A cruise around the island is not often undertaken by most skippers, who seem content to lie in Papeete. Yet such a cruise will show the island in a very different perspective to the adventurous sailor, one that is perhaps truer to the Tahiti of old than what is seen in the busy city of Papeete. It is a little wetter and windier on the south and east coasts; anchorages are deep but uncrowded and the views of Tairapu Peninsula are worth the trip.

Several passes through the reef are suitable for use and though sketches are drawn of their approaches, a running log of openings and pass positions and waypoints should be kept as a backup if clouds obscure the peaks. Most passages behind the reef are well marked with beacons and those near Papeete are lit. Nevertheless, it is best to travel on days with good visibility and to use the most up-to-date charts along with visual methods of navigation when behind the barrier reef.

> When checking in with port authorities ask for the free booklet entitled, *Yacht Guide – Papeete Tahiti*. It is full of useful information such as repair services, medical resources and emergency telephone numbers, etc.

ILES DE LA SOCIETE
ILE TAHITI

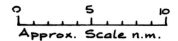

Approx. Scale n.m.

Not to be used for navigation

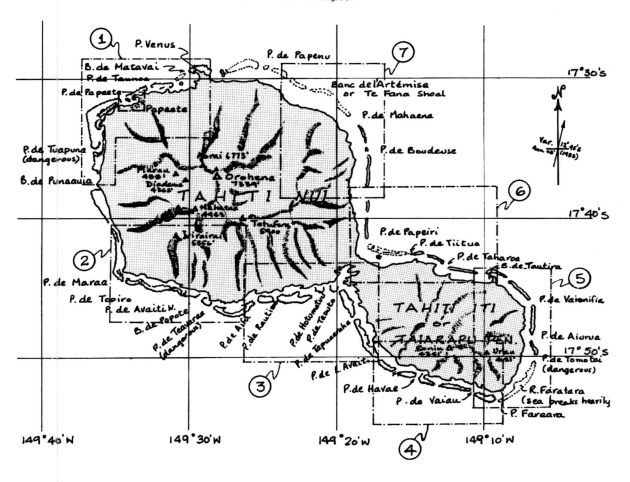

APPROACHING TAHITI APPROX. 7 MILES N. OF POINTE VENUS

PAPEETE

Papeete is the harbor most cruisers visit first when arriving in Tahiti. The most sheltered harbor is Port du Phaeton on the isthmus between Tahiti Nui and Tahiti Iti. For details see page 130, second to the last paragraph. Papeete is on the northwestern coast, about 5 miles west of Pointe Venus (the northern extremity of the island). **Passe de Papeete** is the opening in the barrier reef into the harbor. Though it appears quite wide, the actual dredged opening (capable of accommodating large cruise ships) is about 200 feet wide between the buoys. There is no difficulty for any small, capable vessel entering in good weather, even though currents of up to 5 knots run out of the pass. A heavy northerly swell can cause breakers across the pass and at such times it is best to await calmer seas. Outside the pass the westerly current generally runs at about one knot. Before entering the pass contact Port Control on VHF Ch 12 or SSB 2638 KHz. All vessels must fly the yellow quarantine ("Q") flag when entering the port.

From a distance, the deep cleft of Vallee Fautauna helps identify the approach to the entrance and the sketch shows the view of the harbor when closer in. The Protestant Church on the waterfront toward the west is a prominent feature when approaching the pass and the city of Papeete extends along the shore for a considerable distance. Once the pass is seen and the buoys are visible, an entry can be made on leading lights or marks, on white pylons with red bands on a bearing of 149°T. Once through the pass, you can see leading lights and a range leading to yachts at the moorage.

The Harbormaster (Port Directeur) controls all vessels within the port and around Tahiti. The harbor is divided according to the purposes of the vessels that use it. Moorage (stern-to) is available at **Le Rundel** (formerly known as Quai Bir-Hakeim) along Boulevard Pomare, where it is close to the center of the city, though noise from heavy traffic can be a nuisance. The dockmaster monitors VHF Ch 12. The concrete-faced moorage has floating docks to tie to and sometimes a plank to form a gangway for going ashore. If space is unavailable it may be necessary to anchor off the beach in sand, tying two long stern lines ashore. A good spot is off the little park with a statue of Charles de Gaulle. Neighboring boats are usually helpful in getting newcomers settled and in passing on needed advice. There is usually plenty of space at Le Rundel and adjoining facilities since mooring costs are out of reach for most cruisers. Consequently only two or three charter yachts moor here. Most cruisers moor in or off Marina Taina.

After the boat has been moored, entry procedures include a visit to Customs (Douane) immigration and the port captain, all conveniently located a short walk from the quay. An attempt to speak French is usually rewarded by a helpful response. Be prepared by having crew lists, passports and finances in place for posting the required bond. Take on fuel, water and basic provisions early in your stay to be prepared for the next leg of your journey. Duty free fuel is available in Papeete <u>after</u> obtaining port clearance and a form signed by Customs. It is available only from the Mobile pontoon next to the Moorea ferries, by truck from Shell or from the Total station at Marina Taina. **Caution:** check with other cruisers regarding whether or not the fuel is contaminated. You can obtain clean (jerry can) fuel from the Mobile station near the Protestant church, at the Mobile station close to Marina Taina or at the yacht club at Arue, east of the harbor of Papeete.

All services of a large city are found here such as stores, open-air markets, banks and marine repair services such as welding, refrigeration, engine repair and rigging shops, etc. Papeete is a busy, expensive city to visit, and although some shopkeepers speak limited English, it is wise to keep a French/English phrase book handy. Three museums, accessible by the bus or walking, will broaden your appreciation of Polynesia and are well worth visiting are the Museum of Tahiti and her Islands, the Pearl Museum and the Gauguin Museum. A new and very interesting museum east of Papeete, near Point Venus, is the restored former home of James Norman Hall, co-author of the Bounty trilogy and many other books on the South Pacific.

When checking in with port authorities ask for the free booklet entitled, *Yacht Guide - Papeete Tahiti*. It is full of useful information such as repair services, medical resources, emergency telephone numbers, etc.

Jo Russell

Sunset over Moorea as seen from Tahiti

Holly Scott

Even the surfers had to stop and watch this spectacular sunset in Huahine

The Gran Marche in Papeete – a 'Must See' and a great place to shop for produce

Melinda Young

And fish!

Melinda Young

ILES DE LA SOCIETE
ILE TAHITI
Detail of Papeete Harbor

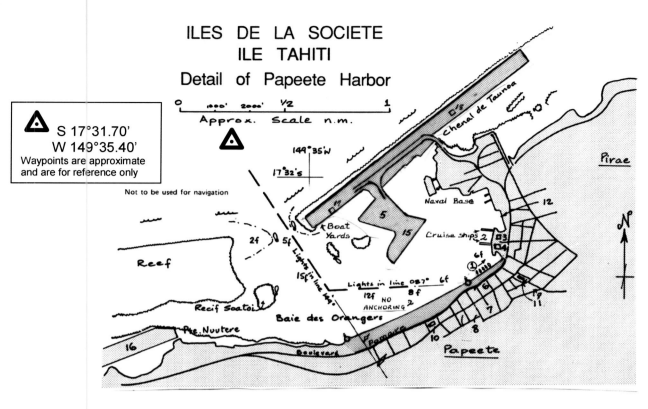

1. Le Rundel (Quai Bir Hakeim)
2. Quai de Paquet
3. Tourist Information
4. Port Captain, Customs, Immigration
5. Motu-Ura, main Customs area
6. Post Office
7. High Commissioner & Assembly
8. Police Station – Surete
9. Hospital
10. Temple Paofoi-Protestant
11. Cathedral
12. Quai de Moorea – Ferries
13. Transit Wharf
14. Inter-island schooner wharf
15. Ocean-going ship wharf
16. Airport
17. Technimarine
18. Gaz de Tahiti -Propane

The following repair agencies have established a reputation for providing good service:

DIESELEC – Checkup and repair of diesel engines and small alternators and starters is done by skilled craftsmen trained at Bosch in Germany and Lucas in France. The use high-tech testing and adjusting devices and speak English, French and German. Tel (689) 42-25-76.

CEGELEC – Excellent and relatively low-priced welding of stainless steel and rewinding and/or reconditioning of very large starters and electric motors is done here. Tel.(689) 41-41-41.

PSA manufactures good quality starting batteries and should be considered since most shippers will not transport open lead/acid batteries. Tel (689) 42-47-22.

TECHNIMARINE – This aluminum welding facility provides haul-out services and long term storage on the hard with good security. The proprietor, B. Paureau and the second in charge, M. Renault are fluent in English.

GAZ de TAHITI – This is an outlet for propane.

TAHITI YACHT CHARTERS, located at the west end of the yacht dock on Boulevard Pomare, is operated by Madame Nicole Paureau. She is fluent in English, very knowledgeable and is generous in sharing information with cruisers. Tel (608) 45-04-00.

All Post Offices offer internet email services.

MEA MA, in front of the airport, provides laundry services.

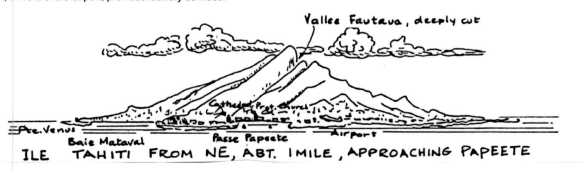

ILE TAHITI FROM NE, ABT. 1 MILE, APPROACHING PAPEETE

ILE TAHITI - NORTHWEST COAST (Pointe Venus to Pointe Nuuroa)

Beginning at Pointe Venus, the guide proceeds in a counter-clockwise direction around the coast of Tahiti. Part of the coast is not detailed as it is too exposed and does not have suitable anchorages.

Pointe Venus is a long, low point easily identified by the 92 foot lighthouse at the tip and a radio pylon about 0.5 miles to the south. The coral reef, awash, extends about 2,000 feet on each side and seaward from the point

Baie de Matavai, with its black sand beach, is west of Pointe Venus. The fringing reef is submerged, but an opening with a depth of 9 fathoms is the entrance. Banc du Dolphin, where there is a beacon, restricts the opening.   Two miles SW of Point Venus at 17°31.3'S and 149° 31.4'W is the buoyed channel leading to Lagon de Arue where there is sheltered anchorage and Tahiti Y.C. facilities.

Passe Taunoa is about 3 miles west of Pointe Venus, and leads into Taunoa and Papawa. It is a 900-foot gap in the reef that is reduced by shoals on each side. An anchorage is in the basin but it is exposed to swell coming through the pass. A slightly less exposed anchorage is near the eastern reef, in black sand. **Chenal Taunoa** is a narrow passage leading to Papeete that is marked by beacons and used by local vessels – overhead clearance is 18 feet.

From the western side of Papeete harbor, **Chenal de Faaa** leads behind the reef and past the airport at Pointe Faaa, after which it turns southward towards Passe Taapuna. Chenal de Faaa is easily negotiated because it is marked by red and green lit beacons and buoys southbound (coming from Papeete harbor, green to starboard, red to port). The currents run northeasterly out of Chenal de Faaa and westerly from Taunoa, all into and then exiting from **Passe de Papeete**. Two anchorages that are comfortable alternatives to Papeete are along this passage; the bus provides quick transportation to downtown Papeete.

The Port Authority has moorings for rent west of Maeva Beach Hotel; 0.25 mile to the south is Carrefour, the largest supermarket in Papeete. Only guests registered at the hotel may use the swimming pool. Do not go through the hotel on your way to the main road, instead use the bridge, and follow the river and the dirt road to the highway. Trash may be deposited in the green garbage cans.

The Carrefour Supermarket includes restaurants, a pharmacy, doctor, port office, and telephone and fax services. Marina Taina is south of Carrefour and is the easiest place in Polynesia to take on fuel and water. The closest laundry, Mea Ma is in front of the airport. The Beachcomber Hotel is friendly to cruisers and will allow boaters to tie dinghies to their dock when permission has been obtained.

Passe Taapuna is about 1.5 miles south of the above anchorages. Although it is marked "dangerous" in the Pilot, it is suitable for auxiliary powered yachts. The pass is 300 feet wide between the reefs – stay mid-channel. The pass has been cleared of obstructions and now the minimum depth at low water is 15 feet. The approach is straight forward and when entering there are three green buoys to starboard and three red buoys to port. Vessels should favor the northern side since the shoal on the south side is only 6 feet deep. The outgoing current can be strong, and if the swell is high, the pass will be white with breakers and transit should not be attempted. Locals say that if there are surfers near the pass, use Passe Papeete instead. As usual with IALA system of buoyage when entering, take the two red markers in the pass on the port side. At the first cardinal buoy (east marker) after entering, the buoyage system changes to "inside the lagoon rules" and from that point onward the green buoys are to be kept to port.

Passe de Taunoa is 0.5 miles WNW of Pointe Ariti and off the eastern end of the coral bank extending in a northeasterly direction from the breakwater protecting Papeete harbor. A prominent landmark marking the pass is the deep Fautaua River gorge beyond which is the saw-tooth summit of Mont Te Tara O Maiao otherwise known as Pic Diademe. This is a straight forward pass with a least depth 14 fathoms and a width of 300 feet. Two flashing beacons on a coral outcrop provide a range (174°T) for entry through the pass. A beautiful black sand beach along the southwestern shore of the basin provides a spectacular playground for locals and guests of the large hotel nearby.

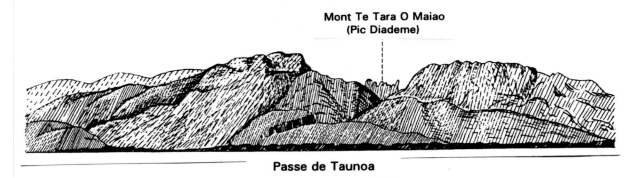

Mont Te Tara O Maiao
(Pic Diademe)

Passe de Taunoa

Anchorage in 2.5 to 7 fathoms, sand can be taken in the east part of Taunoa Basin with protection from easterly winds. If the wind becomes northwesterly, a heavy swell comes through the pass making this anchorage untenable and dangerous. Better protection in all winds can be found off the Tahiti Yacht Club facilities located in Lagon D'Arue and found by following a clearly marked channel to the east. To the west is Chenal Taunoa that connects Taunoa to Fare Ute, an industrial area of Papeete. This channel can only be traversed by vessels with a vertical height less than 17 ft. because a fixed bridge is at the western end of the channel.

The western entrance to Lagon de Arue can be approached from 17°31.4'S, 149°32.7'W; a change of direction of fairway buoyage is indicated by two cardinal markers. The winding channel is marked by numerous buoys and has a minimum depth of 2 fathoms; a lateral beacon is off Pointe Iriti. The eastern entrance to Lagon de Arue is at 17°31.3'S, 149°31.25'W and has lateral beacons that are lit. Pointe Otueaiai is low, covered with thick vegetation and can be identified by the spires of a prominent white church. Nearby is the tomb of Pomare I*, almost hidden by lush plant growth.

* * * *

*Pomare I (also known as Whetoi) was the first leader of a family of chiefs to establish a dynasty that united many of the islands of Polynesia. It has been said that muskets left to him by Captain Bligh enabled him to vanquish many of his enemies and he ruled Tahiti for many years until his death in 1803 or 1805. After the sudden death of his grandson, Pomare III, his sister became Queen Pomare IV. She agreed to let the territory become a French Protectorate in 1842.

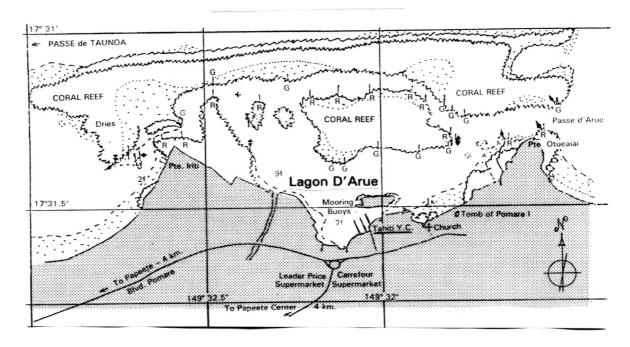

In this well protected setting is the location of the popular, cruiser-friendly Tahiti Yacht Club. Although space is limited for transients at the Yacht Club moorings, two or three spots may become available on weekends when the locals visit Moorea or travel elsewhere. There is limited space to anchor in the vicinity. The friendly manager speaks English and makes a genuine effort to accommodate cruisers; the first night on a mooring is free. Contact is on VHF Channel 6. The fuel dock sells both diesel and gasoline. A noteworthy feature of the yacht club facilities is that this is the only place in the South Pacific with hot water in the showers and laundry. Email yctahiti@mail.pf

A short walk away is the very reasonable Leader Price grocery store and across the street is Carrefour Supermarket with a wide variety of quality merchandise. Several hotels, a post office, banks, pharmacy and restaurants are nearby. The local bus runs to Papeete on a regular schedule.

Southwest of Pointe Venus is an anchorage (shown as a dotted anchor on the sketched chart) that gives good protection from wind and swells from the west through north to SSE. The anchorage is located at approximately 17°29.74'S and 149°29.84'W and the lighthouse bears 080°T. Anchorage may be taken in 2.5 fathoms, good holding mixed black sand and coral bottom. This is a convenient spot to get a rest and prepare for entering Papeete or while waiting for a good wind to sail north to Hawaii or east to the Tuamotus. If a strong southwesterly wind develops a vessel drawing less than 7 ft. may carry through the inshore route east around Point Venus, keeping the first two white markers to port and the following white and black markers to starboard.

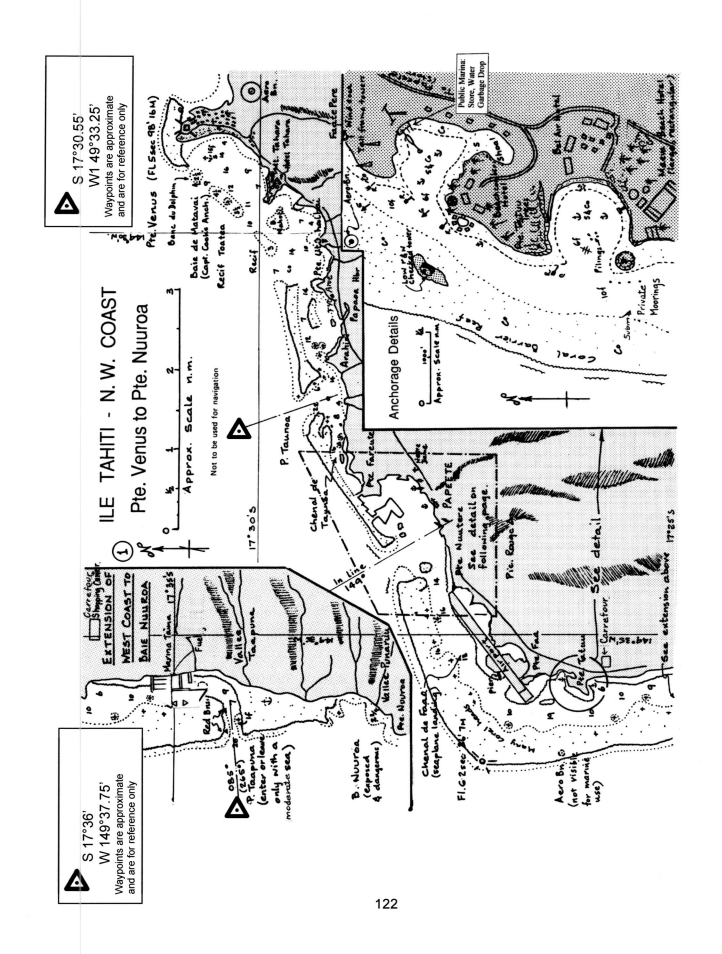

ILE TAHITI - N.W. COAST
Pte. Venus to Pte. Nuuroa

ILE TAHITI - SOUTHWEST COAST (Pointe Maraa to Pointe Mahaitea)

Between Pointe Nuuroa and Paea the coral reef approaches the coast, making Baie Nuuroa so exposed that it should be bypassed. The immense gorge of Vallee de Punaruu extends into the mountains and is a good landmark. Large private estates prohibit public access to this part of the coast. The barrier reef returns at Pointe Nuuroa and off the low point of Pointe Maraa it widens to about 0.75 miles, where the coast then turns eastward.

Passe de Maraa is the westernmost of two passes at the point, separated by a steep hill. It provides entrance to a small bay at the point. Shallow spits extend from both sides of the channel, but beacons mark the navigable water and the clear pass can be easily entered along the centerline. The current sets westerly across the pass and should be taken into account. When southwesterly winter swells cause breaking seas across the entrance it should not be used. Within the pass, anchorage may be taken off the small stream near the point or in front of the steep cliff.

Several basins are behind the reef in the next 3 miles. In good visibility it is possible to thread a route into these basins from the one at the point. The only usable passage for exiting the area is **Passe Maraa** as both Passe Topiro (Fr. name: Passe de Teavaiti), one mile to the east, and Passe West Avaiti (Fr. name: Passe Toapiro), seemingly apparent openings in the reef, are shallow and have coral heads which make them unusable except for small local craft.

The remainder of the coastal reef in this section has no useful passes, though they will be described so that a running check on position can be kept. As the peaks that are often used to define a line through the passes are sometimes obscured, such a running check acts as a navigating backup and the vessel's chartplotter should be set to record the track. The reef is broken in some places, but in general it extends about 2,000 feet from the shore.

Pointe Mahaitea is the highest and most clearly defined of the relatively low points along this coast and is marked by a white building to the north. To the south of the point is **Passe Teavaraa,** a gap in the reef about 900 feet wide. Though it has a depth of 2 fathoms, the swell and surge often cause breakers and lumpy seas, making it dangerous to cross.

* * * * *

NOTE: In this and in sections to follow, the apparently wide passes are reduced in actual width to a narrower navigable area. The breakers that occur across the shallows usually mark the edge of the deep portion of a pass. In a few cases the spits are sufficiently deep that breakers do not occur and so no warning is given. Passes should be entered carefully, especially those slanted toward the coastline, but in most cases a centerline route clears the dangers.

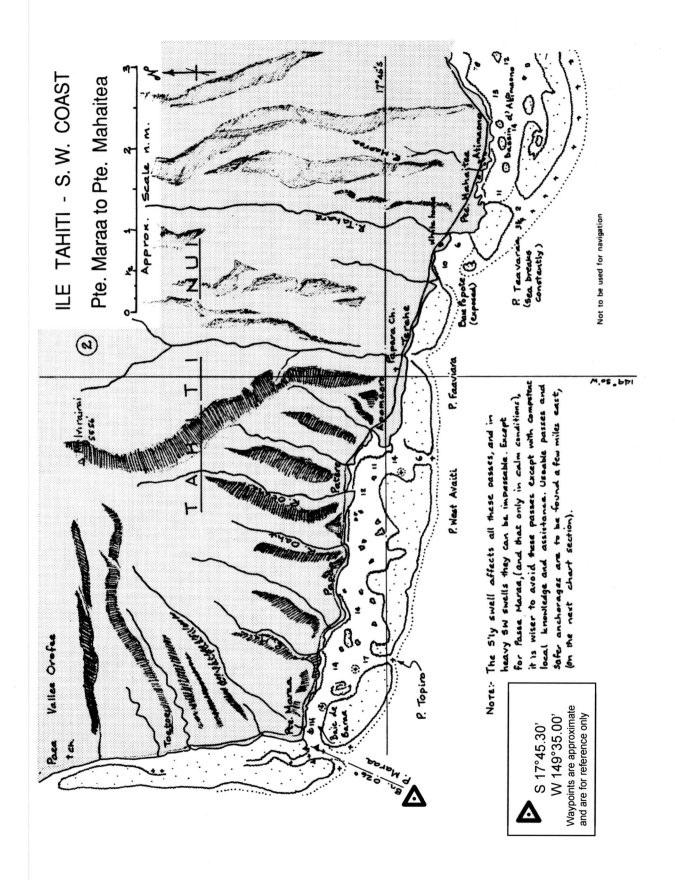

ILE TAHITI - S.W. COAST

Pte. Maraa to Pte. Mahaitea

②

Approx. Scale n.m.

0   ½   1   2   3

N

Not to be used for navigation

NOTE:- The S'ly swell affects all these passes, and in heavy SW swells they can be impassable. Except for Passe Maraa, (and that only in calm conditions), it is wiser to avoid these passes except with competent local knowledge and assistance. Useable passes and safer anchorages are to be found a few miles east, (on the next chart section).

S 17°45.30'
W 149°35.00'
Waypoints are approximate
and are for reference only

124

ILE TAHITI - SOUTH COAST (Passe Aifa to Pointe Patoa)

Beyond Passe Teavaraa the reef bulges out to extend almost 1.5 miles offshore. Behind the reef is a good natural basin, but to enter it you must weather the bulge to reach Passe Aifa which is about 2 miles to the east.

Passe Aifa has an apparent width of 1,000 feet but is reduced by shoals on both sides to a usable passage 300 feet wide. The first wooded islet to appear along the coast, Ile Mapeti, is on the reef on the eastern side of the pass; a small cay is on the western side. Between them are three small reefs awash which leave sufficient room for passage.

The pass is entered on a bearing of 317°T aiming at the small sandy cay and cutting close to the eastern side of the reef. When the south side of Ile Mapeti bears about 40°T, the vessel must turn northward to pass the three small reefs to port and a shallow 3 fathom patch ahead to starboard. The pass leads directly into Baie d'Aifa, then westward into Baie d'Atimaono which is behind the bulge of the reef. It can be used in good weather, and anchorage may be taken in the lagoon in 8 to 10 fathoms.

Passe Rautirare is a deep, clear pass leading directly into Bassin de Papeuriri. It is about 900 feet wide and thus in strong winds it does not provide as much shelter as other less ideal passes. Ilot Pururu stands on the eastern reef well back of the breakers and it provides the best anchorage in good holding, black sand.

Chenal d'Otiaroa is a beacon-marked, 50 yard wide channel leading from Bassin de Papeuriri to spacious Port d'Ataiti. Following the easy passage, anchorage may be taken southeast of the village in 8 to 10 fathoms. Port d'Ataiti is connected to Bassin Papeari on the east by beacon-marked, 50 yard wide Chenal Motuaini. This basin is also accessible via Passe de Temarauri, which is 3 miles east of Pointe Rautirare. Though the eastern side has shoals and reefs, it can be traversed during good visibility.

Passe de Hotumatuu is about 1 mile east of Pointe do Temarauri and it leads into the cul-de-sac of Port de Paul. Anchorage is available for small vessels off the restaurant on Pointe Taunoa that is tucked in the niche behind the reef to the west. A small wharf is nearby, but patches of coral that must be avoided to reach the anchorage also prevent a vessel from mooring to the dock.

Passe de Teputo (Teputa) is one of the entrances leading to Port du Phaeton. Within the opening a large reef (Banc Matuu) divides the pass into two: Passe de Matuu on the west (encumbered by reefs) and Passe de Teputo (deep and clear) which continues along the eastern side. Beacons mark the channel leading to Port du Phaeton, where good anchorage in 4 to 7 fathoms, mud, is available in the large bay, but favor the west side as canoe races are held on the east side. Water and fuel are available at Tahiti Nautic Center (TNC). For shopping, land at the head of the bay at the boulodrome (Petanque Club), where water is also available. It is a short walk to Taravao where there are several large shops, restaurants and two gas stations. TNC is a marina with docks for about 12 vessels, dry storage, a ramp for haul-out and free mooring buoys. For information email tnc@mail.pf, phone (689) 54.76.16. The coordinates are 17°44'S, 149°19.709W.

Passe Tapuaeraha is 3 miles south of Passe de Teputa and leads into Bassin de Tapuaeraha and north to Port du Phaeton or south through Mouillage de Vairo where a naval base is located, to an exit at **Passe East Avaiti (P. Teavaiti).**

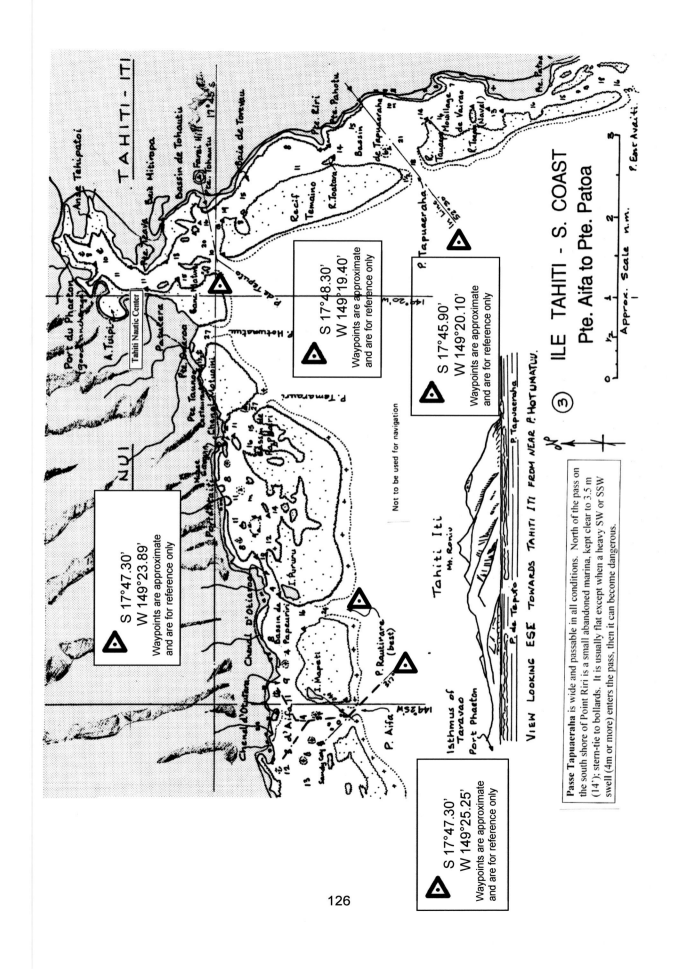

TAHITI - ITI

TAHITI - NUI

Port du Phaeton
(Gendarmerie)
A. Tuipi
Tahiti Nautic Center

Ange Tahiotoi
Baie Nitirapa
Bassin de Tohoutu
Farni Hiff
Opie de Tononui
Pte. Riri
Pte. Pahotu
Bassin
de Tapueraha
Recif Temaino
P. Tautira

Passe Tapuaeraha
P. Tapuaeraha
Tauaramoohage
de Vairao
(Naval)

S 17°48.30'
W 149°19.40'
Waypoints are approximate
and are for reference only

S 17°45.90'
W 149°20.10'
Waypoints are approximate
and are for reference only

S 17°47.30'
W 149°23.89'
Waypoints are approximate
and are for reference only

S 17°47.30'
W 149°25.25'
Waypoints are approximate
and are for reference only

Not to be used for navigation

Isthmus of
Taravao
Port Phaeton

P. Aifa

P. Rautirare (best)

Tahiti Iti
Mt. Roniu

VIEW LOOKING ESE TOWARDS TAHITI ITI FROM NEAR P. HOTUMATUU.

③ ILE TAHITI - S. COAST
Pte. Aifa to Pte. Patoa

Approx. Scale n.m.
0   ½   1   2   3

Passe Tapuaeraha is wide and passable in all conditions. North of the pass on the south shore of Point Riri is a small abandoned marina, kept clear to 3.5 m (14'); stern-tie to bollards. It is usually flat except when a heavy SW or SSW swell (4m or more) enters the pass, then it can become dangerous.

126

ILE TAHITI - SOUTH COAST (Pointe Patoa to Pointa Fareara)

This section of the coast forms the southwestern and southern side of the Taiarapu Peninsula or Tahiti Iti. The land is scored into peaks and valleys making a fantastic skyline and rising to a high plateau at the center of the island. The barrier reef continues around the shore with several usable passes leading to anchorages.

East Avaiti Pass (Passe Teavaiti) is about 1 mile south of Pointe Patoa, and it provides access to Mouillage (Anchorage) de Vairo and Bassin Teahupoo. The pass is 150 yards wide, with least depths of 2 fathoms. In good weather it is usable by small craft but dangerous seas rise across the bar during strong winds. Approach the pass by steering 65T° toward the massive bulk of Mont Tarania, 2,680 feet high, until close-to when the pass can be seen. When within a mile of the pass the alignment can be corrected to a bearing of 60T° on the flat-topped Mont Araope, 899 feet high, and near the coast. Anchorage in 10 fathoms can be found in a basin formed by the projection of a reef, Banc Toa Maere, which projects about 2,000 feet southwest of Pointe Arahuku. Alternatively, slightly more open anchorage is available in Bassin Teahupoo, about 0.5 mile northwest of Pointe Arahuku, close to the coast, sand and coral bottom. Passe Avaino (Passe Teavaino), 1.5 miles to the east is a foul bar with coral heads.

Passe Havae is about 1.5 miles beyond Passe Avaino and is the best of this group. It is straight, deep and clear except for the narrowing of the apparent width of 400 yards to 200 yards by submerged reefs on each side of the opening. A bearing of 30°T on Mont Vaipuu, 2,500 feet high, with the cleft summit of Mont Te Hau 1,273 feet high, leads through the pass. Many yachts use the pass to leave the lagoon traveling from Port du Phaeton.

The coral reef extends from Pointe Fara Mahora, curves eastward and opens at Passe de Puuotohe. The eastern side of the reef extends underwater, reducing the passage to 50 yards. Coral heads within this pass make it dangerous and it should be avoided since a better pass is nearby.

Passe Vaiau has a good, 200 yard wide entrance. A leading line into the pass is at 008T° on the summit of Mont Faretua, 3,190 feet high, a bulky mountain from which three arms extend toward the coast in the form of an "E". It is divided at the inner end into two channels by a reef awash. Either channel may be used, but the western side is preferable. Port de Vaiau is the basin within the reef where anchorage may be found in the cove formed by the coral reef below Pointe Maraetiria.

Passe Tutataroa is not a recommended passage because it is narrow and winding as it goes eastward from Port de Vaiau near underwater reefs and passes Pointe Vareara where the seas are often heavy due to a submerged offshore shoal, Faratara Reef.

The coast turns northeasterly around Pointe Fareara and this portion is called Cote de Pari. Give it a wide berth as the offshore reef is submerged and spectacular breakers can form when there is a heavy swell.

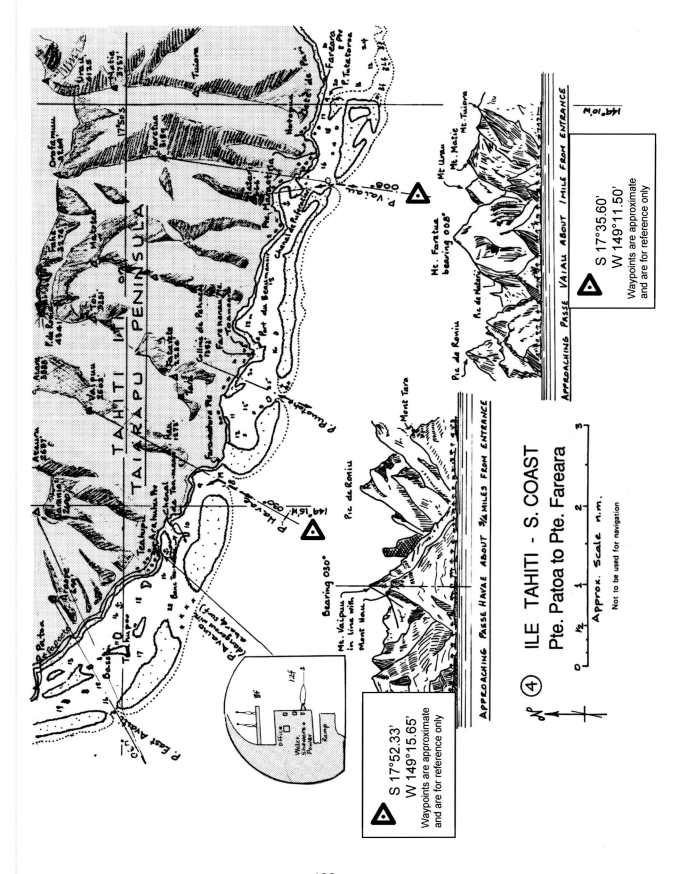

ILE TAHITI - S. COAST
Pte. Patoa to Pte. Fareara

Approx. Scale n.m.

Not to be used for navigation

S 17°52.33'
W 149°15.65'
Waypoints are approximate
and are for reference only

S 17°35.60'
W 149°11.50'
Waypoints are approximate
and are for reference only

ILE TAHITI - SOUTHEAST COAST (Pointe Fareara to Pointe Tautira)

From Pointe Fareara to Pointe Puha, about 3 miles up the coast, the Faratara Reef extends underwater about 4 miles out from the coast. It is submerged to depths varying from 2 to 11 fathoms, and this leaves the coast unprotected. Small vessels must stand clear when sailing up the coast. Because there are no roads in this section until Pointe Tautira, the villages, anchorages, and island views are similar to the Tahiti of old, though the villagers are completely modernized and they speed along in outboard-powered outriggers.

Passe Tomotai, just beyond Pointe Puha, is between the north end of Faratara Reef and the recommencing visible barrier reef that continues up the coast. Ilots Tiere and Fennaino, both covered with palms and clearly visible from seaward, are north of the entrance and help to identify it. Cruisers are advised not to use this pass because of the many hazards near Faratara Reef.

Passe d'Aiurua, located 1 mile north of Pointe Tomotai, is a deep, 200 yard wide pass with easy access to the lagoon behind the reef. A shallow, 2 fathom patch extends southward from the end of the northern reef and requires that the course through the pass be made a little south of the centerline. From seaward a bearing of 276°T on the sharp pinnacle of Mont Teiche takes the vessel on this course. Anchorages are on each side of the pass in coves formed by coral projections extending from the land. The southern anchorage is more exposed, but prettier, and the islets, reefs and motus on the outer reef give some protection. More coral heads are exposed and awash behind the barrier reef, necessitating careful conning while traveling to Pointe Vaitoto if the vessel leaves from Passe Vaionifa.

Passe Vaionifa is about 3 miles north of Passe d'Aiurua and, though reduced from its 200 yard width by shallow spits on each side of the opening, it is an easy pass to transit. It should be approached on a bearing of 233°T taken on the highest peak of the group framed in the deep cut of Vallee de Vaitoto. A shallow patch, marked by a beacon, lies almost on the axis well within the pass and is easily avoided. Le Crabe, marked by a beacon, is a rocky patch awash about 150 yards from the shore and 1 mile northwest of Pointe Vaionifa. Anchorage can be found either midway up Bassin de Tautira, or at the head near Pointe Tautira in about 14 fathoms.

The opening in the reef about 1 mile from the head of the basin is not navigable for it is obstructed by coral heads. There isn't a passage between Pointe Tautira and the reef. In order to travel northward the vessel must exit from Passe Vaionifa, proceed around the reef, and enter Baie Tautira from the north.

Pointe Tautira is a low projection from the mountains that extends northward from the curve of the coastline. The barrier reef bends around the point to end on the west side. The bay is open to the north as there is a 0.5 mile gap in the reef before it begins again. The town of Tautira, an important local center, is extends around the tip of the point.

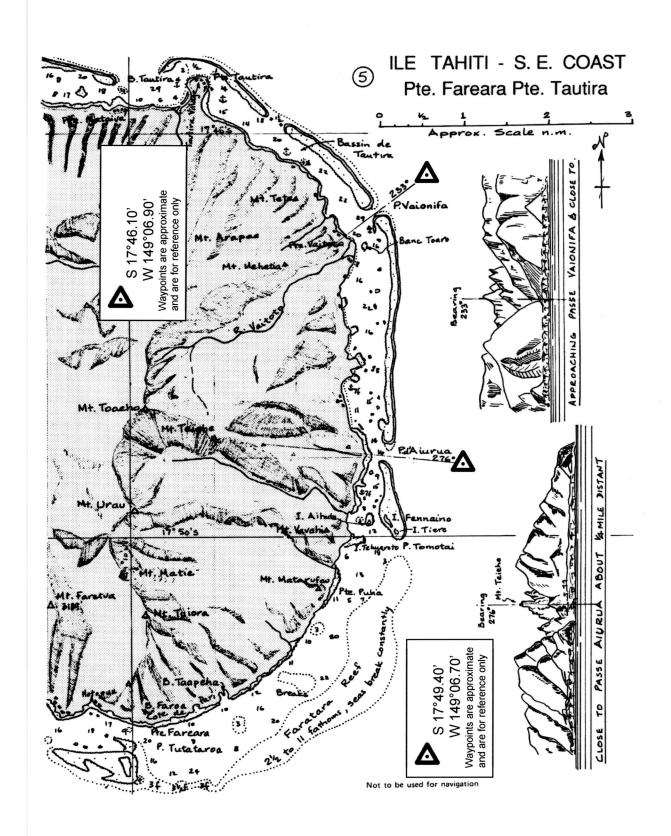

ILE TAHITI - S. E. COAST
⑤ Pte. Fareara Pte. Tautira

S 17°46.10'
W 149°06.90'
Waypoints are approximate
and are for reference only

S 17°49.40'
W 149°06.70'
Waypoints are approximate
and are for reference only

Not to be used for navigation

ILE TAHITI - EAST COAST (Pointe Tautira to Pointe Paritautia)

This portion includes 8 miles of the north coast of Tahiti Iti and the east coast of Tahiti Nui. The scenery from offshore is noteworthy as the hills begin at the shoreline and numerous waterfalls are evident. Vallee Haavini is a spectacular cleft through which peaks at the center of the island can be seen.

Baie de Tautira is within the curve of land along the point and behind the half-mile opening in the reef. It can be entered easily via **Passe Teafa** and anchorage found off the beach near the village, in 6 to 8 fathoms. Winds from the north to WNW make this a lee shore. The fine, black sand beach is one of the few large beaches in Tahiti.

Port de Pihaa is the basin enclosed by the barrier reef that begins west of the opening. It can be entered from either end and is marked by beacons, though a spit of land at the west end, Pointe Pihaa, almost reaches the reef. Several small exposed reefs within the basin can easily be avoided. Anchorage may be taken east of Pointe Pihaa in 14 fathoms, sand and mud.

Passe Taharoa is the next gap in the reef and is about 0.5 mile wide. Banc Tuatua, a shoal covered 3 feet lies on the inside of the pass, dividing it in two. The eastern side is 200 yards wide and some scattered reefs must be negotiated when turning to Port de Pihaa. The western side is clearer and turns almost directly past Pointe Faraari into the next basin, Port de Pueu. A submerged portion of the outer reef could be mistaken for a pass but it is blocked by coral heads and therefore cannot be entered.

Passe de Tiitau is 0.5 mile west of the above false opening. It lies between the end of the barrier reef and a portion of the reef awash, Banc Toapu, which is almost 300 yards across. Ranges on shore give a line through the pass but they are difficult to discern from seaward. There are no problems leaving via this pass.

Baie Taravao is between Pointe Tiitau and the northward turn of the coast. Almost the entire barrier reef in this area is submerged and becomes a series of shoals, except for a few motus. Breaking surf usually identifies the position of underwater reefs. Anchorage here is not recommended for although the holding is good in much of the bay, it is exposed to winds from the north to east and the swell crosses the reef unimpeded.

Passe Papeiri is between the western end of the sunken reef and the visible reef which angles northward. A 6 fathom shoal lies in the entrance. The most popular anchorage is off the village in Port de Vaitoare in good holding, mud and sand; another spot is closer to the offshore reef in slightly less depth. This area can also be entered from the north via **Passe de Faone**. The reef continues for a short distance north of Passe de Faone before the wide opening of Passe d'Utuofai exposes the coast.

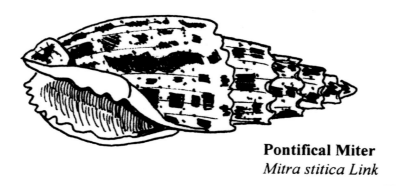

Pontifical Miter
Mitra stitica Link

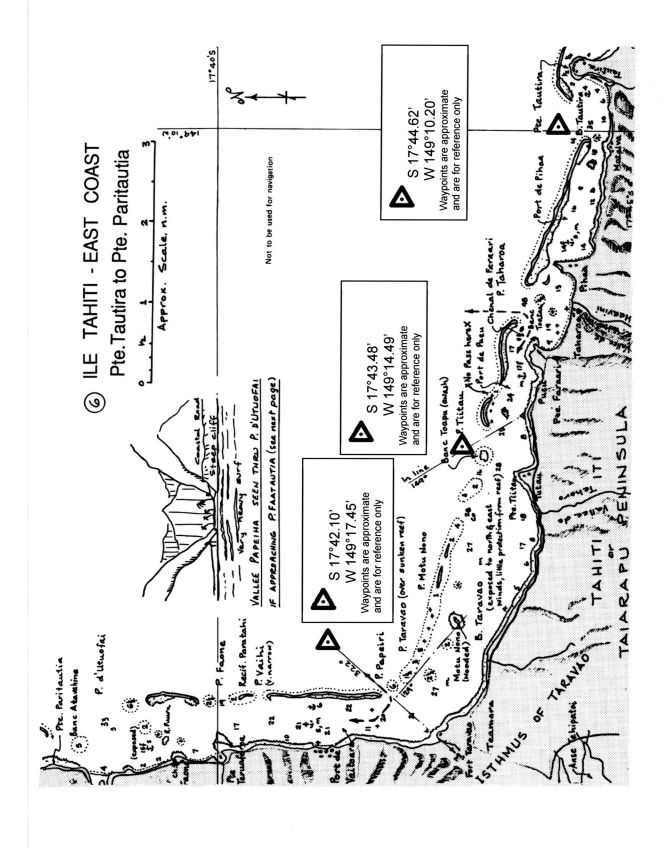

⑥ ILE TAHITI - EAST COAST
Pte.Tautira to Pte. Paritautia

Approx. Scale, n.m.

Not to be used for navigation

S 17°44.62'
W 149°10.20'
Waypoints are approximate
and are for reference only

S 17°43.48'
W 149°14.49'
Waypoints are approximate
and are for reference only

S 17°42.10'
W 149°17.45'
Waypoints are approximate
and are for reference only

VALLEE PAPEIHA SEEN THRU P. D'UTUOFAI
IF APPROACHING P.FAATAUTIA (see next page)

Coastal Road
steep cliff
very heavy surf

132

ILE TAHITI - NORTHEAST COAST (Pointe Paritautia to Pointe de Rauraia)

Pointe Paritautia is an unobtrusive point on the land opposite the recommencing barrier reef at the north end of Passe d'Utofai. The steep cliffs and cleft of Vallee de Papeiha, which is south of the point are more evident as landmarks. This section is the least hospitable for relaxed cruising of any part of a circumnavigation of Tahiti because of some long, dangerous shoals that are found off the coast.

Behind the protection of the reef is a sheltered basin, Porte de Temato (Tamatoe), where good anchorage can be found. The basin is entered through **Passe de Faatautia**, staying within 100 yards of the offshore reef when turning into the anchorage. The small, detached reef on the western side should not be approached closely. Dinghies can land on a black sand beach on the southern side of Pointe d'Hitiaa. The town of Hitiaa lies along the nearby coastal road. A small boat channel is around the coral reef projection at Hitiaa however its depth and suitability for yachts is unknown.

Passe de la Boudeuse is opposite the town of Hitiaa. It is wide although it has some dangerous covered rocks and coral heads on the northern side and vessels should keep close to the edge of the southern reef. Mouillage de Bougainville lies between the island shore and the offshore reef, which is partly submerged. Though this was Bougainville's anchorage, it is not a well-protected basin as wind and swell continue across the reef unabated.

The barrier reef is submerged for the entire 11 miles separating Pointe Mahaena and Pointe Venus. It becomes a chain of dangerous shoals, known as Banc de l'Artemise (locally called, Te Fana), lying from 0.75 to 2 miles offshore. These shoals do not provide protection from the prevailing wind and seas and vessels passing this part of the coast should stand well offshore.

The coast angles northwesterly for the 4 miles between Hitiaa and Pointe Faaru before curving westward. Several deep valleys reach the shore with steep mountain ridges between. Near Pointe de Papenoo, about 9.5 miles from Hitiaa, the great cleft of Vallee of Papenoo extends well into the center of Tahiti. Between this valley and Pointe Venus, only 4 miles away, there are some sandy beaches along the low coast. They are broken by a rocky bluff at Tapahi visible about 1.5 miles from Papenoo. The leper's hospital stands on this bluff and is visible from offshore.

The coast between Pointe de Papenoo and Pointe Venus should be given a wide berth because shoals extend about 600 yards east of Pointe Venus and are 2 miles offshore at Pointe de Papenoo. A vessel coming from the south must stand well to the north (until all of the island of Moorea is open to view beyond Tahiti) before setting a course toward Pointe Venus and Papeete.

The cruise around Tahiti can be made in either direction, but since the western side has light and variable winds, it is easier to follow the pattern described. In this way, the fair, prevailing easterly winds and following seas will take one past the dangerous shoals on the eastern side.

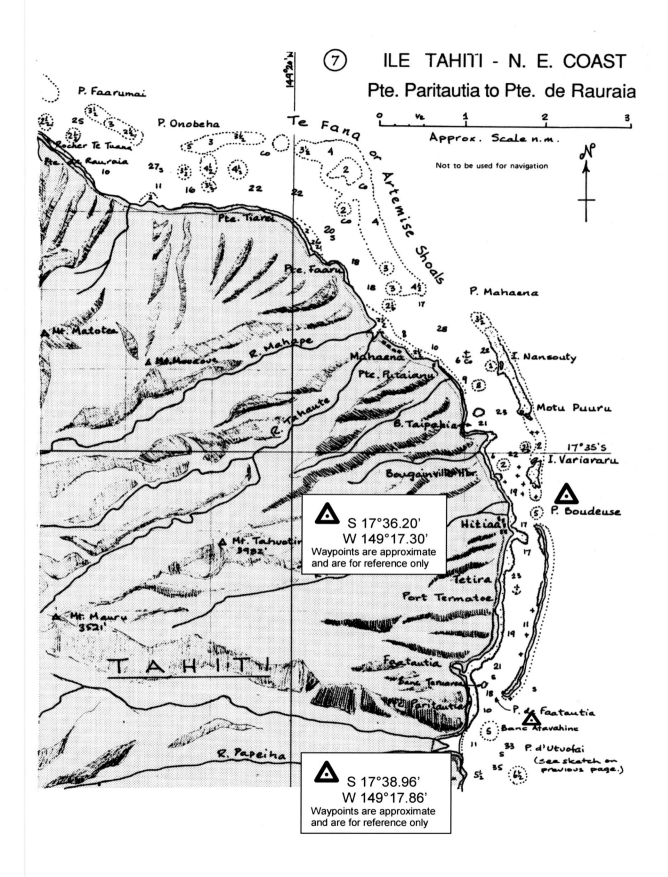

Approx. Scale n.m.

Not to be used for navigation

Te Fana or Artemise Shoals

P. Faarumai

P. Onobeha

Rocher Te Tuana

Pte. de Rauraia

Pte. Tiarei

Pte. Faaru

P. Mahaena

Mt. Matotea

R. Mahape

Mt. Haucoue

Mahaena

Pte. Putaianu

R. Tahaute

I. Nansouty

Motu Puuru

B. Taipahia

17°35'S

I. Variararu

Bougainville Hr.

△ S 17°36.20'
W 149°17.30'
Waypoints are approximate
and are for reference only

P. Boudeuse

Mt. Tahuotir
3992'

Hitiaa

Tetira

Port Termatoe

Mt. Maury
3521'

T A H I T I

Faatautia

Banc Tamarea

P. de Faatautia

Banc Atavahine

R. Papeiha

P. d'Utuofai
(see sketch on
previous page.)

△ S 17°38.96'
W 149°17.86'
Waypoints are approximate
and are for reference only

ILE MOOREA (Excluding Baie de Cook and Baie d'Opunohu)

The usual approach to Moorea takes the swell at an angle and closes the coast near Pointe Faaupo, the easternmost point. As the fringing reef is steep-to and close to the coast, a yacht can sail fairly close to the edge of the reef in good conditions. Proceeding in a counter-clockwise direction around the island, the coast angles northwesterly for about 2 miles until turning south of westerly at Pointe Aroa, which is the northernmost part of Moorea and is marked by a light.

Passe Avaiti is a small pass used by local vessels and is a short distance west of Pointe Aroa. About 1.5 miles further is a slightly wider and usable pass, **Passe Irihonu**, which opens westward into a small lagoon. Anchorage may be taken in front of the Bali Hai Hotel, easily identified by its over-the-water bungalows. A small channel leads westward behind the reef to Baie de Cook, but since the easier entrance of Passe Avaroa is very close, this narrow channel should not be used.

A separate sketch and description is given for the two main bays of Moorea: Baie de Cook and Baie d'Opunohu. Beyond these, the coast continues westward for about 2 miles to Passe Taotoi (Passe Taotai). This entrance can be used in good weather, but it only leads into a long, narrow passage behind the two islets at the western end of Moorea. The channel shallows as it opens into a bay where Club Med is located. The bay and its approaches are shallow and beset with coral heads.

The western coast of Moorea runs southeasterly towards Haapiti and the southern tip of the island. Several hotels are behind the sandy beaches and though a beacon-marked channel runs in front of them, the channel is used mainly by fishing craft. About 6 miles along the curve of the reef from Passe Tautoi is Passe Taota, and a mile further, is Passe Avamotu. Both are narrow and lead into small lagoon cul-de-sacs. Husky rollers are usually seen at the entrance bars of these passes and they should not be entered.

Passe Matauvau is a mile beyond Passe Avamotu and it leads into an extensive lagoon behind the reef where the pretty village of Haapiti is located. During calm conditions this pass can be used but it can be rough and dangerous when a southwesterly swell is running. Passe Avarapa, about 2.5 miles further south, is a rough pass leading to a small lagoon and can be ignored. The southernmost part of Moorea is a mile east of Pointe Avarapa, after which the coast begins to turn northeasterly toward Pointe Faaupo.

Passe de Teruaupu and Passe Tupapaurau both lead into a lagoon that borders the villages of Maatea and Afareaitu. Though rollers invade both entrances, Passe Tupapaurau is preferred since the turbulence is less pronounced. Numerous markers have been established in Passe Teruaupu, making it mandatory to reference the latest French charts for anchorage in Baie Aharoa.   Anchorage can be taken near Afareaitu, the largest village in Moorea.

Three miles northeast of Passe Tupapaurau is **Passe Vaiere**, which can be rough but is usable for cruising vessels and anchorage is available. Several high-speed ferries and a cargo ship use this pass when making frequent scheduled runs from Papeete to a wharf and port at the head of the bay. A new marina south of the ferry dock has room for about 30 yachts but is often filled with local vessels.

ILES DE LA SOCIETE
ILE MOOREA

0   1   2   3
Approx. Scale n.m.

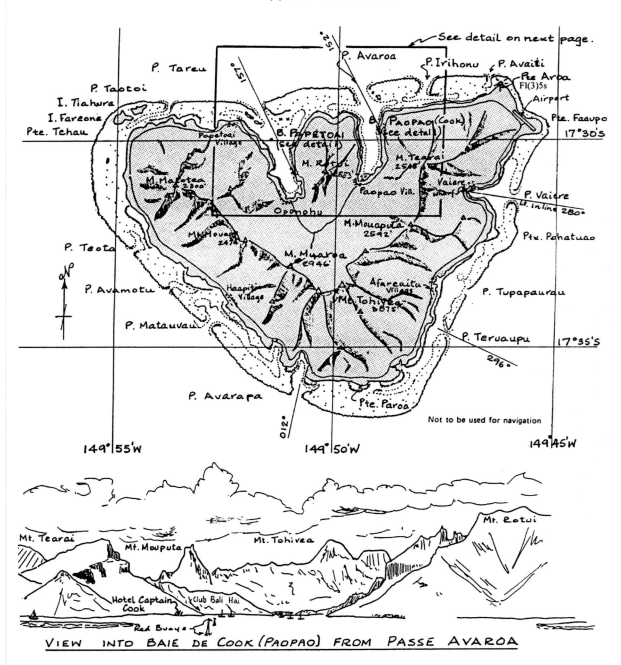

See detail on next page.

P. Tareu

P. Taotoi
I. Tiahura
I. Fareone
Pte. Tehau

P. Avaroa
P. Irihonu
P. Avaiti
Pte Aroa
Fl(3)5s
Airport
Pte. Faaupo
17°30'S

Papetoai Village
B. PAPETOAI
(See detail)
B. PAOPAO (Cook)
(See detail)

M. Rotui
M. Tearai 2548'
Paopao Vill.
Vaiare Wharf
P. Vaiere
Lt. Inline 280°

M. Mouaroa 2800'
Opunohu

M. Mouaputa 2542'
Pte. Pahatuao

P. Teota
M. Muaroa 2946'

P. Avamotu
Haapiti Village
Afareaitu Village
P. Tupapaurau

P. Matauvau
M. Tohivea 3975'

P. Teruaupu
17°35'S
296°

P. Avarapa
Pte. Paroa
012°

Not to be used for navigation

149°55'W   149°50'W   149°45'W

Mt. Tearai
Mt. Mouputa
Mt. Tohivea
Mt. Rotui

Hotel Captain Cook
Club Bali Hai
Red Buoys

VIEW INTO BAIE DE COOK (PAOPAO) FROM PASSE AVAROA

ILE MOOREA (Baie de Cook / Baie de Paopao and Baie d'Opunohu / Baie Papetoai)

Even more than Tahiti, these two bays have probably come to represent the sailor's idea of Polynesia because they have been photographed so often. The spectacular view of the peaks behind them is one of the reasons that Moorea is known as one of the most scenic islands in the world. High speed ferries and a cargo ship make frequent scheduled runs to Papeete from the Vaiare ferry dock. A marina south of the ferry dock can accommodate about 20 yachts. Grocery and hardware stores are nearby.

Baie de Cook is entered through the wide, well-marked pass of **Passe Avaroa**. It is easy to negotiate as the wind and sea have little effect in the partial lee of the island's mountains. Once through the reef, the water's colors indicate the deep portions leading to anchorages on either side of the entrance behind the reef or to passage further into the bay.

On the east side of the entrance to the bay is the former Hotel Captain Cook, a prominent landmark that is closed. The most popular anchorages are off Club Bali Hai Hotel which is midway along the eastern side or at the head of the bay before the village and clear of the shallows. A small fuel dock is located next to Club Bali Hai Hotel. Numerous grocery stores, restaurants, a pharmacy, dive operators, and bike/scooter/car rental firms are located around the bay. The spire of Mont Mouaputa is at the end of the bay; a hole through it near the top resembles a patch of snow visible from the north and northwest. Another hole-pierced mountain is on the eastern side of the bay.

Baie d'Opunohu is entered using **Passe Tareu**, which is 2.5 miles west of Passe Avaroa. It is wide and clear and numerous markers make it mandatory to use the latest French chart. Since the route is slanted to the line of the reef it requires caution to negotiate. A wreck, which resembles a pile of rocks, lies on the western side of the pass. Vessels should proceed well into the bay and clear extensions of the reef before turning to anchor. Pretty anchorages are on each side of the pass behind the reef. Anchorage in 2 – 6 fathoms is available on the east side, off a sandy beach below the bulk of Mont Rotui (the mountain between the bays). On the western side a channel leads to the village of Papetoai where anchorage may be taken in front of the octagonal church. It has been reported that some cruisers have been discouraged from anchoring here. A short distance beyond is a small boat basin used by local boats and its depth may not be adequate for large yachts. Water is available in the basin and grocery stores, small restaurants and a post office are nearby. It is possible to tie to the outer harbor wall to take on water.

Other anchorages are further up the bay, the first being the little cove at Orufara on the western side, where an anchor can be laid in the bay and stern line tied to the palms. Robinson's Cove, on the eastern side, is a short distance past the white board structures that give a leading line through the pass. Unfortunately two commercial tour boats monopolize it with mooring lines that make it impossible for cruisers to use as an anchorage. An old house in a lovely garden is on the point to the south which helps to form the cove. Anchorage may also be taken at the head of the bay, closer to the village, and a limited number of vessels can use the smaller coves.

The view behind the bay includes the massive bulk of Mont Tohieva and the spire of Mont Mouaroa, famous not only from sailing stories but also as the backdrop in the film version of *South Pacific*. There is an excellent view of both Opunohu and Cook Bays from the "Belvedere," a lookout above Opunohu experimental farms. Two miles up the Opunohu valley is a collection of marae (temples) and other archeological sites.

ILES DE LA SOCIETE
ILE MOOREA
Baies de Cook & D'Opunohu

O 1000' ½ 1 2
Approx. Scale n.m.

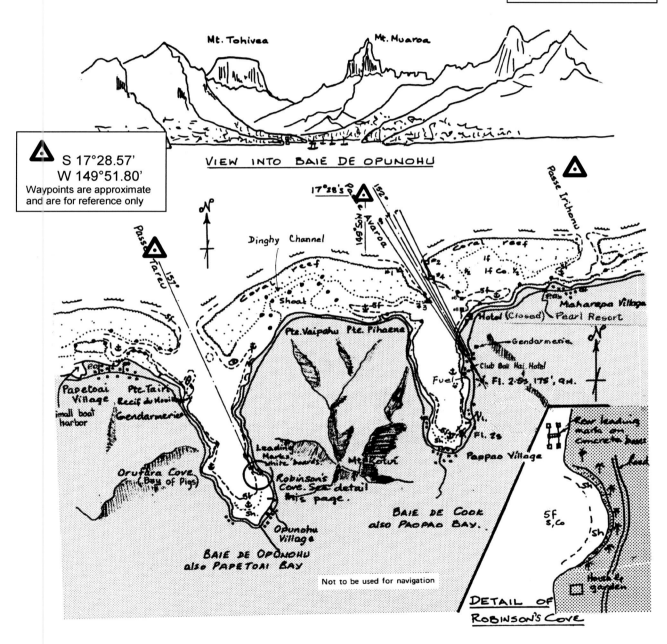

VIEW INTO BAIE DE OPUNOHU

Not to be used for navigation

DETAIL OF
ROBINSON'S COVE

SMALLER ISLANDS of the ILES DU VENT

This group consists of the islands of Mehetia, Tetiaroa, and Maiao (Tubuai Manu). They are described for information only as they are not recommended for visits by yachts since they have neither entry to lagoons nor anchorages.

ILE MEHETIA

This high little island is 60 miles east of Tahiti, and is the easternmost of the Society Island Group. It is 180 miles south of Mataiva, the westernmost island of the Tuamotus. It is formed by a remarkable, peaked cone, Fareura (1,427 feet) which descends in steep cliffs to the sea on all sides except the south. The island is usually uninhabited and going ashore is very difficult. It is a good sighting landmark to use when approaching Tahiti from the east.

ILE MAIAO (also known as TUBUAI MANU)

This is the westernmost island of the group and lies 40 miles west of Moorea. The fringing reef closely surrounds two interlocked islands that enclose shallow lagoons. At the center are two hills, the higher one reaching 440 feet. The hills are visible from seaward before the island itself is clearly defined. A small cut in the reef in the southern end is sometimes used by local vessels for landing; an indifferent, deep, exposed anchorage is just offshore. Landing is hazardous on this inhabited island.

ILE TETIAROA

This is the only atoll of the Iles du Vent, and is composed of twelve islets enclosing a protected lagoon. It lies about 30 miles north of Tahiti, and should be kept in mind by navigators when laying a course to a destination point north of Pointe Venus on Tahiti. The southern tip of the island is marked by a light. Superb snorkeling and diving can be enjoyed in the 100' depths of the lagoon. It is a very beautiful atoll having brilliant white beaches and is a nesting site for thousands of sea birds which congregate on Birds Island in the southern part of the lagoon. There is no entrance into the lagoon for other than very small boats; the wharf-like structure on the reef at the southwest corner is used by trading vessels. Check with local cruisers for information on landing.

The island was once owned by Marlon Brando, who purchased it when he played Fletcher Christian in the 1966 version of "*Mutiny on the Bounty*." In 1973 the island was opened to tourists, who were flown in to the airstrip on Motu Onetahi. Hotel development here has now stopped.

Historically, the island was a resort for Tahitian Chiefs and the Pomare royal family. Long ago the motu of Rimatuu, where they resided, was planted with royal 'tuu' trees. The female members of important families were sent there to 'fatten' and get fashionable lighter skin before their marriages. In 1904 the royal family gave the atoll to a Canadian dentist who eventually put it on the market.

Public restroom in Huahine - Modern conveniences in a traditional setting!

Personal transportation, Island style – Traditional and modern versions

The only thing missing here is <u>YOUR</u> boat!

Humpback Whale at Niue

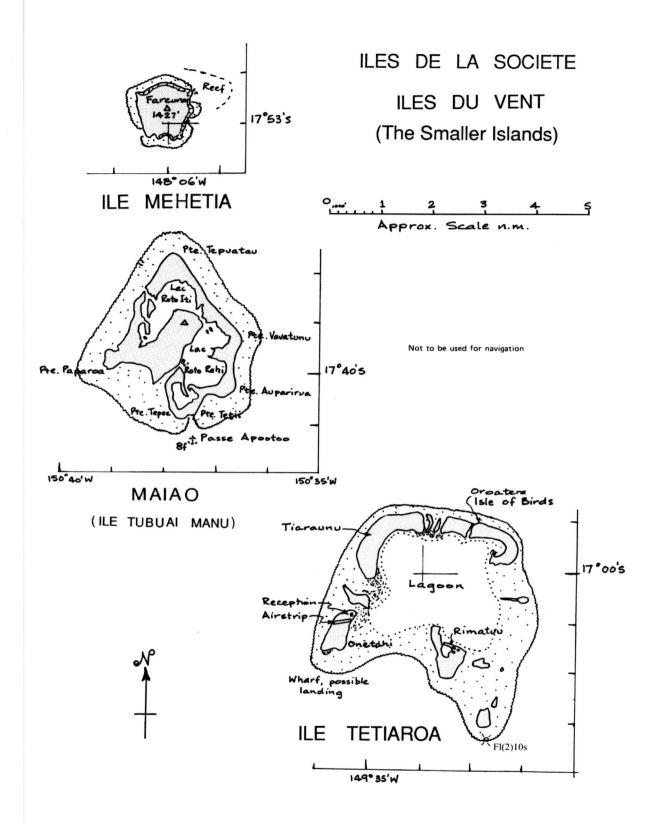

ILES DE LA SOCIETE

ILES DU VENT

(The Smaller Islands)

ILE MEHETIA

17°53'S

148°06'W

Farewa 1427'

Reef

Approx. Scale n.m.

0   1   2   3   4   5

Not to be used for navigation

MAIAO

(ILE TUBUAI MANU)

Pte. Tepvatau

Lac Roto Iti

Pte. Vavatunu

Pte. Paparoa

17°40'S

Lac Roto Rahi

Pte. Auparirua

Pte. Tepee

Pte. Tetii

Passe Apootoo

8f

150°40'W

150°35'W

N

ILE TETIAROA

Oroatera (Isle of Birds

Tiaraunu

Lagoon

17°00'S

Reception
Airstrip

Rimatuu

Onetahi

Wharf, possible
landing

149°35'W

Fl(2)10s

ILE HUAHINE

Huahine is the closest of the leeward island group to Tahiti, lying 90 miles to the northwest. The passage from Tahiti should be arranged so the approach to Huahine is made in daylight. Plan for landfall after sunrise by leaving Moorea just before dusk, keeping the boat speed to about 5 knots since the current gives a boost when approaching the island.

The mass of Huahine is made up of two mountainous islands, Huahine Nui and Huahine Iti, connected by a narrow isthmus and bridge. The islands are enclosed by a common barrier reef that is close to the northern coast but extends as much as a mile offshore elsewhere. There are five passes through the reef and the four most useful to yachts are described below.

Passe Avamoa, on the northwest side, the major pass to Huahine, is easy to negotiate, and gives entry to the village of Fare. Its apparent width of 400 yards is reduced to 120 yards by shoals on either side. Buoys mark the deep water of the pass and ranges with lights give a line through the entrance. Fare lies along the southeastern shore. A pier at the waterfront is used by trading vessels; yachts anchor southeast of it or off the Bali Hai Hotel, which is on the seaward side of the pier. This is not an all-weather anchorage, and every year the combination of gusty winds and reversing tidal currents causes boats to drag ashore onto coral heads. Water is available from faucets southeast of the main commercial wharf. Check the clarity of the water before filling your tanks; following heavy rain it will be turbid from sediment. There is very good shopping in Fare, with a large supermarket, bank, several restaurants and internet services. It is possible to hire a car to explore this fascinating island. Show an anchor light as one or two large ships call nightly and the yacht anchorage is near the channel.

Passe Avapeihi is 1 mile south of Passe Avamoa. Though slightly narrower than Passe Avamoa it is almost as easy to use. Range lights visible for 4 miles, bearing 94°T, and green buoys mark both the pass and a passage between the two passes behind the reef. Anchorage can be taken near the end of Baie Haavai though it is deep and narrow. Several good, but deep anchorage spots are also found in the basin of Port du Bourayne, which is reached using the clear passage behind the barrier reef south of the passes. Use the deep, marked northern channel past Motu Vaiorea when entering as the southern entrance is shallow. A dinghy can be taken through the marked Passage Honoava.

A first rate anchorage is at Avae (Pointe Tiva) at 16°49.66'S, 150°59.74'W. The marked channel along the west side of the island is clear. A small shop and restaurants can be found here.

Passe Farerea is deep and straight, though the curve of the reef from Motu Topati toward the coast reduces the pass to a width of 100 yards. It should be used only in good weather as strong trade winds can make the pass very difficult to negotiate. A bearing of 262°T taken on the range on the north side of the entrance to Baie de Maroe leads through the pass. Beacons mark the passage and vessels should favor the northern side. The best anchorage is off the village of Maroe where landing can be done at the pier. Squalls can blow off the steep mountains around the bay. Use French Chart 6434 if anchoring other than at Fare or Haavai.

Passe Tiare is about 1.5 miles north of Passe Farerea. It is deep, narrow and should only be used in calm weather after being checked by dinghy. A small boat harbor dredged to a least depth of 6 feet is in the bay's northeast corner and good anchorages are in the lee of Motu Vavaratea.

ILE HUAHINE FROM THE N. ABOUT 6 MILES

ILES DE LA SOCIETE
ILE HUAHINE

Not to be used for navigation

0   1   2   3 n.m.

Approx. Scale n.m.

🔺 S 16°42.30'
W 151°03.20'
Waypoints are approximate
and are for reference only

🔺 S 16°43.50'
W 151°03.40'
Waypoints are approximate
and are for reference only

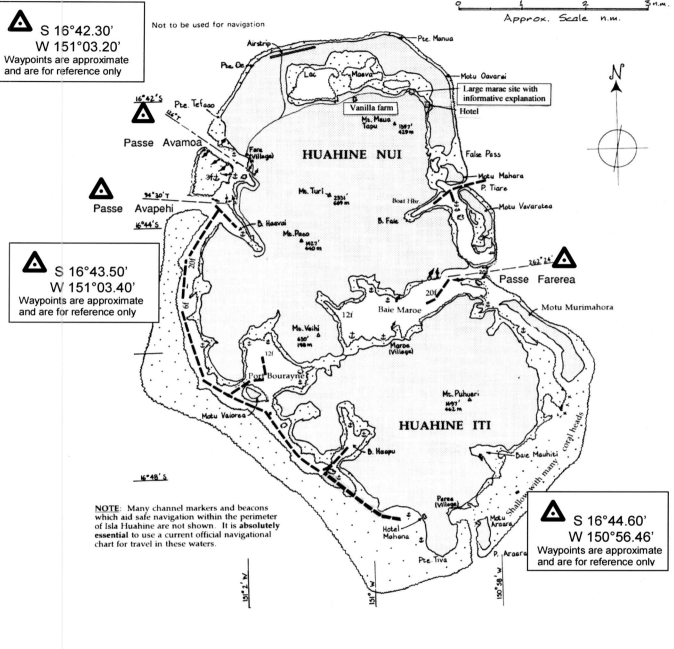

🔺 S 16°44.60'
W 150°56.46'
Waypoints are approximate
and are for reference only

NOTE: Many channel markers and beacons
which aid safe navigation within the perimeter
of Isla Huahine are not shown. It is absolutely
essential to use a current official navigational
chart for travel in these waters.

APPROACHING HUAHINE FROM TAHITI,
i.e. FROM S.E.

ILE RAIATEA AND ILE TAHAA

Raiatea and Tahaa lie within the same coral reef, about 20 miles west of Ile Huahine. Both are mountainous with spurs radiating from central ranges to the coast forming an indented shoreline. The many maraes in Raiatea attest to the long period when it was the cultural and religious center of the Societies and it is well worth visiting these fascinating and revered sites.

The surrounding barrier reef is awash in some places and submerged in others. Eight passes lead through the reef around Raiatea and two into Tahaa. Deep and navigable water between the reef and the islands makes it possible to travel entirely around Tahaa and about two-thirds of the way around Raiatea. Shoals and coral heads are scattered in the inner waters but the routes between them pose no difficulty if traveled in sunlight with a person aloft.

Passe Teavapiti is the normal entry for vessels from Huahine or Tahiti and can be used during all weather conditions. Approach it by heading toward the square-topped bulk of Mont Tapioi, 998 feet high, at the north end of Raiatea. As the pass is closed, align the leading lights and marks ashore on a bearing of 269°T or if not visible, the depression between a pair of skyline peaks south of Mont Tapioi can be used. The opening in the reef has two channels separated by Ile Taoru. The southern channel is **Passe Teavarua**, the northern is Passe Teavapiti with a width of 200 yards. On each side of the opening the reef is partly submerged, but its extent is clearly indicated by islets and surf. The north side of the pass should be favored (where the reef is steep-to) as any current in the pass is usually southerly.

Beacons mark the channel leading from Passe Teavapiti to Uturoa. The town is spread along the coast but the center is near Pointe du Roi Tomatoa. A concrete wharf used by freighters and ferries extends along the shore southeast of the point. A fuel dock suitable for stern-to mooring is next to the main Uturoa wharf and an excellent supermarket is next door. A municipal marina with a capacity of 50 boats is 0.25 miles north of the fuel dock and sometimes has room for cruisers. Good anchorage can be taken in the channel northeast or southeast of the wharf in 15 to 18 fathoms, sand and mud. A pier at the northern end of the main wharf can be used as a dinghy dock. Two blocks from the wharf is a market with many shops and the famous "Cafe au Motu."

Passe Teavarua is the southern channel of Passe Teavapiti and it is used if the vessel's course turns southward behind the reef. Beacons mark the channel but care is needed for it has many coral heads to avoid. The open bays along the coast at Vairahi, Averaiti and Averarahi provide safe anchorages. They are open to the trade winds but protected from the sea by the reef.

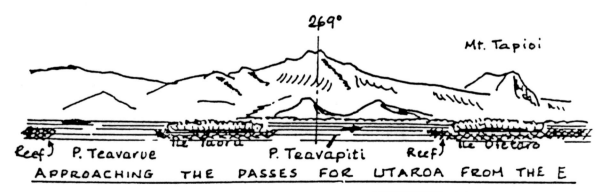

APPROACHING THE PASSES FOR UTAROA FROM THE E

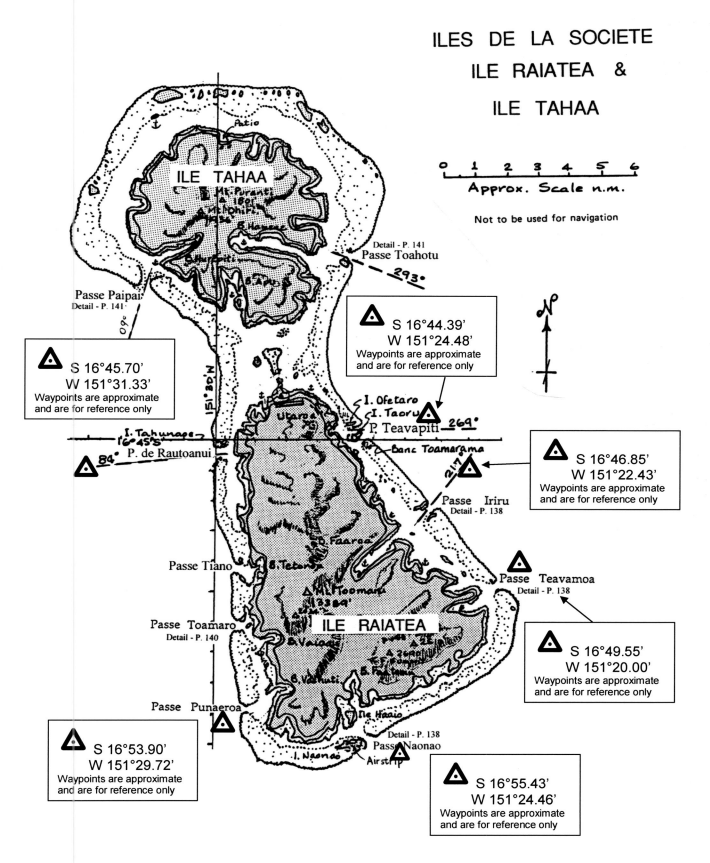

ILES DE LA SOCIETE
ILE RAIATEA &
ILE TAHAA

0 1 2 3 4 5 6
Approx. Scale n.m.

Not to be used for navigation

ILE TAHAA

Patio

Mt.Purauti
1801'

Passe Paipai
Detail - P. 141

Detail - P. 141
Passe Toahotu
293°

S 16°44.39'
W 151°24.48'
Waypoints are approximate
and are for reference only

S 16°45.70'
W 151°31.33'
Waypoints are approximate
and are for reference only

I. Ofetaro
I. Taoru
P. Teavapiti 269°

Banc Toamarama

I. Tahunape
16°45'S
P. de Rautoanui

84°

217°

S 16°46.85'
W 151°22.43'
Waypoints are approximate
and are for reference only

Utaroa

Passe Iriru
Detail - P. 138

Passe Tiano

Mt.Toomaru
2389'

Passe Toamaro
Detail - P. 140

ILE RAIATEA

Passe Teavamoa
Detail - P. 138

S 16°49.55'
W 151°20.00'
Waypoints are approximate
and are for reference only

Passe Punaeroa

Ile Haaio

Detail - P. 138
Passe Naonao
Airstrip

I. Naonao

S 16°53.90'
W 151°29.72'
Waypoints are approximate
and are for reference only

S 16°55.43'
W 151°24.46'
Waypoints are approximate
and are for reference only

146

Passe Iriru (Maire) is about 3 miles southeast of Passe Teavapiti and is clearly identifiable by the two islets on the coral reef bordering each side of the pass which is 150 yards wide. An entry on a bearing of 217°T taken on the sharp peak of Mont Maufenua (that lies E. south of Baie Faaroa) leads through the reef near the southern side where the sea is quieter. Good anchorage is available near the head of Baie Faaroa in 8 to 12 fathoms, mud. Sunsail Charters has about 20 moorings and with permission it is possible to land at their dock halfway along the north shore. An interesting dinghy trip is up the Aoppomau River at the head of the bay. The passage behind the reef between Passe Iriru and Passe Teavamoa can be traversed but careful conning is needed to avoid many shoals and coral heads.

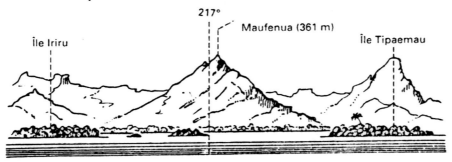

Passe Iriru

Pacific Islands Pilot, Volume III – U.K.

Passe Teavamoa is deep, narrow, fairly short, and can be easily entered. Care is needed on entry to avoid the coastal reef that projects at the outer ends of the bay, especially from the south. The pass leads to a very nice anchorage in Baie Hotopuu, about midway up the bay in 15 fathoms, mud. A short walk to the northwest leads to Marae Taputaputea, the most important religious and historical site in Polynesia.

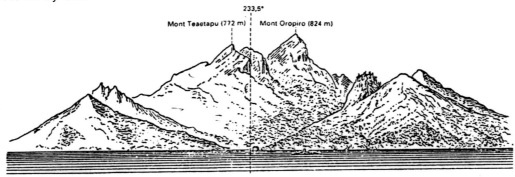

Passe Teavamoa

Pacific Islands Pilot, Volume III – U. K.

Passe Naonao is about 100 yards wide and a bar at the narrows causes the sea to break if southerly swell is running, so it is not recommended in unsettled weather. There are attractive but deep anchorages in the lee of Iles Naonao and Haaio. A small store is in the village of Tautara. Anchorage may be taken off the west end of Motu Nao Nao at 16°55.05S, 151° 26.20W. The airstrip has been abandoned for some time.

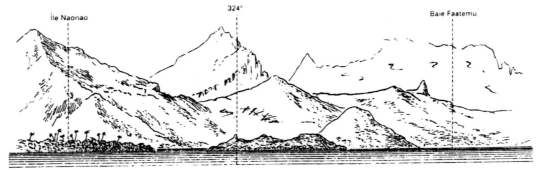

Passe Naonao

Pacific Islands Pilot, Volume III – U. K.

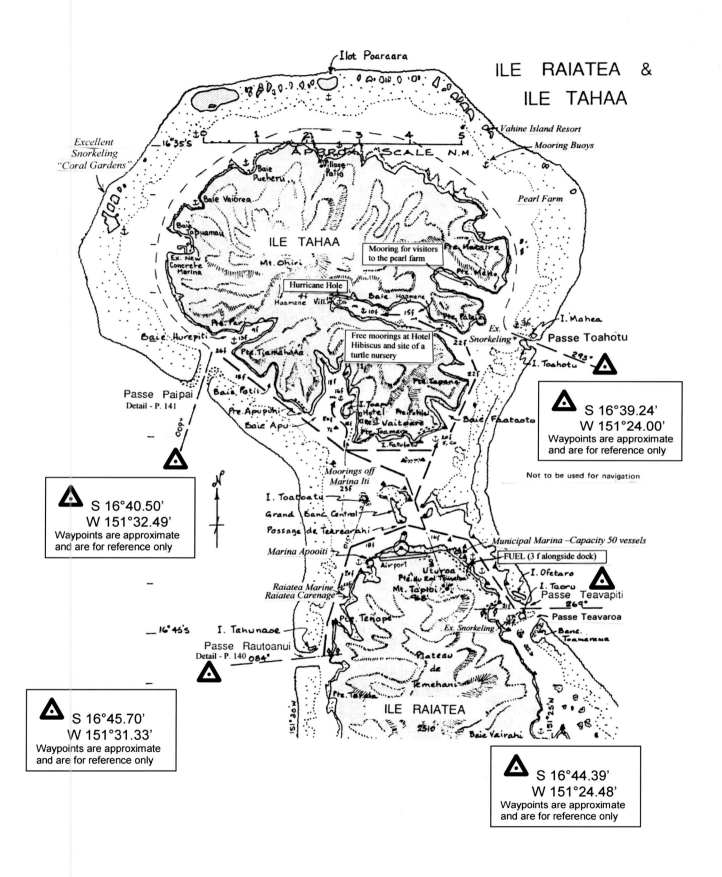

ILE RAIATEA &
ILE TAHAA

Ilot Poaraara

Excellent Snorkeling "Coral Gardens"

Vahine Island Resort

Mooring Buoys

16°35'S

1 2 3 4 5
APPROX SCALE N.M.

Pearl Farm

Baie Pueheru

Village Patio

Baie Vaiorea

ILE TAHAA

Baie Tapuamau

Mt. Ohiri

Pte. Mataira

Ex. New Concrete Marina

Mooring for visitors to the pearl farm

Hurricane Hole

Haamene Vill.

Baie Haamene

Pte. Patii

Pte. Faru

Baie Hurepiti

Pte. Tiamahana

Free moorings at Hotel Hibiscus and site of a turtle nursery

Ex. Snorkeling

I. Mahea

Passe Toahotu

I. Toahotu

295°

Passe Paipai
Detail - P. 141

Baie Patii

Pte. Apupihi

Baie Apu

I. Toau
Hotel Vaiteare
Pte. Teamere

Pte. Topana

Baie Faataoto

I. Fatula

▲ S 16°39.24'
W 151°24.00'
Waypoints are approximate and are for reference only

Not to be used for navigation

Moorings off Marina Iti

I. Toaoatu

Grand Banc Central

Passage de Tearearahi

Marina Apooiti

▲ S 16°40.50'
W 151°32.49'
Waypoints are approximate and are for reference only

Airport

Uturoa
Pte. Hu Rai Tinehe
Mt. Tapioi

Municipal Marina –Capacity 50 vessels

FUEL (3 f alongside dock)

I. Ofetaro
I. Taoru
Passe Teavapiti
269°

Passe Teavaroa

Raiatea Marine
Raiatea Carenage

Banc Toamarama

Pte. Tenepe

I. Tahunaoe

Ex. Snorkeling

16°45'S

Passe Rautoanui
Detail - P. 140 084°

▲ S 16°45.70'
W 151°31.33'
Waypoints are approximate and are for reference only

Pte. Taipu

Plateau de Temehani

ILE RAIATEA

2510

151°30'W

151°25'W

Baie Vairahi

▲ S 16°44.39'
W 151°24.48'
Waypoints are approximate and are for reference only

148

Passes Punaeroa, Toamaro, and Tiano are along the lower western side of the island. The first two can be used in good weather, but they lead to separate lagoon pockets not joined to the lagoon around Raiatea. In good weather with the sun overhead it is possible to sail inside the reef from Ile Naonao, around the southern end of Raiatea and exit at Passe Punaeroa or Passe Taomaro. Good anchorage can be taken in 2.5 fathoms sand, NE of Ile Toamaru at 16°05.73S, 151°29.18W. Passe Tiano is not recommended.

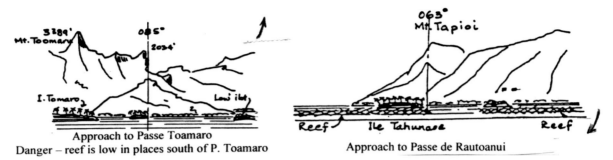

Approach to Passe Toamaro
Danger – reef is low in places south of P. Toamaro

Approach to Passe de Rautoanui

Passe Rautoanui is the main pass on the western side and is an all-weather entrance for the port of Uturoa. It is over 300 yards wide and is easy to navigate with leading lights and marks. An equally wide passage to the north, marked by beacons, makes connections to Uturoa or Tahaa. Near the western end of the airport is Marina Apooiti where temporary moorage, a sail loft, fuel, water and ice are available. Anchorage outside the basin is also possible. About a half mile south of Marina Apooiti is the entrance to the boatyards at Le Carenage at 16° 44.12S, 151°29.21W; these operations are not related to the marina. The two adjacent yards are: Chantier Naval des Iles (CNI; email raiatea.marine@mail.pf, or cni@mail.pf) and Le Carenage (associated with The Moorings, email: raiateacarenage@mail.pf). Equipped with travelifts and a marine railway, their services include long-term dry storage, painting, engine, sail, and equipment repairs. Raiatea Marine is a small chandlery. The best hurricane hole in the area is the cul-de-sac of Hamamene Bay in Tahaa.

Pointe Motutapu is the northernmost part of Raiatea and the coastal reef extends northward from it for about 650 yards. The gap between this reef and Grand Banc Central (a large reef between Raiatea and Tahaa) is about 325 yards wide. Marked on both sides by beacons, Passage de Tearearahi is deep and provides the shortest route across the lagoon as well as access to Tahaa's anchorages and passes via channels on both east and west sides of the Banc. **Passe Tohahotu**, on the eastern reef can be used in good weather to access Tahaa.

On the north coast of Tahaa is the main village of Patio where the bank, Gendarmerie, post office and largest shops on the island are located. An excellent anchorage is located 1.25 miles north of Patio (south of Ilot Poaraara) in 6.5 fathoms, sand. On the southeastern coast near Baie Faataoto is the village of Vaitoare where anchorage may be taken or further to the north in Baie Haamene, near its head in 8 to 10 fathoms. Another spot is at Baie Apu, on the SW coast behind Ile Toapui. A safe hurricane moorage is a marina in Baie Tapuamu on the NW coast where water, fuel and fresh bread are available. Anchorage can be taken in the bay in 10 fathoms but stay clear of the wharf, as the inter-island freighter calls frequently. Haamene Bay shoals to 4 fathoms and provides safe anchorage 100 yards off the village of Haamene. A dentist, physician, pharmacy, post office, bank, and store (magazin) are in the village. Hotel Hibiscus on the north shore is a turtle sanctuary that nurses turtles until they are fit to be set free again. Cruisers are welcomed and free mooring buoys and bicycles are available. The helpful owner is fluent in English, French and German.

Passe Paipai is located on the southwestern side of Tahaa and gives access to Hurepiti Bay, Apu Bay and Tahaa village. It is about 300 yards wide and about 0.5 miles long. The entrance, marked with beacons, is deep and free of dangers except for a shoal extending about 200 yards from the SE tip of the NW edge of the encircling reef. The shoal is marked by a heavy swell. Do not use this entrance in southerly weather when a very heavy swell sweeps the pass, making it dangerous. Currents in the pass are reported to be strong.

Good holding anchorage can be found about halfway into Hurepiti Bay just beyond the reef extending from a small projection on the north shore. The entire north shore of Hurepiti Bay is lined with coral reaching almost halfway across the bay beyond the anchorage. Three moorings of "Vanilla Tours" are nearby, for information call Alain on VHF Ch. 9. Anchorage near the buoys can be taken at 16°38.62'S, 151°33.46'W. A luxury hotel is on Motu Tautau. Excellent anchorage is also available about 0.2 miles north of the southernmost tip (Pointe Toamaru) of Baie Apu. The resort has several moorings along the shore.

A cruise around Tahaa can be easily done for reef projections are marked with beacons. On the north coast is the main village of Patio where there is a bank, post office, shops and a Gendarmerie. Good anchorage can be taken east of the village or 1.25 miles north of Patio, south of Ilot Poaraara in 7 fathoms, sand.

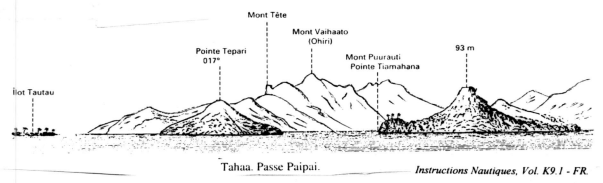

Tahaa. Passe Paipai.   *Instructions Nautiques, Vol. K9.1 - FR.*

Passe Toahotu is easily recognized by two islets, Mahea and Toahotu, marking the northern and southern tips of the reef. It is about 300 yards wide and free of dangers. When entering the pass bring Mont Purauti on a range of 293°T with the hill on Pointe Patai. The anchorage at the northwestern end of Baie Haamene is so secure that it is considered a hurricane hole. Take care to avoid coral banks lining the bay; some extending well into the bay and marked by beacons.

In the next bay to the north, Baie Faaaha, the Motu Pearl farm is located on the north shore. Moorings are provided for patrons of the farm where prices for pearls and mother of pearl crafts are much less expensive than in Tahiti.

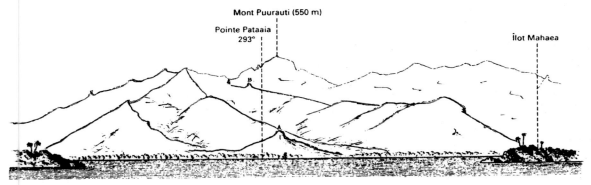

Tahaa. Passe Tohahotu.

Instructions Nautiques, Vol. K9.1 - FR.

ILE BORA-BORA

The spectacular volcanic peaks surrounded by an extensive lagoon of varied hues of blue make this one of the world's most beautiful islands.

Passe Teavanui is the only entrance into the lagoon and is wide, clearly marked and easily traversed. A prominent lit beacon on a white concrete port is on the SE corner of the outer reef. A leading line of 104°T taken on shore markers leads through the pass. The front marker is a conspicuous red column with a white top 33 feet high and the rear marker, not easily seen amidst the trees high on the hillside, is about 90 feet high. Lighted buoys mark the channel and the edge of the reef can be seen on either side. The current is almost always ebbing.

Directly beyond the pass is the Bora-Bora Yacht Club (a nice restaurant) where anchorage may be taken. There is charge for tying to the mooring buoys. Water is available at the short dock for a nominal charge. **Warning**: Just outside the mooring field of the Yacht Club is a sunken wreck in 83 ft. of water. The (unmarked?) wreck is approximately 28 ft. long and the mast lays horizontally at 16°29.287S and 151°45.704W.

The town of Vaitape is in the next bay to the south where another favorite anchorage is located in 15 fathoms, sand. It is possible to temporarily tie to the south side of the large commercial wharf when taking on fuel or supplies. The gendarmerie is located at the head of the wharf, and banks, a grocery store, post office and hospital are located nearby. Try to avoid visiting the town when cruise ships arrive as the crowds of tourists are overwhelming. The concrete wharves where inter-island freighters land cargo are around the point of land to the north. Directly across from the wharf in **Baie de Faanui** is an excellent, but small, hurricane harbor.

Vessels having a draft of less than 8 feet can follow a well-marked channel which takes you around the northern end of the island and down the east coast as far as Club Med. Use **French Chart #6002** to follow the marked route which threads through coral patches and passes through an area where coral was blasted to make a channel When circling an island within a lagoon, red cylindrical markers are on the island side of the channel and green cones are on the sea side of the channel. In settled weather anchorage within the lagoon may be taken in 2 - 3 fathoms in areas free of coral found off the motus to the east.

Other anchorages have some limitations. Free mooring buoys are available for patrons of *Bloody Mary's*, an excellent, expensive and unique restaurant. On the southern point of Baie de Povai is the luxurious Bora-Bora Hotel off which is an exposed anchorage. Patrons of the bar may use their dinghy dock. A sprawling tourist development has taken over the southern shore of Toopua and part of Toopua-Iti and another hotel is located at the north end of Toopua. Further south, around Pointe Matira, the barrier reef is attached to a point of land and forms a secluded little bay where anchorage may be taken in 5 fathoms, sand. Entry to this spot is through a narrow corridor in the coral heads that must be negotiated only in the best visibility, thus requiring an overnight stay. It is best to locate the channel by dinghy prior to entering.

A well-marked channel leads all the way around Toopua and Toopua Iti and vessels can anchor on their western sides. Idyllic anchorages in 5 to 7 fathoms are just within the reef on either side of the pass. Between Motu Tapu and two semi-exposed coral areas to the east is a gap showing deep, blue water leading to a fair expanse of sandy bottom which is encircled by coral where temporary, day anchorage can be taken near excellent snorkeling. A similar spot lies between the southern end of Ile Teveiroa and Motu Ahuna on the north side of the pass, which is shallower and less constricted by coral.

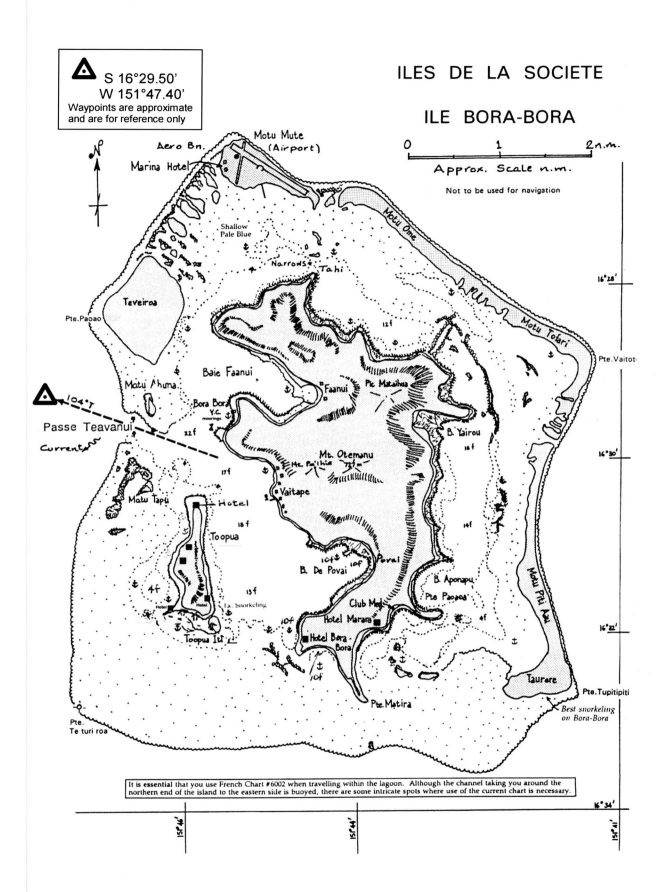

ILES DE LA SOCIETE

ILE BORA-BORA

S 16°29.50'
W 151°47.40'
Waypoints are approximate
and are for reference only

0   1   2 n.m.
Approx. Scale n.m.
Not to be used for navigation

Aero Bn.
Motu Mute
(Airport)
Marina Hotel

Motu Ome

Shallow
Pale Blue

Narrows Tahi

Motu Tofari

16°28'

Teveiroa

Pte.Paoao

12 f

Pte.Vaitot

Baie Faanui

Motu Ahuna

Faanui

Pte. Mataihua

Bora Bora
Y.C.
moorings

22 f

104°T

B. Vairou

16 f

Passe Teavanui

Currents

16°30'

Motu Tapu

17 f

Mt. Pa'hia

Mt. Otemanu
727 m

Vaitape

Hotel

18 f

14 f

Toopua

B. De Povai

10 f 10 f

Povai

B. Aponapu

Pte.Paopao

13 f

4 f

Club Med

4 f

Hotel Marara

10 f

Ex. Snorkeling

Toopua Iti

10 f

Hotel Bora-
Bora

16°32'

Taurere

Pte.Tupitipiti

Pte.
Te turi roa

10 f

Pte.Matira

Best snorkeling
on Bora-Bora

It is essential that you use French Chart #6002 when travelling within the lagoon. Although the channel taking you around the northern end of the island to the eastern side is buoyed, there are some intricate spots where use of the current chart is necessary.

151°46'

151°44'

16°34'

151°41'

ILE MAUPITI

This isolated, lofty island is the westernmost of the Society Group, and lies 27 miles northwest of Bora-Bora. It is a remnant of a volcanic peak that now has steep, vertical cliffs in a semicircle on the southwestern side. The highest point, at 1,250 feet, is near the center of the island. A barrier reef completely encircles the island, the northern side having one short and two long motus. At the southernmost point is Passe Onoiau, located between two small islets, Pitiahe (Motu-Iti-Ahe) and Tiapaa (Motu-Te-Apaa). The population is about 1,200.

Passe Onoiau has a poor reputation because in rough conditions it is hazardous to enter and numerous vessels have come to grief here. Not only is it winding and narrow but a strong outgoing current also adds to the difficulties in negotiating the channel. With a southerly swell large amounts of water come over the low and poorly defined reef on the southwest side. This water flows out of the pass constantly, reaching speeds of up to 9 knots. This results in heavy breakers across the entrance and some vessels have been trapped within the lagoon for up to two weeks. Breakers on the southern reef of Bora-Bora are a good indication of conditions at Maupiti.

Considering the tide, departure from Bora-Bora must be planned to arrive at the optimum time for entering the pass. Passe Onoiau is about 75 yards wide at the entrance but the navigable channel is greatly reduced by a submerged projection of the reef's eastern edge. The sea usually breaks over this projection, which has 2 fathoms of water where it drops off. When approaching the entrance you should line up the passage from a short distance out to sea, through the clear portion of the opening to the two islets where the entrance is marked with white beacons with a red band. The channel to the wharf at the village is marked with beacons and depths vary from 1.5 to 5 fathoms.

The village of Vai'ea on the eastern shore of the island has a concrete wharf and basin for speed boats; a wide, level, coral playing field is alongside. Anchorage can be taken in a fairly clear area south of the wharf or obtain permission to tie stern-to the wharf. There are about 2 fathoms alongside, but care is needed as the bottom shoals rapidly on its northern side. Water and fuel are available by jerry jug from the gas station on the edge of the basin. Numerous small stores are scattered throughout the town and some produce (mainly watermelons and cantaloupe) are available. Fresh bread is available before 0700 at the blue-roofed bakery south of the wharf. The post office is open from 0730 to 1230. The island is linked to Papeete with thrice weekly air service via Raiatea or Bora-Bora and weekly service by the passenger ferry *Meherio II* from Raiatea.

East of the village is a wide, whitish expanse of very shallow water beyond which is the curve of Motu Tuanai (Tuanae) where the airstrip connecting Maupiti to the rest of the Societies is located. A hike to the Haranae Valley in the northeastern part of the island leads to some interesting petroglyphs of turtles. The western side of the island has the remains of a marae.

The beauty of the island is twofold: the lovely shades of blue water and the pale colors of the shoal create a delightful contrast to the green palms, and the warm, friendly people always make visitors feel very welcome.

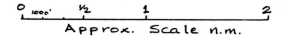

ILES DE LA SOCIETE

ILE MAUPITI

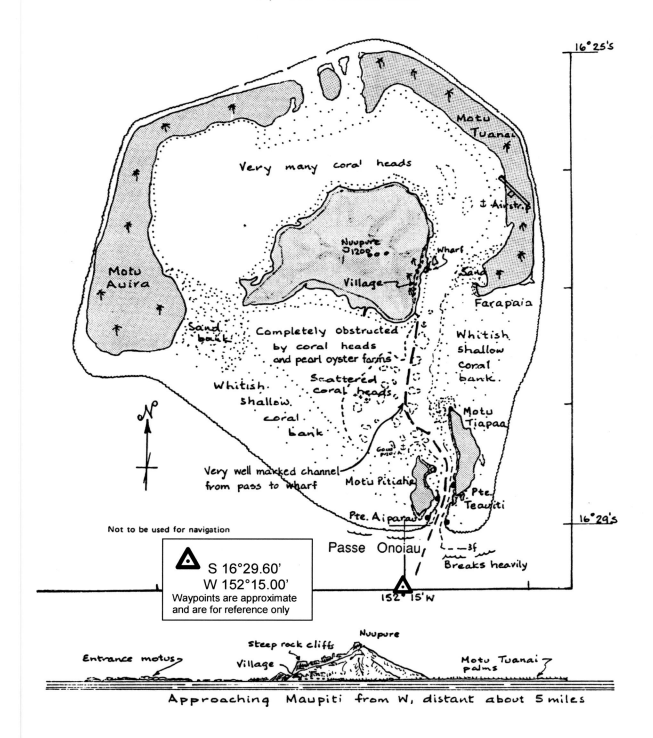

Approx. Scale n.m.

16°25'S

Motu Tuanai

Very many coral heads

‡ Airstrip

Nuupure △1200

Wharf

Village

Sand

Motu Auira

Farapaia

Sand bank

Completely obstructed by coral heads and pearl oyster farms

Whitish shallow coral bank.

Scattered coral heads

Whitish Shallow coral bank

Motu Tiapaa

Very well marked channel from pass to wharf

Motu Pitiahe

Pte. Teauiti

Pte. Aiparau

16°29'S

Not to be used for navigation

⚠ S 16°29.60'
W 152°15.00'
Waypoints are approximate and are for reference only

Passe Onoiau

Breaks heavily

—3f

152°15'W

Nuupure

Steep rock cliffs

Entrance motus

Village

Motu Tuanai palms

Approaching Maupiti from W, distant about 5 miles

154

ILE MAUPIHAA (Mopelia)

This island lies 100 miles west of Ile Maupiti. Since it is an atoll that cannot be seen until close by, the approach should be timed to occur in daylight. Allowance must be made for the set of the current, and this can be established by using Maupiti as a mark as long as it is visible combined with GPS data. The atoll is roughly circular in shape, about 5 miles across.

In 1998 Cyclone Martin swept over the island, destroying 75% of the trees and vegetation and completely destroyed all but one of the houses. Life has returned to normal and there are a few inhabitants involved in pearl shell cultivation. Three houses and a cistern are visible a mile south of the northern end of the island and several houses can be seen near the southern end of the motu. On the northwestern side of the atoll is the only pass which leads into the extensive, deep lagoon. The minimum depth in the pass is about 2.5 fathoms. A break in the coral shelf and agitated water indicates the location of the pass. Each side of the entrance is marked by a white posts set in the reef on the sides of the entrance pass commencing about 30 yards inside the pass. A monthly supply ship from Maupiti services the island.

Passe Taihaaru Vahine is one of the trickiest passes in French Polynesia because it is very narrow and the constantly ebbing current can reach 6 knots or more at times, making a reliable engine and calm nerves necessary. Whirlpools occur in the vicinity of the coral patches where ebb currents meet inside the entrance. If there is a strong southerly swell or southeast trade wind blowing, water entering the lagoon on the south side will funnel out of the pass creating too much current for most yachts to negotiate safely. On the other hand, a northwesterly wind causes the waves to break across the pass and rips caused by opposing currents make the entrance impassable. During moderate easterly winds the current can decrease to 3 knots. Posts mark the outer edges of the pass.

It is important to time your entry around noon when high tide occurs and the coral is plainly visible. The Pilot reports the pass to be 30 yards wide but it seems much narrower and a bow look-out should be posted.

Three anchorages are available inside of the lagoon. The course must be set by visual means, with the clarity of the water making identification of coral heads relatively easy. Oyster floats are scattered throughout the lagoon at depths of over 8 fathoms. Careful conning with good visibility is needed to find a route to the anchorage at the southeastern corner of the lagoon. Stay parallel to the beach in about 4 to 6 fathoms to avoid oyster floats. During south and southeasterly winds this is the best anchorage.

Thousands of seabirds inhabit the small motus and the lagoon abounds with sharks, turtles and colorful tropical fish.

ILES DE LA SOCIETE

ILE MAUPIHAA (MOPELIA)

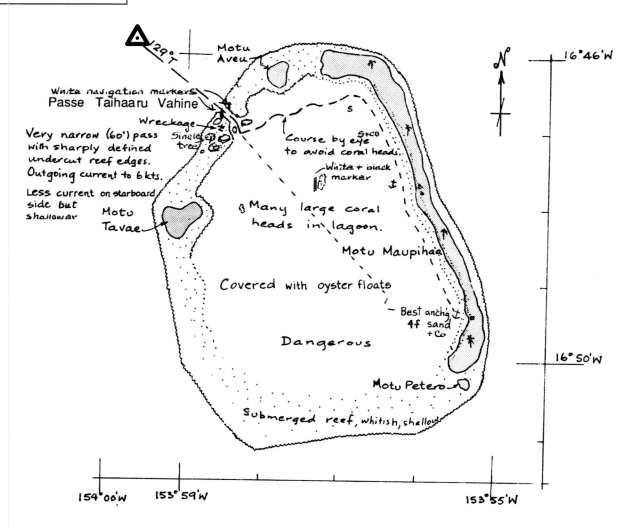

0   ½   1   2   3
Approx. Scale n.m.

Motu Aveu

White navigation markers
Passe Taihaaru Vahine

Wreckage

Very narrow (60') pass
with sharply defined
undercut reef edges.
Outgoing current to 6 kts.

Less current on starboard
side but
shallower

Single
tree

Course by eye
to avoid coral heads.

White + black
marker

Many large coral
heads in lagoon.

Motu Tavae

Motu Maupihaa

Covered with oyster floats

Best anch'g
4f sand
+ co

Dangerous

Motu Petero

Submerged reef, whitish, shallow

16°46'W

16°50'W

154°00'W   153°59'W   153°55'W

Not to be used for navigation

156

WESTERN ATOLLS of ILES SOUS LE VENT

The three atolls of Ile Tupai, Ile Manuae, and Motu One are described for information only since they are isolated and are not normally visited by cruising vessels due to the difficulty of landing and lack of anchorages and facilities.

ILE TUPAI (Motu Iti)

This is a pretty atoll, covered with palm trees, and about 8 miles NNW of Bora-Bora. Since the traffic from Bora-Bora heads south or west, the island is seldom visited. Though it is approachable without danger, the fringing reef encloses the two islets of the atoll without an entry into the lagoon. A landing place with a small passage in the northwestern corner is used by small local vessels. About 50 people on the island support themselves with copra production. A small private airfield is on the island.

Legend has it that Chilean crew aboard the warship *Araucano* mutinied in 1822, pillaged coastal towns in Peru, and later buried their treasure in a marae on the eastern side of the Ile Tupai.

ILE MAUNAE (Scilly Island or Fenua Ura)

This is the westernmost island of the Iles Sous Le Vent group and it is about 40 miles WNW of Ile Maupihaa. The lagoon is about 6 miles in diameter and is accessible only to small boats through a pass located about 0.4 miles WSW of the northern point. Another pass used by small local vessels in calm conditions is on the east coast near a village. A reef borders the eastern coast which is composed of wooded motus; coral reefs are on the western and southern sides. The western coast is a dune more than 10 miles long and only about 1.5 feet high and is often inundated by seas washing over the reef. This is a dangerous atoll and should be avoided as it is visible mainly because of the surf on the western and southern sides.

Only a few people live on the island and support themselves with the harvest of copra. A visible wreck is located at 16°34.2'S, 154° 43.0'W.

MOTU ONE

This is the smallest atoll in the Iles Sous-le-Vent and is about 40 miles WNW of Ile Manuae. It is composed of four wooded islets surrounding a shallow lagoon with depths of less than a fathom. The perimeter of the atoll is marked with rocks. There is no pass giving access to the lagoon, though small local boats land on the west and south side of the atoll. Off these landing spots precarious anchorage can be taken in 10 to 20 fathoms. The small village is occasionally inhabited by seasonal workers harvesting copra.

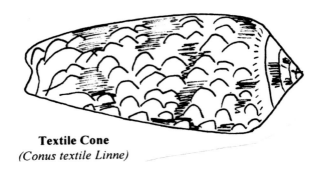

Textile Cone
(Conus textile Linne)

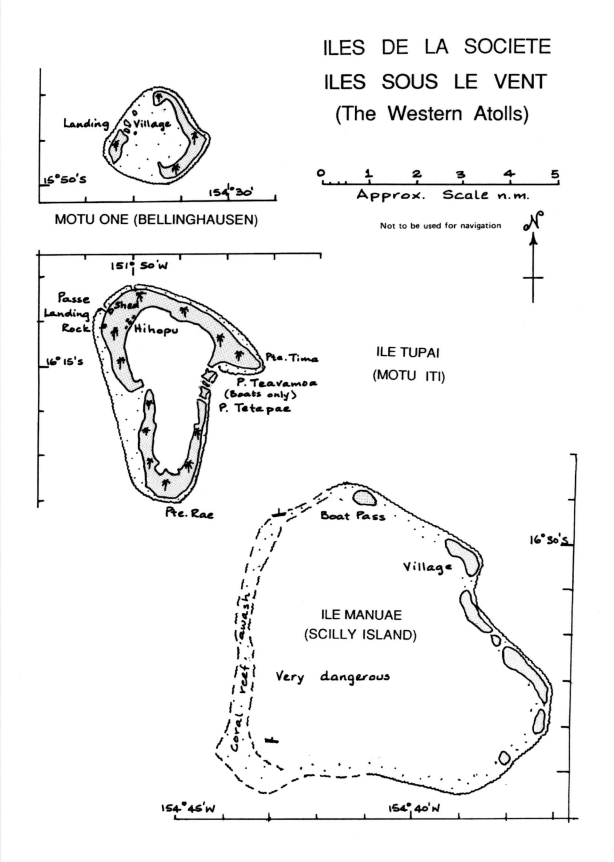

ILES DE LA SOCIETE

ILES SOUS LE VENT

(The Western Atolls)

0   1   2   3   4   5
Approx. Scale n.m.

Not to be used for navigation

MOTU ONE (BELLINGHAUSEN)

15°50'S

154°30'

Landing   Village

151° 50'W

Passe
Landing
Rock

Shed

Hihopu

16°15'S

Pte. Tima

P. Teavamoa
(Boats only)

P. Tetapae

Pte. Rae

ILE TUPAI
(MOTU ITI)

Boat Pass

Village

16°30'S

ILE MANUAE
(SCILLY ISLAND)

Coral reef awash

Very dangerous

154°45'W

154°40'W

ILES AUSTRALES (ARCHIPEL TUBUAI)

This group of islands spreads over 800 miles in a WNW-ESE line across the Tropic of Capricorn, between 145°and 155°W longitude. It includes the islands of Maria, Rimatara, Rurutu, Tubuai and Raivavae. Ile de Rapa and Ilots Marotiri, located 300 miles southeast of Raivavae, are under the jurisdiction of Tubuai. With the exception of Maria, which is an atoll, the islands are volcanically formed and resemble the Societies except for the lower altitude of their peaks. Approximately 5,200 people inhabit these islands.

Caution: Many of the beacons marking passages through the reefs around these islands are missing. Since the water is not clear, great caution must be exercised to avoid the numerous scattered coral patches.

These are high, volcanic islands, surrounded by fringing coral reefs close to the islands. There is no shelter behind the reefs, except at Tubuai and Raivavae. The islands are within the trade wind belt and have weather conditions similar to the rest of French Polynesia though they are slightly more humid. Their more southerly position gives them a wider temperature range, dropping to 10°C (50°F) in winter. The strongest trade winds occur in July.

Permission to visit the group should be obtained in Papeete, and special permission must be obtained to visit Ile Rapa. An informal entry can be made at Tubuai or Raivavae. The main islands are fertile and support wild coffee and orange plantations. There are no facilities, and neither provisions nor fuel can be obtained in quantity. These are the most isolated of the French Polynesian Islands, although they are being brought out of this separation by air service to Tahiti.

The islands have had a turbulent past which is belied by today's quiet way of life. Agriculture was once well developed to support the warlike villages and a strong and aggressive population once lived here. Sadly, they were decimated by disease and only a few survived. Because of this, unfortunately they now have very little cultural ties to their past. For example, Raivavae once had a social structure to rival Tahiti and had similar influence on the migrations of Polynesians. Tubuai once violently rejected the Bounty's mutineers and Rapa, the most exotic of all, still has the remains of abandoned fortified villages on some mountain peaks.

Comb of Venus
(Murex pecten Lightfoot)

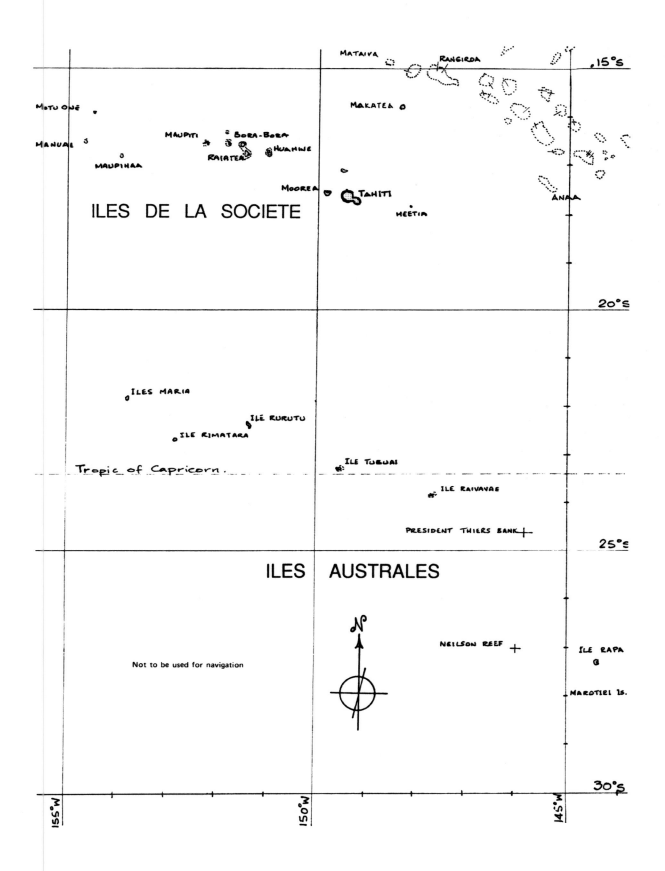

MATAIVA   RANGIROA

MOTU ONE

MAKATEA ○

MANUAE

MAUPITI   BORA-BORA

RAIATEA   HUAHINE

MAUPIHAA

MOOREA   TAHITI

MEETIA

ANAA

ILES DE LA SOCIETE

○ ILES MARIA

ILE RURUTU

○ ILE RIMATARA

Tropic of Capricorn.

ILE TUBUAI

ILE RAIVAVAE

PRESIDENT THIERS BANK +

ILES   AUSTRALES

N

NEILSON REEF +

ILE RAPA

Not to be used for navigation

MAROTIRI Is.

.15°S

20°S

25°S

30°S

155°W

150°W

145°W

ILE RURUTU

A fringing coral reef closely encircles this island and provides no protected anchorage within. The passages through the reef allow only small boats to have access to the shore. Vessels anchored outside the reef sometimes tie stern-to the stakes that mark the passages. On a northerly approach the main village of Moerai is prominent though its church is hidden by vegetation until close in. Two miles SSE of Moerai the red roof of the church in Hauti is clearly visible, as is the church in the village of Avera on the west coast.

The island has a population of about 2,000 and the Government Administrator and gendarme reside here. Anchorage is possible off the passage at the village of Moerai but the holding is poor on hard, flat coral bottom, and strong trade winds make it an unsafe anchorage. There is a tiny harbor in front of the gendarmerie that can accommodate one yacht in calm conditions. Lighters unload cargo from the trading ships at the small harbor and pier 0.5 mile northwest of the gendarmerie, in front of a large, white church. Although there is a lot of surge during E to SE winds, vessels can tie to the dock until the bi-weekly island freighter arrives. Water and some produce can be obtained. An airstrip gives the island access to Papeete.

The village of Avera is midway along the western side of the island, where safe anchorage can be taken. Since the southwesterly swell causes high surf on this side, landing can be difficult making landing at Moerai preferable. Woven mats and bags with scallops and open work made from dried pandanus leaves are unique to the island.

ILE RIMATARA

This small island rises to about 272 feet and has a population of about 1,000. It is encircled by a coral reef, cut by a few passages used for landings, but it does not have any sheltered anchorages. From seaward all that can be seen is a large graveyard (with tombs dating back to the 19th century) next to a green cement block boathouse above the beach. On the eastern side is the main village of Amaru which has a gendarmerie, radio station, stores, bakery and a school. The largest marae site in the Australs is found on this island.

Anchorage off the passage near Amaru is unwise due to poor holding. Better anchorage is found directly north of Passe Tahine in about 6 - 7 fathoms, sand. In settled easterly weather, landing can be made at the concrete landing in the middle of the beach or on the sandy beach at Passe Tahine.

Anapoto is a village on the northwestern side of the island and its large church, school and concrete wharf are visible from offshore. Anchorage may be taken in the lee of the island in 5 fathoms, sand and coral. Dinghy landing can be made at the wharf used by lighters to unload trading ships. Passe Hitiau, leading to Anapoto, may be the only usable pass in strong prevailing winds. An average of one or two yachts per year visit Rimatara.

ILE MARIA

This is a group of four small wooded islets within a coral reef. Two shallow passes on the western side are used by copra harvesters from Rimatara and Rurutu. Reports indicate that anchorage may be taken about a mile NW and SW of the reef in 6 - 15 fathoms, sand.

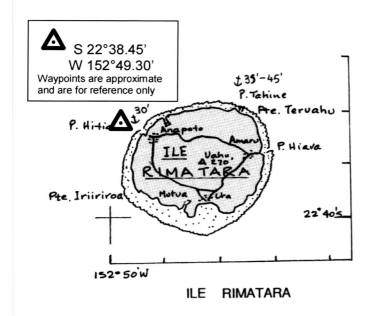

S 22°38.45'
W 152°49.30'
Waypoints are approximate
and are for reference only

ILES AUSTRALES

ILE RIMATARA

& ILE RURUTU

0   1   2   3

Approx. Scale n.m.

P. Hitia   30'

P.Tahine
‡ 35'-45'
Pte. Teruahu
Anapoto
P. Hiava
ILE
Amaru
Uahu 270
RIMATARA
Pte. Iriiriroa   Mutua   Ura
22° 40's

152° 50'W

ILE RIMATARA

Not to be used for navigation

Surge

Fish Boats

Moerai

S 22°28.80'
W 151°21.60'
Waypoints are approximate
and are for reference only

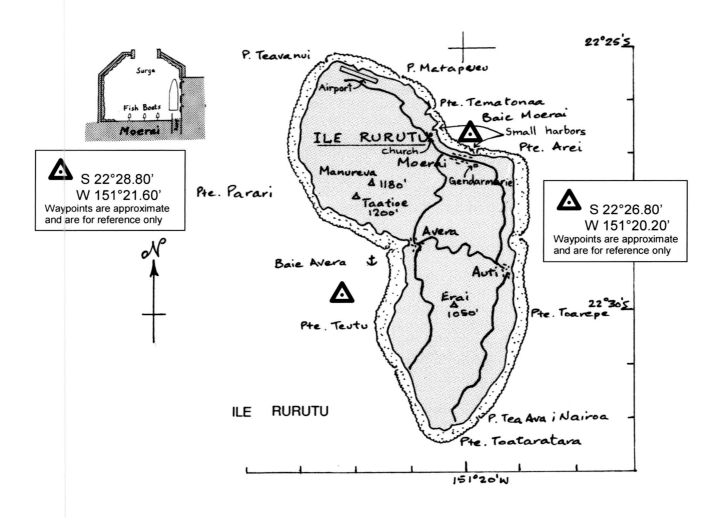

22°25'S

P. Teavanui

P. Matapeveu

Airport

Pte. Tematonaa

Baie Moerai

ILE RURUTU

Small harbors

church

Pte. Arei

Moerai

Pte. Parari

Manureva
△1180'

Taatioe
1200'

Gendarmerie

S 22°26.80'
W 151°20.20'
Waypoints are approximate
and are for reference only

N

Avera

Auti

Baie Avera   ‡

Erai
△ 1050'

Pte. Toarepe
22°30'S

Pte. Teutu

P. Tea Ava i Nairoa

ILE RURUTU

Pte. Toataratara

151°20'W

162

ILE TUBUAI

This volcanic island lies about 115 miles ESE of Rurutu, and 100 miles WNW of Raivavae. The largest of the Iles Australes with a population of almost 2,000, it is the administrative center for Ile Tubuai, Raivavae and Rapa. From seaward it appears to be two separate islands as the mountains at each end, Mount Taita (1,390 feet) and Mount Hanareho (1,024 feet), are separated by a low-lying intermediate strip of land. The barrier reef lies up to 3 miles offshore. The channel through the reef is well marked. The lagoon is shallow and numerous coral heads prevent travel within the encircling reef. Keep a sharp lookout for FADS (Fish Aggregating Devices).

Passe Te Ara Moana on the northern side is the main pass; the use of Passe Rotea just to the east is discouraged. Entry is made on a bearing of 159°T taken on green leading lights in the range, both flashing green 4 sec. All other markers in the fairway are either lit (indicating a course change) or fitted with radar reflectors and reflecting foil. A current of approximately 0.8 to 1 knot runs from east to west in the marked channel leading to the jetty inside the reef. Once within the reef, a well-marked route to the east leads to the village where anchorage may be taken in about 3 fathoms.

If space is available and tradewinds are blowing, the vessel may be tied to the concrete wharf east of the center of town. You must check the schedule at the Meteorological Office for the arrival of the freighter *Tuha'a Pae III,* which comes every 2 weeks, to avoid being tied up when it arrives. Gendarmes warn cruisers not to tie alongside the wharf because vandalism from inebriated locals has been known. Rather than tying alongside, surge may make it more prudent to anchor in the lee of the wharf where the bottom consists of rock and coral rubble left from dredging. After threading a route through the coral heads anchorage may also be taken at a spot off Motu Roa.

The Government Administrator and local Gendarme in Mataura can authorize entry. Two white markers indicate a channel through the reef east of the wharf leading to a convenient spot for a dinghy landing. About 2,000 people inhabit the island's villages and a road circles the island linking the communities together. The airport gives the island access to the rest of Polynesia and the inhabitants have all conveniences such as electricity, television and telephones.

Excellent drinking water is available from a tap close to the warehouse at the base of the jetty. Shower facilities and a restroom are in a nearby building. Though expensive, fuel is available from the Total station across the street from the boat harbor using jerry cans. Daily weather forecasts and Weather fax can be obtained from the Meteorological Office. Just across the street, Don Travers has excellent photographs of the Australs for viewing and possible purchase. There are two banks in the village as well as a supermarket, which is close to the post office. Local farmers also sell quality potatoes, carrots and other fresh produce from sheds along the road and coffee is available in season. Several well-stocked stores, a bakery and an infirmary are in Mataura. A worthwhile, 4-hour hike to the top of Mount Taitaa rewards you with some spectacular views.

Good anchorage can also be found by turning to the southwest after clearing the entrance, traveling south of Pointe Tepuu and anchoring between the southwestern end of the airport runway and the village of Anua. A well-stocked store is near the airport. Air service from Papeete operates regularly. It is recommended that you check schedules ahead before planning on utilizing these services.

The mutineers on H.M.S. Bounty attempted to land on Tubuai in May, 1789 but were forced back to the ship by a hail of stones from the inhabitants. Fletcher Christian returned to Tahiti, where some crew were left ashore. He tried to land here a second time, failed, then went to Pitcairn Island where he founded a colony.

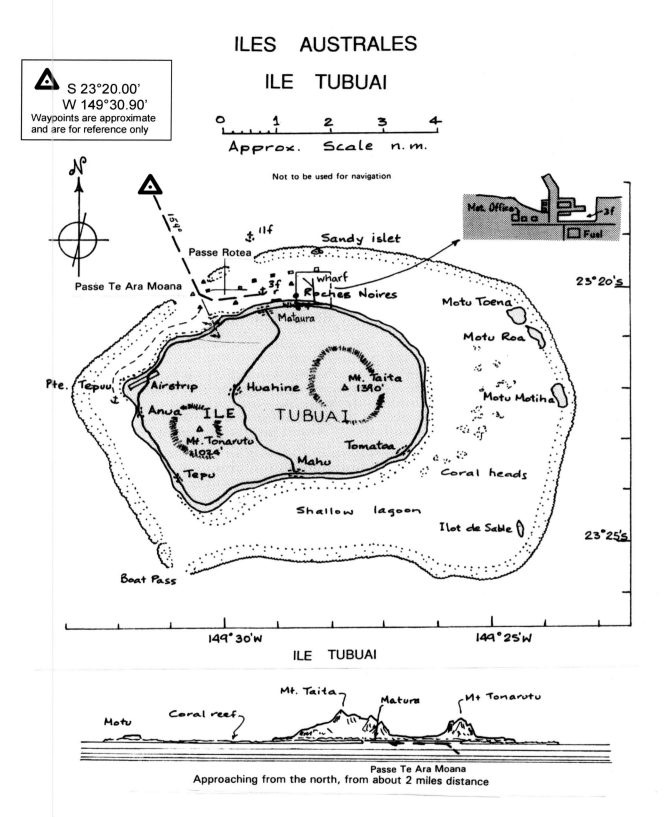

ILES AUSTRALES

ILE TUBUAI

S 23°20.00'
W 149°30.90'
Waypoints are approximate
and are for reference only

0 1 2 3 4
Approx. Scale n.m.

Not to be used for navigation

Mar. Office

Fuel

Passe Rotea

Sandy islet

Passe Te Ara Moana

wharf

Roches Noires

Mataura

23°20's

Motu Toena

Motu Roa

Pte. Tepuu

Airstrip

Huahine

Mt. Taita
△ 1390'

Motu Motiha

Anua

ILE   TUBUAI

Mt. Tonarutu
△1024'

Tomatoa

Tepu

Mahu

Coral heads

Shallow   lagoon

Ilot de Sable

23°25's

Boat Pass

149°30'W

149°25'W

ILE   TUBUAI

Motu   Coral reef   Mt. Taita   Matura   Mt Tonarutu

Passe Te Ara Moana
Approaching from the north, from about 2 miles distance

164

ILE RAIVAVAE

Raivavae lies about 100 miles ESE of Ile Tubuai and Ile Rapa is 200 miles further to the southeast. Near the northeastern end of the island is the highest point, Mont Hiro, (1,430 feet) and to the southwest is Mont Taraia, (1,000 feet). The peaks are steep and precipitous, reaching out in two spurs at Pic Rouge and Presqu'ile Vainnana to enclose the main anchorage at Baie Rairue. Often described as one of the most beautiful islands in Polynesia, it has a barrier reef that is mostly awash and lies up to 2 miles offshore. When approaching from the south its streetlights are visible from 7 to 10 miles offshore. The island is a good radar target for up to 25 miles.

Raivavae provides the best anchorages in the Australes, though visibility within the lagoon is not always as good as in the Tuamotu and Society Islands. The main entrance through the reef is **Passe Mahanatoa**; alongside to the east is Passe Teavarua, which should not be used because the beacons have been removed. Two other openings in the reef, Passe Teaoa on the south and Passe Teruapupuhi at the northeast corners are encumbered with coral heads and are not recommended.

Passe Mahanatoa has a marked channel through the reef on the north side of the island. The current is almost always outflowing and a sharp lookout is advised to avoid shoal heads scattered about. The centerline is marked by lighted lateral beacons aligned with a range ashore bearing 167°T. The entrance range consists of a tall white mast with a white square beyond. The minimum depth in the entrance is 15.5 feet reducing to 14.0 feet at the inner end for a distance of 115 feet on each side of the centerline. After passing the beacons marking Roches Totoro proceed on a bearing of 261°T on the white turret on Motu Tuitui. After passing Pointe Matoaitanata, follow the route shown on the sketch. This is an all-weather entrance.

The best anchorage area is in the eastern part of Rairua Bay in 5 fathoms, mud a little inshore of the line between the first red marker and the big satellite dish close to the harbor warehouse. The westernmost end of the wharf then has a bearing of 215°T. This area has minimal fetch and gives more protection when the wind shifts to the northeast during passing frontal systems. A prudent sailor will securely set two anchors 30° apart as very heavy squalls often sweep down the hills. Vessels may tie to the wharf until the supply ship *Tuhaa Pae II* makes her visit every 2-3 weeks. When the wind becomes northerly, moorage at the wharf becomes very uncomfortable and anchoring is preferable as the barrier reef gives good protection.

Another anchorage is off the village of Mahanatoa, but this location is exposed to the pass and it suffers from northerly winds. A safer anchorage is further to the east off the village of Anatonu. Report to the gendarme after the anchor is set even if you have arrived from Papeete.

Although rainfall is abundant, water is in short supply. There is no official water tap at the wharf but in an emergency you can take a small amount quietly from a tap at the French Telecom building next to the wharf's warehouse. Edmond, a Frenchman who came to Raivavae 30 years ago, lives near the main pass range marker and enjoys supplying yachts with fruit and vegetables from his extensive gardens. The baker delivers fresh bread to the wharf at 0700 if it is ordered the day before. Satellite phone service is available at the post office and the infirmary is staffed by a French doctor. There are no garbage facilities. Beer is sold but hard liquor and wine are not available.

For years the inhabitants turned down France's offer to build an airport but one was finally constructed on the north shore in 2002 and now there are twice weekly flights from Papeete. The road circling the island provides a long, scenic hike or a 45-minute walk takes you over the middle of the island.

Only one large stone tike remains of the many that graced the maraes of the past. Located near Rairua, many believe that this tiki still has magical power (mana).

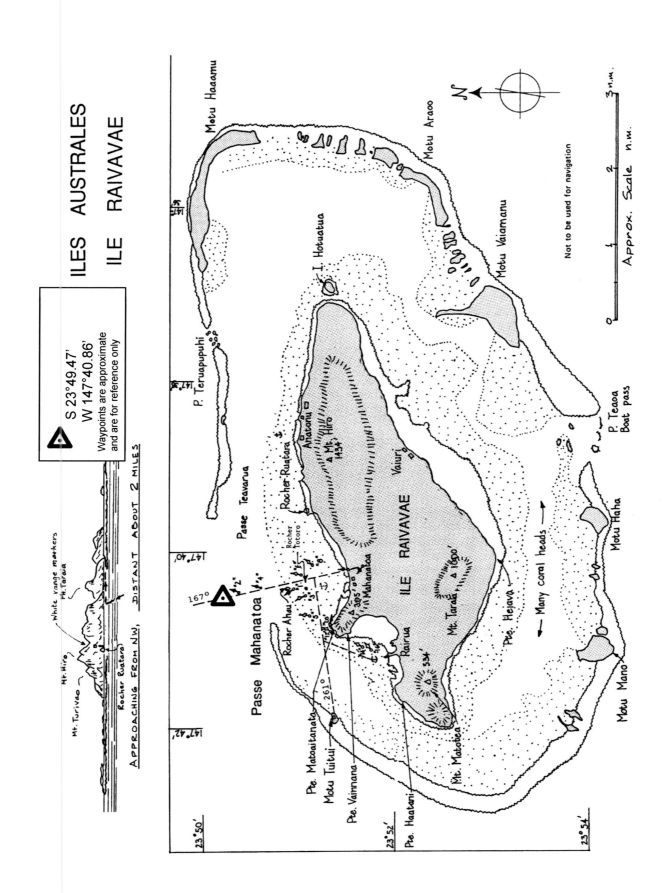

ILES AUSTRALES
ILE RAIVAVAE

S 23°49.47'
W 147°40.86'
Waypoints are approximate
and are for reference only

Mt. Turivao
Mt. Hiro
White range markers
Mt. Tarau
Rocher Ruatara

APPROACHING FROM NW, DISTANT ABOUT 2 MILES

Motu Haaamu

P. Teruapupuhi

Passe Teavarua

Rocher Ruatara
Anatonu
Mt. Hiro
1434
Rocher Totoro
Mahanatoa
Passe Mahanatoa

167°

261°

Pe. Matoaitanata
Motu Tuitui
Pe. Vainnana
Pe. Haatoni

Rairua
Mt. Mataotea

ILE RAIVAVAE
Vaiuri
Mt. Tarau
1690
Pte. Hejava

Many coral heads

I. Hotuatua

Motu Araoo
Motu Vaiamanu

Motu Mano

Motu Aha

P. Teaoa
Boat pass

N

3 n.m.
0   1   2
Approx. Scale n.m.

Not to be used for navigation

147°44'
147°42'
147°40'
23°50'
23°52'
23°54'

166

ILE RAPA

This spectacular, but somewhat forbidding island lies well to the south of the rest of Iles Australes, about 300 miles from Ile Raivave, and is administered by officials in Ile Tubuai. The island is composed of several steep, high, and jagged mountain peaks that drop to the sea in cliffs around much of the coast. The highest peak is Mont Perau, at 2,130 feet. Many of the other peaks exceed 1,200 feet. The climate is temperate and humid, with frequent rain and sometimes fog. From October to April the prevailing winds are easterly though about once a month from December to February brief westerlies occur. The strongest winds from the west occur during July and August.

The steep coast has few offshore underwater dangers, except in the approaches to Baie de Ahurei, where the main villages and anchorages are located. The approach to, and actual entry into the bay is complex, and as the clarity of the water is not as good as elsewhere in Polynesia, the passage needs to be taken with care. Shoals and spits block off much of the bay and extend well out from each of the seaward points, narrowing the entrance. This bay is impressive for it is the crater of a volcano which has been breached open to the sea.

Cruisers tie to the wharf to check in with the local official, a policeman (muto'i) who, when asked, will stamp your passport as proof of having visited the island. The bay is either very deep or shoal, making care and good sunlight necessary to find spots suitable for anchoring. The coral is mainly soft staghorn so damage to the vessel is negligible if you ground. Set the anchor well in the good holding coral, mud and rock, as boisterous squalls have been known to funnel down the steep hillsides into the bay.

The island's 550 residents live on the most isolated spot in Polynesia and the supply boat, *Tuhaa Pae*, only visits the island every 6 to 8 weeks. The 3 or 4 small stores run low on inventory between shipments; "Fare Toa" usually has the best selection. Water is available behind the building on the main wharf. Crayfish are plentiful but the climate is not suitable for coconuts or other tropical fruits. Spear fishing is not allowed inside the harbor.

Since there is no road linking the two villages of Area and Ahurei, contact is by crossing the bay in long boats. For a small fee cruisers may be offered a ride ashore. A telephone is located near the post office on the main wharf. It requires a phone card, which is available at the post office. Money can also be changed at the post office if the bank is closed. Electricity is available from 0800 to 1200, from 1600 to 2400 and all day Saturday. The island is served by cable TV.

The trail to the forts is west from Ahurei village, past the soccer field. Proceed around the back of a bulldozed hill, turn left to an abandoned weather station and follow the trail. By turning right you will be on a longer walk but will arrive at a more interesting site, the restored fortress of Morongo Uta.

The island has had a colorful, and at times, violent history as evidenced by the fortifications and other remains on its green-clad, pointed hills. Wherever the hills appear terraced near the peak, it indicates the remains of fortified mountain village strongholds that are now overgrown. These forts, built and faced with rock, were the homes of warrior tribes that controlled the agriculture in the neighboring fertile lowlands. As elsewhere, the usual pattern of European exploration and exploitation eventually unfolded. The missionaries brought the people down from the healthy lifestyle in the forts, exposed them to disease, while the whalers and traders took the men and forced them to work elsewhere, until the island was one composed almost entirely of women. During this period, women became the work force and Rapa became known as the "Island of Amazons."

ILE RAPA

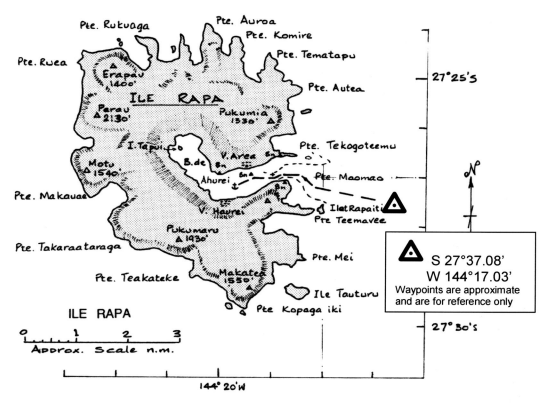

Pte. Rukuaga
Pte. Auroa
Pte. Komire
Pte. Ruea
Pte. Tematapu
Erapau 1400'
ILE RAPA
Pte. Autea
Parau 2130'
Pukumia 1530'
I. Tapui
Pte. Tekogoteemu
V. Area
B. de
Pte. Maomao
Ahurei
Motu 1540'
Pte. Makauae
Ilot Rapaiti
Pte. Teemavee
V. Haurei
Pukumaru 1930'
Pte. Takaraataraga
Pte. Mei
Pte. Teakateke
Makatea 1550'
Ile Tauturu
Pte. Kopaga iki

27°25'S

27°30'S

N

🔺 S 27°37.08'
W 144°17.03'
Waypoints are approximate
and are for reference only

ILE RAPA

```
0    1    2    3
Approx. Scale n.m.
```

144° 20'W

Not to be used for navigation

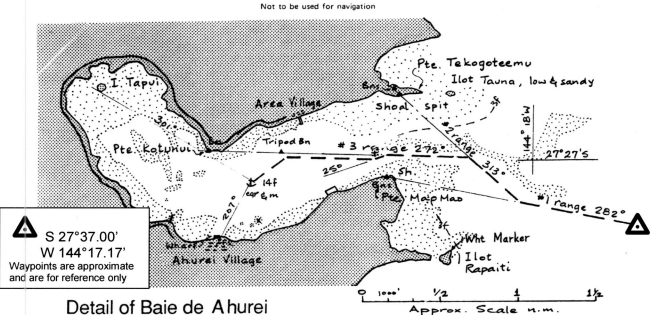

I. Tapui
Pte. Tekogoteemu
Ilot Tauna, low & sandy
Area Village
Shoal Spit
Tripod Bn
#3 range 272°
Pte. Kotunui
250°
#2 range 313°
144° 18'W
27°27'S
14f
Sh.
#1 range 282°
Pte. Mao Mao
Wht Marker
Ilot Rapaiti

🔺 S 27°37.00'
W 144°17.17'
Waypoints are approximate
and are for reference only

Detail of Baie de Ahurei

```
0   1000'   ½    1    1½
Approx. Scale n.m.
```

168

COOK ISLANDS

The flag of the Cook Islands has 15 white stars in a circle on a blue field, which represents the 15 small islands that lie scattered over a large area. The boundaries of the country include the land and sea between Latitudes 8°S and 23°S and Longitudes 156°W and 167°W. This is an area of over 750,000 square miles with a total land area of 93 square miles. The islands are flanked to the west by the Kingdom of Tonga and Samoa and to the east, French Polynesia. The weather is warm and sunny throughout the year with June to August being the cooler months. Rainfall is heaviest from November to March, the hottest season. Many of the islands were explored by Captain Cook, after whom the islands are named.

The islands are divided into two geographic groups. The Southern, Lower Cook Islands, have volcanic origins with fringing coral reefs and include Rarotonga, Mangaia, Manke, Atiu, Mitiaro, Takutea and Manuae (Hervey Islands). The vegetation is sparse in comparison with the luxuriant growth of the Society Islands. The Northern Group are low-lying atolls and include Palmerston, Suvarov, Nassau, Pukapuka, Rakahanga, Manihiki and Penrhyn.

Entry formalities are handled at Rarotonga, Aitutaki, Penrhyn and Pukapuka (Danger Is.); permission to visit other islands can be requested on entry. On a trial basis, Palmerston has been designated as a **Port of Entry**, permitting yachts to arrive directly from Bora-Bora, with the same entry fees applying. A yacht arriving from another Cook Island will be charged only a $5NZ 'landing fee'. Yachts arriving from Aitutaki or Rarotonga should clear out of the country at those ports rather than at Palmerston. The unit of currency is the New Zealand Dollar, supplemented by Cook Island currency that is not negotiable outside the Cook Islands. Entry rules and regulations are a result of the government's efforts to control the influx of disease and pests that might damage the country's agrarian economy. The boat will be visited by the harbormaster, customs and agriculture and unless the vessel is arriving from New Zealand, it will be sprayed for pests. Note: Avoid entering or leaving the outer islands on a Sunday since it is strictly observed as the Sabbath.

The history of man's habitation on the islands is relatively brief. It is estimated that the first Polynesians probably arrived about 500 AD. The major migration to New Zealand, which culminated in the Maori culture, began elsewhere in Polynesia. It was from Ngatangiia in about 1350 AD that the intrepid seafarers set out in their great canoes on the last leg of the journey to Aetorea (modern day New Zealand).

Since 1965 the Cook Islands have been a self-governing democratic commonwealth affiliated with New Zealand, which handles foreign affairs and defense, and subsidizes finances. Cook Islanders enjoy New Zealand citizenship and move freely to and from that country. The main language is Cook Island Maori, but English is also spoken with a strong New Zealand accent.

Cook Islanders are true, fun-loving Polynesians who are enthusiastic participants in both sports and dances. It is well worth attending one of their feasts, sure to have entertainment in the form of dancing. Although there are many similarities in dance and language to those found in Tahiti, the Cook Island style is more closely related to the Maoris of New Zealand.

The London Missionary Society, now operating as the Cook Islands Christian Church, has had a major influence on the lives of the people. They avidly attend church and religion is a dominant factor in their lives. So as not to offend these friendly people, visitors should respect their dress code and dress modestly. Swimwear should not be worn when visiting towns or villages. Tipping is contrary to local custom.

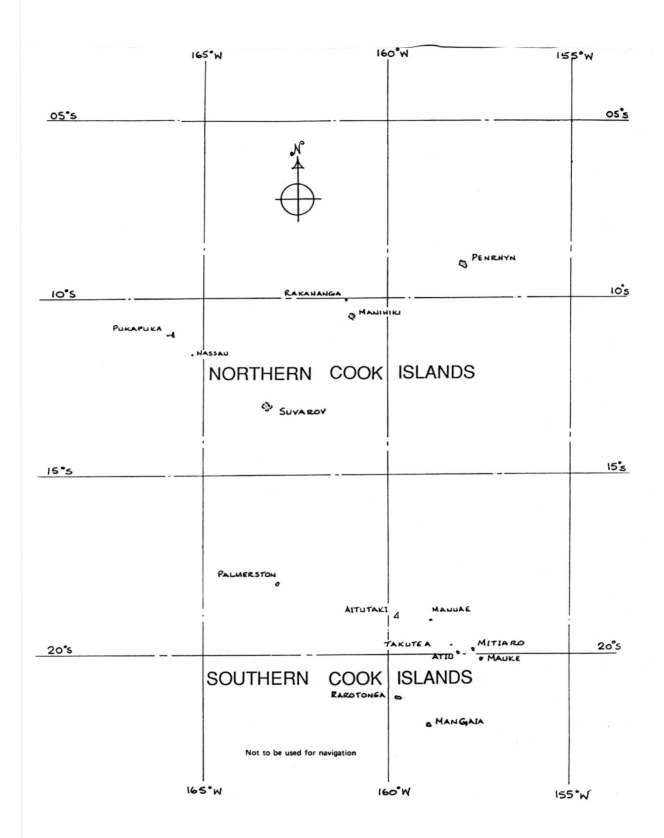

Not to be used for navigation

RAROTONGA

Rarotonga is a luxuriantly green, mountainous island within an encircling barrier reef and is about 25 square miles in area. The rugged peaks of the interior reach to about 2,000 feet, creating a sharp outline and are a spectacular sight from offshore. This is the most important of the Cook Islands, as over half of the population resides here and it is the center of government. The main **Port of Entry** for the Cook Islands is at Avatiu. The island is a good radar target for up to 40 miles.

Avatiu, the only harbor on the island, is located in the middle of the north shore. It is extremely limited in space and access, for the small, square basin is cut out of the reef with partially reclaimed areas on each side. Entrance during daylight is straightforward and there is a lighted range of vertical green and red lights. Daily charge for mooring are NZ$2.00 per meter per day for monohulls and NZ$2.75 per meter per day for multihulls. Local vessels have priority in the harbor. This can be a dangerous harbor to visit as deep-sea vessels maneuvering in the confined space sometimes collide with and damage yachts tied ashore. Cruising vessels must moor Med-style and be ready to move with short notice in the event of a ship arriving or strong winds from a northerly quarter that can make the harbor untenable. During the cyclone season, from the end of November to the end of March cruisers are not allowed to remain in the islands. A small craft harbor for vessels less than 32 ft. is available west of the Avatiu harbor.

The Harbormaster handles Customs and Immigration. When a vessel is within VHF range, contact the harbormaster on VHF Ch 16 or through ZKR, Radio Rarotonga and request berthing instructions. Vessels should fly the yellow Quarantine Flag while awaiting the Port Health officer, who may spray the vessel with the same insecticide that is used for aircraft arriving from foreign countries. Upon arrival a 31-day visa is granted; an extension can be obtained only at the immigration office in Rarotonga. To prevent the import of produce-borne bacteria, all fresh fruits and vegetables will be seized. When departing the Cook Islands a $25NZ per person exit fee is charged, payable before port clearance papers are issued.

The harbor at Avatiu is in the middle of the residential and commercial area of the town of Avarua and stores and other facilities are within walking distance. The public market has a good selection of local vegetables and refrigerated and dried foods from New Zealand. Diesel and kerosene are available in Avarua. If large quantities of fuel are needed, arrangements can be made for a fuel truck to deliver it to Avatiu Harbor. Telephone cards are available in the harbor office and just across the road is a laundry. Many cruisers congregate here for the annual 10-day Constitution Day celebrations at the beginning of August. Propane is available next to the Harbormaster's office. There are several international flights per week to Tahiti, Auckland, Fiji, Los Angeles and Honolulu.

At Cooks Corner island buses depart every half-hour, one traveling clockwise and the other counter-clockwise for the 50-minute trip of 20 miles around the island. The church at Arorangi and nearby Tinomana's Palace are interesting spots to visit.

A shallow entrance to the lagoon for vessels drawing less than 5 feet is on the eastern side of Ngatangiia. Permission must be obtained to use this pass for it is constricted with fish traps. It is advisable to sound depths by dinghy or snorkeling before entry. It is best to anchor bow and stern in front of the condos. A heavy south or southeast swell produces a strong ebb current, making maneuvering difficult at best. It is from the Ngatangiia Harbor that the Maoris migrated to New Zealand in long canoes in 1350. A local sailing club sails small dinghies in Muri Lagoon, a little further south.

SOUTHERN COOK ISLANDS
RAROTONGA ISLAND

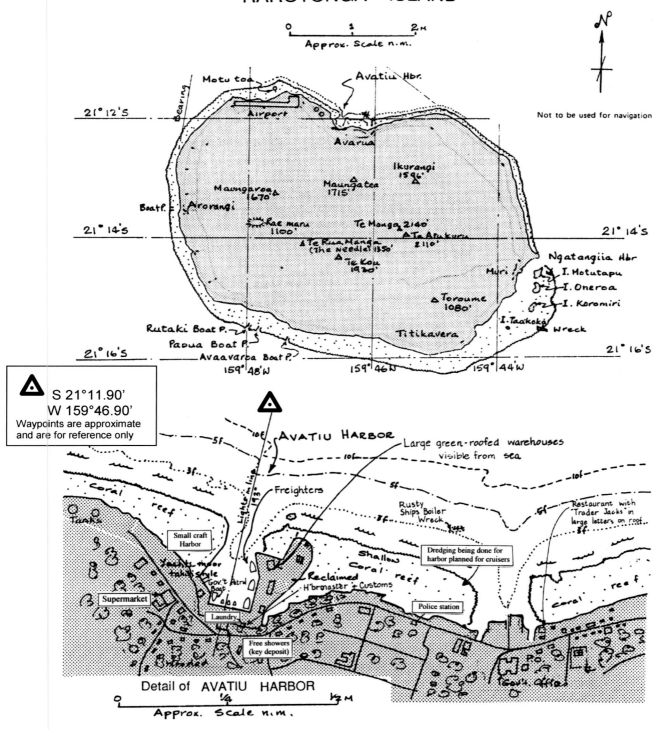

Not to be used for navigation

S 21°11.90'
W 159°46.90'
Waypoints are approximate
and are for reference only

Detail of AVATIU HARBOR

AITUTAKI

This is the northernmost island of the Lower Cook Islands and it lies 150 miles north of Rarotonga and about 55 miles northwest of the Hervey Islands. Its highest point is Mount Maungapu, at 390 feet high, where a light is located at the peak. A fringing reef borders the northern end of the island; on the south is a barrier reef on which a few tree-covered islets are scattered. A large, shallow lagoon, about 1.5 feet, with numerous coral heads is within the reef, creating a beautiful area that is reminiscent of Bora-Bora. Strong westerly setting currents south and east of the southern tip of the island must be considered when in the vicinity. Several yachts have been shipwrecked near Motikitiu while approaching the island during poor visibility.

Arutunga Pass provides the only navigable channel through the reef. The current is almost always outgoing at 1 to 4 knots. The pass was created during WWII by the US military by blasting a route through the coral. It is a well-marked, long, narrow passage leading to a small basin on the western side of the island. The passage is less than 32 feet wide and there is a shallow section where the maximum depth that can be carried at spring tides is 5.5 feet. Coming from seaward, the shallowest spot is about one-third of the way into the pass, where a vessel is obliged briefly to detour from otherwise hugging the steel posts that mark the northern edge of the pass. Current Tide Tables for Central and Western Pacific Ocean are required to determine the time of high slack water. Because of very limited swinging space, it is best to anchor fore and aft or take a line ashore to a palm tree in the natural pool south of the harbor, in 2.5 fathoms. Other spots are stern tied to the shoreline in the harbor, only with the harbormaster's permission and when no freighter is due or in an area SW of the inner end of the pass where you must negotiate coral heads with care and lay a stern anchor, however this area is subject to cross-currents and can become uncomfortable if a squall with a W component develops. Catamarans can anchor in a shallow area E of the tip of the wharf. There is a $5NZ daily fee for anchoring. Avoid the rock in the southern part of the harbor, covered 2 feet.

The Port Captain occasionally monitors VHF Ch 16 during working hours and vessels may enter and clear through this **Port of Entry**. The Port Administration Authority Office is adjacent to the small basin. A visa valid for 31 days is issued on arrival and can be extended for an additional period in Rarotonga. Dogs are forbidden from landing on Aitutaki. Water is available on the main shipping wharf. Spider and Co., an internet café, is about 1 mile north of the harbor. One ATM is next to the post office at Westpac Bank on the main road near the harbor and a second one is about 1.25 mile north of town at Mango Traders (ANZ bank). Nearby is Café Tupuna where mail can be sent (for a small fee) to richards@aitutaki.net.ck This can also be a mail drop--postal address: "Name of Boat," C/O Cafe Tupuna, P.O. Box 57, Aitutaki, Cook Islands, South Pacific.

There are several bike and car rental agencies. A bakery is next door to the large white church, built in 1828 and visible on approach. *Orongo II,* a 37 foot tugboat, is based here and there is also a 19-ton mobile crane. The Blue Nun Café is a popular restaurant and nightspot.

The island's main hotels take turns in organizing "Island nights" which include traditional dancing and a buffet dinner. It is sometimes possible to attend only for the price of a beer. A German-Swiss longtime resident who owns the ABC store on the north side of the village welcomes cruisers and maintains guest logs of visiting yachts. Air service links the island to Rarotonga. Motus at the SE tip of the lagoon are breeding grounds for Red-Billed Tropicbirds. This is a popular area for kite-surfing.

The first European to weigh anchor here was Captain Bligh in the *Bounty,* just two weeks before the infamous mutiny in the waters off Samoa. In 1821 John Williams of the London Missionary Society arrived and immediately began converting the islands to Christianity. Though he met an ignominious end - stewed in a pot by the Big Nambas of Vanuatu - his church survives to this day as the Cook Islands Christian Church.

APPROACHING AITUTAKI FROM E. DISTANT ABOUT 7 MILES

SOUTHERN COOK ISLANDS
AITUTAKI ISLAND

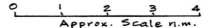

Approx. Scale n.m.

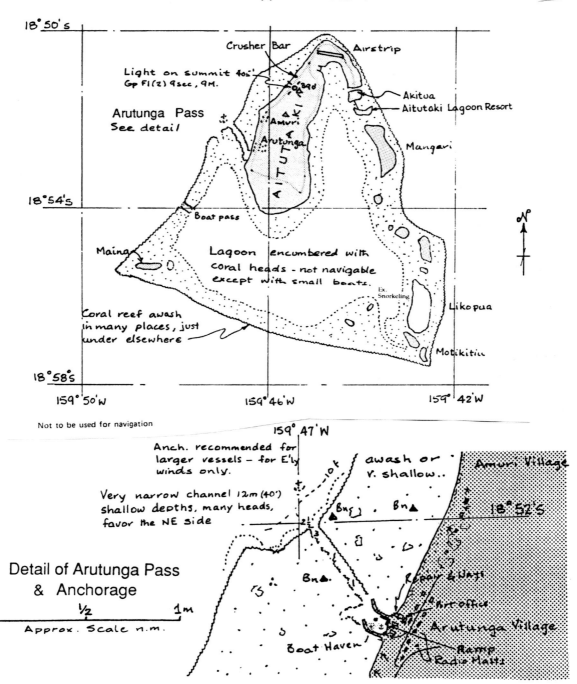

Crusher Bar   Airstrip

Light on summit 40'
Gp Fl(2) 9sec, 9M.

Arutunga Pass
See detail

Akitua
Aitutaki Lagoon Resort

Amuri

Arutunga

Mangari

18° 50' S

18° 54' S

Boat pass

Maina

Lagoon encumbered with
coral heads - not navigable
except with small boats.

Ex.
Snorkeling

Likopua

Coral reef awash
in many places, just
under elsewhere

Motikitiu

18° 58' S

159° 50' W   159° 46' W   159° 42' W

159° 47' W

Anch. recommended for
larger vessels — for E'ly
winds only.

awash or
v. shallow..

Amuri Village

Very narrow channel 12m (40')
shallow depths, many heads,
favor the NE side

Bn

Bn

18° 52' S

Bn

Detail of Arutunga Pass
& Anchorage

Approx. Scale n.m.

Repair & Haul
Port office

Arutunga Village

Boat Haven

Ramp
Radio Mast

174

MANGAIA ISLAND

The most southerly of the Cook Islands, Mangaia Island is 110 miles ESE of Rarotonga. The island rises to a height of 554 ft. in the center but it is dominated by makatea, a formation of raised coral cliffs named after the high atoll in French Polynesia. The cliffs virtually encircle the island but are most prominent on the northern side, where they vary between 150 and 230 ft. In places the raised wall is over one mile wide, and the coastal road around the island has to adjust to this feature. Caves once used as burial sites can be found in this formation.

A fringing coral reef, generally visible and extending up to 0.25 mile offshore, surrounds the island. There are no harbors, though boat passages or landings cut through the reef are used by small local vessels. Southwesterly swells affect these landings and at such times the northerly landing can be used. Someone must stay aboard the vessel at all times since anchorage is not possible at any of the landings. Currents in the area typically set to the west at about 0.5 knots.

Oneroa, the island's main village, is on the western side of the island and is clearly visible from a distance. A passage is located here but a better landing is at Avarua, about one mile to the north where a boat passage leading to a small wharf has been blasted out of the reef. A large shed marks the landing, and a light is sometimes shown if a cargo ship is expected. The swell and surge are such that it is best to use local vessels to go ashore.

The Lower Cook Islands are administered for the New Zealand government by a Resident Commissioner at Avarua in Rarotonga. Each island has a Resident Agent who is assisted by the Island Council.

MAUKE ISLAND

This is the most easterly of the Lower Cook Islands, and is about 150 miles ENE of Rarotonga. There is some makatea in the island's formation though its highest elevation is about 150 ft., including the trees. It is encircled by a fringing coral reef that extends up to 0.25 mile offshore and is steep-to, allowing vessels to approach fairly closely if a landing party is to go ashore. There are no anchorages available. The island does have an airstrip and is reported to be visible on radar from a distance of 17 miles.

A good landing place is at Taunganui, at the northwestern end of the island, located by sighting the village and its flagstaff. If the southerly swell is strong, an alternative landing is on the northern side of Angataura. There are other locations but they are more difficult to negotiate. During shore visits someone should be left aboard the vessel and the trip ashore made in local boats.

Ancient Fish Hooks of Pearl Shell

SOUTHERN COOK ISLANDS
MANGAIA ISLAND & MAUKE ISLAND

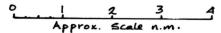

Approx. scale n.m.

Not to be used for navigation

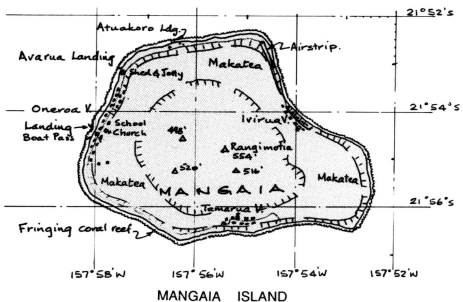

MANGAIA ISLAND

No anchorage is available; boats must remain hove-to near the coast and landing is best made with local small boat help.

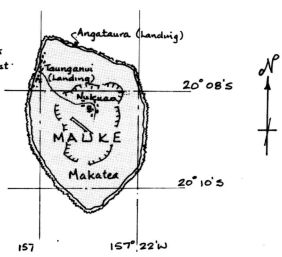

Mauke Is. may lie 2½m further eastward than this position taken from the chart.

MAUKE ISLAND

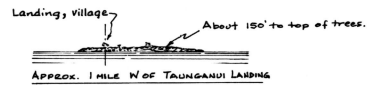

Landing, village ⌐
About 150' to top of trees.

APPROX. 1 MILE W OF TAUNGANUI LANDING

176

HERVEY ISLANDS

These two small, low islands, Manuae and Auoto, are within one encircling coral reef located 55 miles southeast of Aitutaki. There is no passage into the lagoon, though a landing can be made on Manuae Island through Turakina Boat Passage. In the northwest part of Manuae there is a very small settlement augmented by people engaged in copra collection who work out of Aitutaki. An airstrip on the island provides connections to the rest of the Cook Islands.

MITIARO ISLAND (Mitiero Island)

This small, slightly raised coral island with traces of makatea, is about 22 miles northwest of Mauke. It is a green and fertile island with a small population. Although it is encircled by a fringing coral reef there is a landing place on the western side at Omutu, off the village of Atai. An interesting feature of the island is the brackish lake in the interior, where you can find edible eels.

ATIU ISLAND

Composed of raised coral and resembling Mangaia with its makatea, the small island of Atiu is 20 miles WSW of Mitiaro Island. The main villages are in the center of the island where the plateau has an elevation of 394 ft. The village church is prominent from seaward. This is a subsidiary **Port of Entry** where clearance may be obtained when customs officers are present, otherwise you may have to pay for their transportation costs from Rarotonga.

The bold, raised, cliff-edged coast has several small bays where landing is possible. The fringing coral reef lies fairly close to the island, but landings are possible at Taunganui on the northwestern side or in suitable conditions, at Iotua Ika on the north. Other landings can be seen, but they are more difficult to use. The yacht must remain manned, and shore visits are best taken in local boats. Small amounts of fresh water may be obtained and some fresh produce is available in season. The island has a population of about 1,300 inhabitants and the Resident Agent resides at Taunganui.

TAKUTEA (Fenua Iti)

This is a very small, low, wooded island lying about 10 miles northwest of Atiu. It has a white coral sand beach and is surrounded by a fringing coral reef. A reef extends about 2 miles southeast from the southeastern end of the island, and occasionally the sea breaks heavily across it. There is also a shoal extending about 0.3 miles west of the western end of the island. Strong tide rips occur north of this shoal.

A possible landing site is on the north side but it is best avoided because of the dangers inherent in keeping a yacht in this area during a landing. The island is a bird and wild life sanctuary, though islanders from Atiu come here to harvest coconuts.

Interrupted Cone
Conus Ximenes (Gray)

SOUTHERN COOK ISLANDS

NOTE:- Hervey Is. may be about 5 miles
further N'ward then shown below
taken from charts.

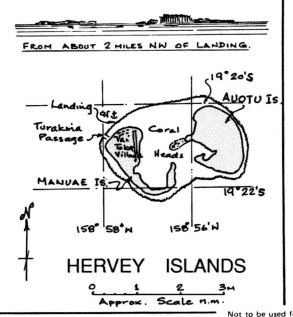

FROM ABOUT 2 MILES NW OF LANDING.

HERVEY ISLANDS

0   1   2   3M
Approx. Scale n.m.

Village — ← Low-lying, about 90' high

FROM ABOUT 2 MILES W OF VILLAGE LANDING

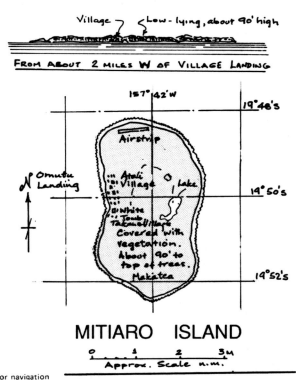

MITIARO ISLAND

0   1   2   3M
Approx. Scale n.m.

Not to be used for navigation

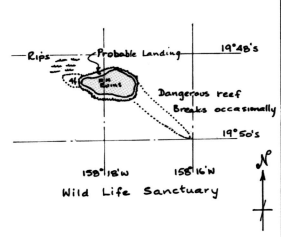

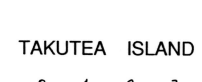

Wild Life Sanctuary

TAKUTEA ISLAND

0   1   2   3M
Approx. Scale n.m.

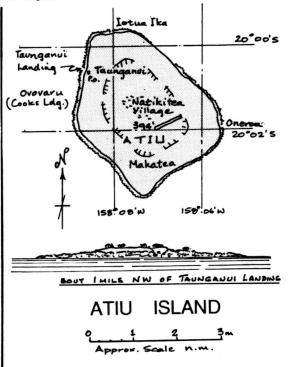

BOUT 1 MILE NW OF TAUNGANUI LANDING

ATIU ISLAND

0   1   2   3m
Approx. Scale n.m.

178

PALMERSTON ATOLL

This atoll lies about 200 miles WNW of Aitutaki and measures about 6 miles by 4 miles, with half a dozen motus, one of them inhabited. Six sandy islets are scattered along the coral reef surrounding the lagoon. All islands are covered with coconut palms and some ancient mahogany trees are in the center of the largest one; the overall height of the island is barely over 50 ft. On the northwesterly side of the most westerly islet is a settlement that is prominent from the west. A stranded wreck on the reef shows well on radar. Heavy gales from the northeast to east are common in January and February, usually lasting 24 to 36 hours. The atoll is dangerous to approach at night.

There are several small boat passages into the lagoon, the largest of which is Big Passage on the western side. Yachts are not permitted to enter the lagoon or to land with their own dinghies as all entrance passes are extremely dangerous. Islanders maintain six mooring buoys in the preferred anchorage spot that are suitable in settled conditions for average-sized yachts; however these should not be relied upon if the wind turns westerly, upon which immediate departure is recommended. In settled trade wind weather, temporary day anchorage is possible a little to the south of Big Passage. The anchorage is on coral, affording a poor grip and the possibility of fouling. The reef drops off very quickly, leaving only a very narrow shelf on which to anchor. An anchor watch must be maintained for this anchorage is safe only as long as an easterly wind holds the vessel away from the reef. Nevertheless many yachts have been lost here for when the wind subsides, the current can set a vessel on the reef.

Visiting yachts are given a warm welcome especially since the supply ship comes in only once every three or four months and families take turns to host the crew. Yachts are greeted and "adopted" by islanders, who may be quite competitive in seeking to guide them to "their" mooring buoy or anchorage spot. The family will discuss landing arrangements and will host them during their stay. It is neither practical nor desirable for a yacht to "go their own way" and decline such hospitality, which is offered with no ulterior motive. It is courteous for yachts to return the hospitality with gifts of staples such as flour, fishing gear, outboard fuel, fresh produce or school supplies. The islanders have refused offers of an airstrip or visits from cruise ships as they treasure their self-imposed isolation. Parrotfish fillets are the island's only export and form a major component of the local diet. Cyclones pass quite often and the traditional and time-honored order to inhabitants is to lash themselves to trees to prevent their being washed away.

The island's inhabitants have a unique history. They are the descendants of a patriarchal figure, William Marsters, a Lancashire sea captain who settled here with three Penrhyn Island wives in 1862. He fathered 26 children, divided the islands and reefs into sections for each of the three "families" and established strict rules regarding intermarriage. The one-mile long island is divided into three segments, with each occupied by the descendants of Marsters and respectively one of his three wives; the "middle' family is traditionally the dominant one. Incidentally, it is neither polite nor wise to point out the contradiction between William Marsters' patriarchal dictates and his having three wives. He is still referred to as "Father" and long ago he decreed that English was to be the language of his descendants. The original home was built using massive beams salvaged from shipwrecks washed ashore and although it still stands, it bears the scars of many hurricanes. The church bell is all that remains of the wreck of HMS *Thistle*.

In 2009 the island had a population of about 50 inhabitants including 23 children, all of which are descended from "Father" Marsters. The island "government" is run by Tere Marsters and his wife Yvonne and employs fifteen people (half of the adult population).

NORTHERN COOK ISLANDS

PALMERSTON ISLANDS

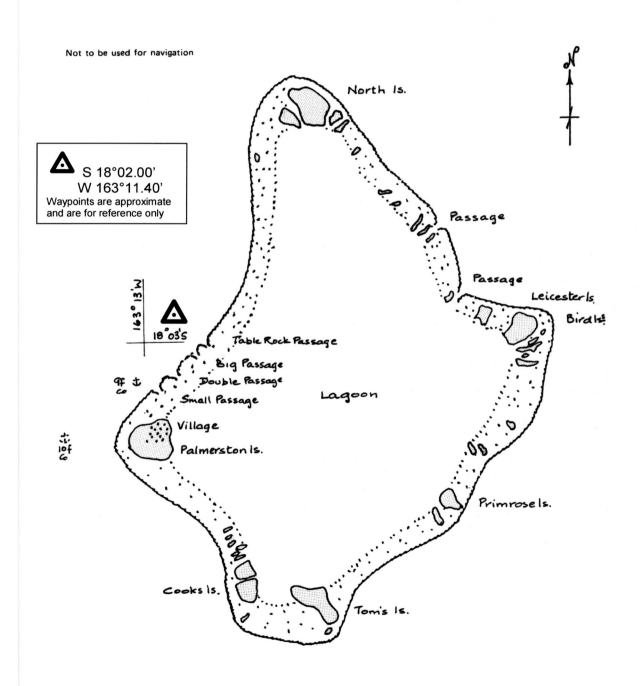

Approx. Scale N.M.

Not to be used for navigation

S 18°02.00'
W 163°11.40'
Waypoints are approximate
and are for reference only

North Is.

Passage

Passage

Leicester Is

Bird Is.

163° 13'W

18° 03'S

Table Rock Passage

Big Passage

Double Passage

Small Passage

Lagoon

Village

Palmerston Is.

Primrose Is.

Cooks Is.

Tom's Is.

SUWARROW ISLANDS (SUVAROV)

Suwarrow is a fairly large atoll, about 11 miles across. A few small islands are scattered around the northern part of the reef, the largest being Anchorage Island, visible from a distance of almost 7 miles. The southern part of the atoll is submerged and very dangerous to approach. A conspicuous wreck is situated near Seven Islands. Many vessels have been lost here and several have sunk within the lagoon where their wreckage is still visible on the bottom. The anchorage is dangerous in anything but stable trade wind conditions.

The only pass into the lagoon is on the northeastern coast, between Anchorage Island and Northeast Reef. Several large coral heads (East Reef and South Reef) extend across part of the passage near Northeast Reef. A 2 fathom shoal extends southwest from Northeast Reef and this causes the entry to be slightly complicated though it is 0.3 miles wide.

Entry should be made only in good weather with a calm sea because the seas break over the shoal with any swell causing turbulence in the entrance. A bearing of 175°T taken across the center of South Reef to Entrance Island on the southeast side of the barrier reef will lead past the shoal at the tip of Northeast Reef. Care must be taken to counter the effect of the ever-present current which has a strong set toward Anchorage Island. The vessel can pass on either side of South Reef, make the turn to the northwest, and enter the anchorage area. Tom's Place, a wooden shack and a small pier he repaired, are midway along the island shore.

Suwarrow is a National Park and permission to visit the park must be obtained from the resident park administrator who resides on Anchorage Island from April to the end of October. A fee is charged for entrance/anchorage. If vessels have not already cleared into the Cook Islands at a designated Port of Entry an additional fee may be charged. Permission is not normally given to anchor anywhere but off the pier at Anchorage Island, though sometimes the caretaker will allow visiting cruisers to anchor elsewhere in the lagoon such as in the lee of Seven Islands. However, this corner of the atoll has many coral heads which must be avoided when seeking an anchorage. By quietly rowing to the largest islet you will be rewarded by a view of thousands of birds in the air, on the ground, and in the trees. With permission, it may be possible to obtain small amounts of water from the cistern.

The lagoon has many scattered coral heads. The clarity of the water and multitude of colorful fish make for excellent diving however one must always be aware, as this the this lagoon is known to have a large shark population. . The caretaker (equipped with a spear gun) will sometimes accompany divers. .

This atoll has also had a unique figure in its past, for it was here that New Zealander Tom Neale lived as a hermit for a number of years, from 1952 until his death from cancer in 1978. Many yachts visited during his time on the atoll and their crews were charmed by him. He wrote a book describing his experiences entitled, *An Island to Oneself*.

The first European to visit the atoll was the Russian explorer, Lazarev. He arrived in 1814 aboard the *Suvarov* and the island was so named. After the Cook Islands gained independence the name was changed to "Suwarrow" so that it was more in tune with the Cook Island language. Many years ago the atoll became infested with termites and can no longer be used for copra production.

NORTHERN COOK ISLANDS
SUVAROV ISLANDS
(SUWARROW)

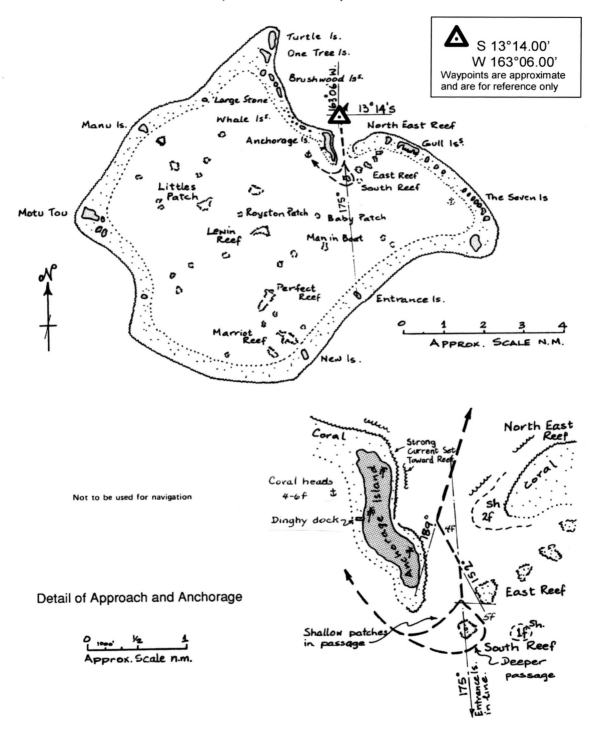

S 13°14.00'
W 163°06.00'
Waypoints are approximate
and are for reference only

Turtle Is.
One Tree Is.
Brushwood Is⁵.
Large Stone
Whale Is⁵.
Manu Is.
Anchorage Is.
13°14'S
North East Reef
Gull Is⁵.
East Reef
South Reef
Littles Patch
The Seven Is
Motu Tou
Royston Patch
Baby Patch
Lewin Reef
Man in Boat
Perfect Reef
Entrance Is.
Marriot Reef
New Is.

0 1 2 3 4
APPROX. SCALE N.M.

Not to be used for navigation

Detail of Approach and Anchorage

0 1000' ½ 1
Approx. Scale n.m.

Coral
North East Reef
Strong Current Set Toward Reef
Coral heads 4-6f
Coral
Sh 2f
Dinghy dock
189°
4f
152°
Anchorage Island
East Reef
Shallow patches in passage
5f
1f Sh.
South Reef
Deeper passage
175° Entrance Is. in line.

182

PUKAPUKA ATOLL (DANGER ISLANDS)

Pukapuka is the most western and isolated of this group and is a **Port of Entry**. It is a narrow atoll with a long, partially submerged coral reef (Terai Reef) extending from its western side for almost 3 miles. The palms on Motu Kotawa grow to about 125 feet, while those on Pukapuka and Motu Ko reach about 100 feet. A 3 to 5 knot current sets on to the eastern side of the atoll. This turns the stream so that it sets southward across Terai Reef on the ebb and northward on the flood. The reef and currents are the reason for its popular name of Danger Islands. Many downed airmen were carried by currents to the island during World War II. The island is featured in books by R. D. Frisbee and Professor Beaglehole.

A small whaleboat passage at the northern end near the village of Yato can be dangerous as the swell makes landing difficult unless you are using an inflatable. During easterly winds the anchor may be set in the pass with the aid of aluminum skiffs, with the current holding the vessel off. Otherwise you can anchor in the lee of the island on the western side where the current set must be kept in mind. Someone must be aboard the vessel at all times, maintaining a watch.

MANIHIKI ATOLL

This low-lying atoll has islets heavily treed with 70 foot coconut palms scattered around much of the perimeter. The village of Tauhunu, on the west side is marked by a sign, "Welcome to Manihiki," painted in huge letters on a corrugated iron shed at the head of a jetty. In settled conditions it is possible to land a dinghy at the jetty. There is no boat pass into the lagoon, though anchorage (using two bow anchors) may be taken north of the landing in 7 to 10 fathoms, coral or off the village of Tukao. Anchors may become fouled in the coral, making it necessary to dive in order to free the ground tackle. Vessels must be ready to leave at once if the wind leaves the easterly quadrant.

Since the atoll occasionally experiences droughts, water is used sparingly. With permission, water jugs may be filled at the cisterns behind the church. Bi-weekly air service links the island to Rarotonga and telephone service operates by means of satellite connections. The atoll has a population of about 500 inhabitants. The lagoon is the site of pearl farming activities and the local men are renowned divers.

RAKAHANGA

This atoll is 29 miles NNW of Manihiki. The main village, anchorage and boat pass lie near the SW end of the island. Because of its close proximity to the reef, this anchorage is safe to use only in periods of calm or settled easterly trade wind conditions and an anchor watch should be kept at all times.

NASSAU ISLAND

This small island with its fringing reef is 155 miles northwest of the Suwarrow Islands. The only landing is on the reef at the northwestern corner of the island, and local advice is essential in getting ashore. A dangerous hazard in the area is Tema Reef, about 25 miles NNW of Nassau Island. The location of the reef is indicated by heavily breaking seas.

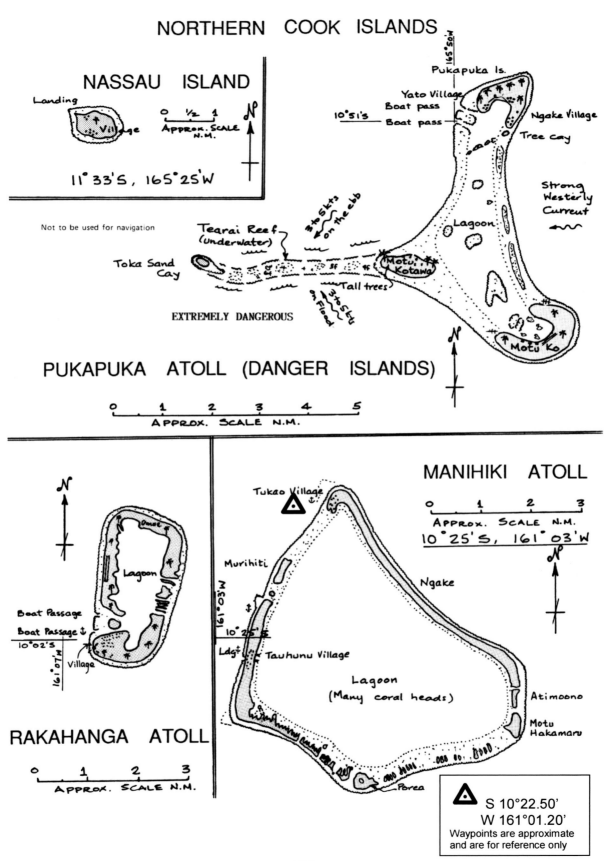

NORTHERN COOK ISLANDS

NASSAU ISLAND

Landing

Village

0   ½   1
APPROX. SCALE N.M.

N

11°33'S, 165°25'W

Not to be used for navigation

Pukapuka Is.

165°50'W

Yato Village
Boat pass
10°51'S   Boat pass

Ngake Village

Tree cay

Strong Westerly Current

3 to 5 kts on the ebb

Tearai Reef (underwater)

Lagoon

Toka Sand Cay

Motu Kotawa

Tall trees

3 to 5 kt on Flood

EXTREMELY DANGEROUS

Motu Ko

N

PUKAPUKA ATOLL (DANGER ISLANDS)

0   1   2   3   4   5
APPROX. SCALE N.M.

MANIHIKI ATOLL

N

Tukao Village

0   1   2   3
APPROX. SCALE N.M.

10°25'S, 161°03'W

N

Murihiti

161°03'W

Ngake

10°25'S

Ldg

Tauhunu Village

Lagoon
(Many coral heads)

Atimoono

Motu Hakamaru

Porea

Boat Passage
Boat Passage
10°02'S

161°07'W

Village

Lagoon

Canal

RAKAHANGA ATOLL

0   1   2   3
APPROX. SCALE N.M.

S 10°22.50'
W 161°01.20'
Waypoints are approximate
and are for reference only

PENRHYN ISLAND (TONGAREVA)

This is the northernmost of the Cook Islands, lying almost 745 miles NNE of Rarotonga and about 400 miles northeast of Suwarrow. It is an atoll with many low islets, most of which are topped with coconut palms. Three passes lead into a lagoon that has many large, visible coral heads and detached reefs with navigable water between. Black pearl farming in the lagoon makes it important to watch for and avoid the floats and lines of pearl shells, sometimes tethered just below the surface. Good anchorages are found in the lagoon.

Taruia Pass (West Pass), on the western side, is the best pass for use by cruising vessels. The channel has a depth of 19 feet and is about 300 feet wide at its narrowest part (where reef extensions on either side are visible). Tidal rips extending from the pass indicate the strength of the tidal currents, which can reach up to 5 knots. The easiest entry is at slack water or with the first of the flood. The pass is entered on a bearing of 087°T on Te Tautua village, on the eastern side of the lagoon. If the village is not clearly seen, the gap in the palms at the northern end of the village islet (between the long island and the smaller ones to the north) can be used. After entering the lagoon locate an anchorage either northeastward in the lagoon or southward off Omoka by visual navigation. **Siki Rangi (Northwest Pass)** is usable but shallower, and has a bank extending northwesterly that can cause rough seas.

The channel leading to Omoka turns to the south just east of the coral reef and a little islet, then leads through a clear passage between coral heads in the lagoon and the reef. Passage is easy in good light. Most of the coral heads are marked by poles topped by a semaphore in the shape of the number four. The poles are placed at one end of the coral head and the arm generally points to the other end. Travel within the lagoon is restricted because of black pearl aquaculture and cruisers must anchor off one of the two villages. Anchorage off Omoka can be unpleasant and dangerous during easterly winds and an uncomfortable chop often develops during northeast to southeast winds. Anchorage off the beach is preferable to tying to the rough rock wharf that has a depth of 14 feet alongside. The 90 foot coral fill dock is only 4 feet deep alongside.

Other anchorages include Ruahara, which is about midway along the north side of the atoll, about 4.5 miles northeast of Omoka; use caution because there are many coral pinnacles in this area. Many cruisers consider the spot across the lagoon, off the village of Te Tautua, to be the best anchorage in the Cook Islands as there are fewer coral heads and less chop. Black pearl farming was initiated in the lagoon in 1994. It is important to watch for floats and strings of pearl oysters that are sometimes tethered just below the surface of the water. The local inhabitants are very friendly and enjoy visiting with cruisers. They often want to trade pearls for such hard to get items as sheets, towels, knives, tools and fishing gear. Takuna Pass is not recommended (except in calm conditions) because it is narrow and sometimes has breakers across the entrance.

Omoka is an official **Port of Entry** and you must check in with Health, Customs, and Agriculture officials, each of whom may wish to board the vessel. The Customs officer may keep the crew's passports until the vessel checks out and all fees have been paid. A nominal daily fee is charged for anchorage in the lagoon as well as for spraying the vessel for insects by Agriculture officials. If the vessel is leaving the country an exit fee of about $25 (NZ or Cook Is. currency) per person is charged. Weekly flights and sporadic shipping service connect the island to Rarotonga and worldwide telephone service operates by means of satellite connections. Breadfruit, watermelon and fish are readily traded for. Fresh bread can be ordered from Christine early in the day for pickup at 1700 hrs.

NORTHERN COOK ISLANDS

PENRHYN ISLAND (TONGAREVA)

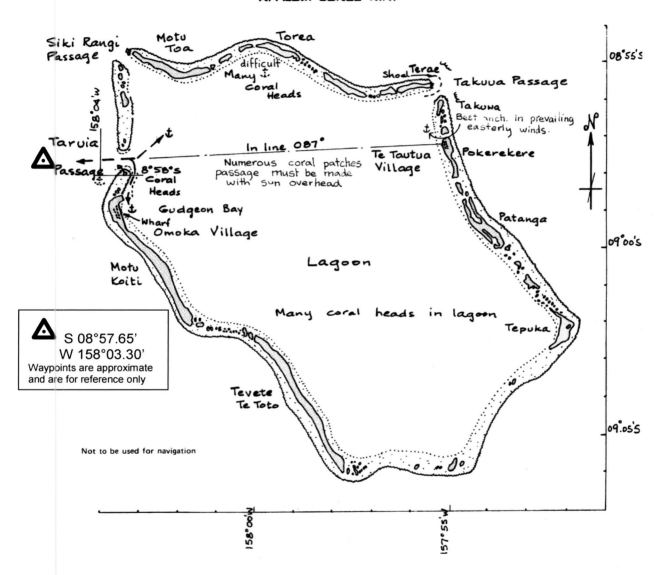

The islanders are devout Christians who welcome visitors to Sunday services which are worth attending to hear the haunting harmonies of their hymns. Photographs may not be taken inside the church and a dress code is strictly adhered to—women wearing dresses and hats, men in shirts and long pants.

NIUE

*Note: Niue lies west of the 165° West longitude boundary of *Charlie's Charts of Polynesia*, but after hearing the glowing reports of cruisers about this lovely spot it has been included in the guide.

First sighted by Captain Cook in 1774, this isolated island is situated 600 nautical miles WNW from Rarotonga and 1,100 miles west of Bora-Bora. It is composed of coral limestone, shaped like a two-tiered saucer that rises steeply from the sea to 100 feet and then again to 200 feet. The interior is the remains of a lagoon, and is therefore flat but heavily forested. Affectionately known as "The Rock", Niue has no surrounding lagoon and only a brief skirt of limestone reef protecting the island. On land the coral has produced many caves, caverns and arches and without streams or rivers the rainwater filters through the coral and passes into the sea completely devoid of any sediment. This allows the surrounding ocean to be crystal clear, with visibility often up to 230 feet. The dry season is from April to November and the cyclone season is from November to April

Niue is an independent nation in free association with New Zealand. The 1,100 inhabitants have dual citizenship although the island administers its own affairs. English and Niuean are spoken and the currency is the New Zealand dollar. The promised installation of ATM's is yet to eventuate. At present, Visa is the only credit card accepted by the Bank of South Pacific however don't expect to use your credit card for everyday purchases. Only major car rental firms and Matavai Resort accept Visa. There is only one flight per week, an Air New Zealand Airbus leaves Auckland Saturday morning, arrives Niue Friday at 1300 and returns to Auckland an hour later. The flight time is 3.5 hours.

The main town of Alofi is an open roadstead with a concrete wharf. The Niue Yacht Club (VHF Ch16 - you will then be directed to Ch 10) has 20 new moorings for the 2011 season. The moorings are constructed with polyester rope and each has a pickup float with reflective tape for night approach. Mooring fees of $NZ15 per night are payable to the Niue Yacht Club. This is the main source of income for this voluntary organization to develop and maintain their facilities. Anchoring is difficult because of the seabed topography and is discouraged as anchors can get lodged in rock fissures. If the mooring field is full, call the Niue Yacht Club for possible anchoring locations.

There is no protection from westerly winds and yachts must be prepared to put to sea when a passing cold front turns the normal SE trades to the west. As Alofi has is no sheltered harbor or beach landing, small boats are lifted in and out of the water by a crane located on the south side of the wharf. Dinghies from visiting yachts are also handled in this manner so they need to be rigged with a lifting bridle. Please use the Yacht Club tender trolley on the wharf to park your tender clear of the wharf access and return the lifting hook back over the water and lower for the next vessel to come in.

Niue Radio monitors VHF Ch16 24/7 and notifies Customs of yachts arrival. Please do not come ashore until notified about clearance arrangements with Customs. An Entry Permit is granted on arrival and is valid for 30 days; extensions are available from the Immigration Department. A Niuean Government departure tax is $34 per person (no charge for children under 12). This is payable to Customs at clearance.

The town of Alofi is small but most services are available including a hospital, bank, post office, tourist office, internet access, cafes, bakery, supermarket, hotels, and car rentals. Internet access may be possible from your yacht for a one-time $NZ25 access fee. This will give you 24/7 Wi-Fi access. Strength of signal depends on your yacht's antennae and / or position in the mooring field. Scan for Wi-Fi nodes. If you are getting a strong signal from "Alofi" or "LDS" it could be worthwhile signing up with the ISP. Send an email to support@nyc.nu or call NYC on Ch 16 for details. Please note Niue's Wi-Fi is not "blistering fast" but Skipping is possible at times. The Niue Yacht Club HQ is 100 meters South from the Police Station and Immigration office. Please register your yacht with Ira. For 2011, NYC is setting up a free Wi-Fi access for cruisers if you bring your own laptop. Friday is market day but to get the best choice of goods plan to arrive at 0600. A small produce market is also held on Tuesday morning. There is no public transport but vans, cars, scooters and bicycles can be rented from Alofi Rentals (Tel 683-4017), e-mail: alofirentals@niue.nu It's a full day's drive around the island, especially if you want to explore the caves and chasms. If you'd like to get an overview of the island the Tourist Office can recommend a selection of interesting guided excursions. Niue is renowned for its spectacular diving and many cruisers utilize the professional services of Dive Niue niuedive@dive.nu Strict fishing regulations apply and there are some restricted areas, so you will need to ask at the Tourism Office or Dive Niue for the current information. Humpback whales visit Niue to calve from June to September and can often be seen basking on the surface within the mooring field. There are strict rules for interactions with these huge mammals so please check with NYC, Niue Dive or the Tourism Office about what is allowed.

Potable water is available in a faucet at the base of the electric winch on the wharf. Water is safe to drink anywhere on Niue, and fresh water is provided at many of the tourist spots.

The Yacht Club has two washrooms situated just above the wharf. Solar heated showers, a large stainless steel washing tub and a head is available in each of the facilities. Obtain a key from NYC HQ for use during your stay. A $NZ20 deposit is required and is refunded on return of the key.

The Niue Yacht Club (VHF Ch16) is helpful in providing information on local services and for NZ$20 you can become a member. There is a Seven Seas Cruising Association cruising Station on Niue. The Host is Keith Vial. He is eager to help SSCA members as well as other cruisers. His contact information is: Keith Vial, Niue Yacht Club, Box 50, Alofi, Niue, or commodore@niue.nu or support@nyc.nu and www.niueyachtclub.com or www.nyc.nu For information on joining Seven Seas Cruising Association, visit their web site at www.ssca.org

NIUE MOORINGS

Inner mooring line
#1 S19°03'11" W169°55'21" to **#8** S19°03'20" W169°55'30"   - depth 8 - 12 fathoms

Outer mooring line
#11 S19°03'12"   W169°55'26" to **#17** S19°03'23"   W169°55'34" - depth 10 – 20 fathoms

There are also four moorings north of the wharf in approximately 12 fathoms.

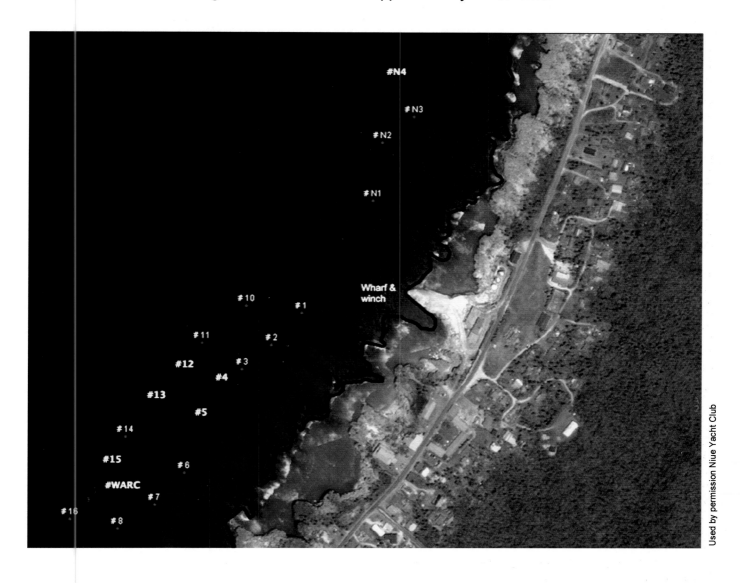

The newly renovated Niue mooring field

Aerial view of Niue Wharf

NIUE

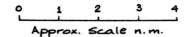

0   1   2   3   4

Approx. Scale n.m.

Not to be used for navigation

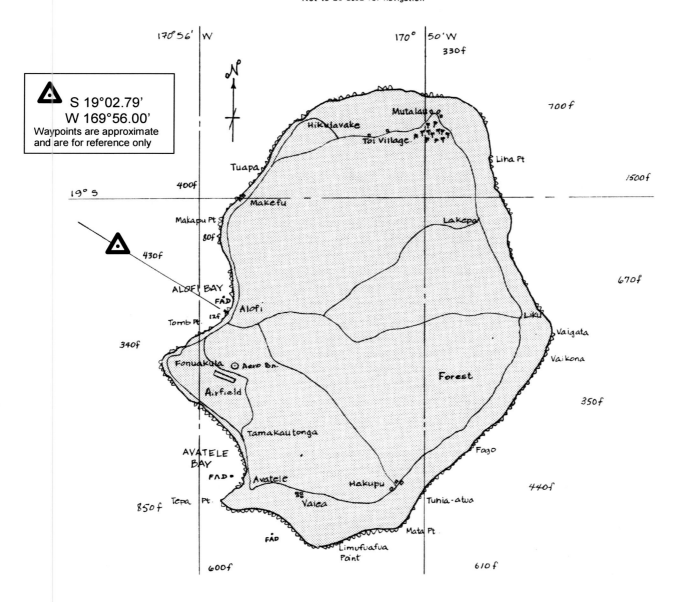

S 19°02.79'
W 169°56.00'
Waypoints are approximate
and are for reference only

170°56' W

170° 50'W

330f

700f

Mutalau

Hikulavake

Toi Village

Liha Pt

Tuapa

1500f

19° S   400f

Makefu

Makapu Pt

Lakepa

80f

430f

670f

ALOFI BAY

FAD   Alofi

Tomb Pt   12f

Liku

Vaigata

340f

Vaikona

Fonuakula   Aero Bn

Forest

350f

Airfield

Tamakautonga

Fago

AVATELE
BAY

FAD   Avatele

Hakupu

440f

850f   Tepa Pt.

Vaiea

Tuhia-atua

FAD

Mata Pt

Limufuafua
Point

600f

610f

190

THE HAWAIIAN ISLANDS

The Hawaiian Islands lie well north of the equator but from a cultural, historic, and in an oceanic voyaging sense, they are linked to Polynesia and are therefore included in this guide. The information presented in the following section is an abbreviated version of *Charlie's Charts of the Hawaiian Islands.* Only islands having Ports of Entry are included here.

The chain of Hawaiian Islands is an extensive archipelago extending 1,500 miles and consisting of 132 islands. Over 99% of the land mass is concentrated in 8 islands at the southeastern end, and of these, the island of Hawaii (the Big Island) is 60% of the total. The northwestern part has a few tiny islands with many shoals and reefs and is a wildlife preserve. Midway, a military base is the most northwesterly island.

The islands are a result of volcanic action that continues at a spot on the Pacific Plate now occupied by the Big Island. Since 1983, Kilauea's eruptions on Mauna Loa have often resulted in extensive lava flows that have reached the coast with dramatic consequences. About 35 miles due south of Kilauea, the Loihi seamount rises more than 3,000m above the ocean floor but is still far below sea level. In 1996 Loihi experienced a major eruption and has been intermittently active ever since. As the earth's crust has slid over this spot the other islands have moved northwesterly. Now only the Island of Hawaii is growing and in Mauna Kea and Mauna Loa its height exceeds 13,000 feet. If measured from the ocean floor, their true origin, these are the tallest mountains on earth, well over 30,000 feet high.

The prevailing winds are the northeast trades, which tend to be predominantly easterly. The trades are more consistent during summer months, though their velocity and direction can be affected by hurricanes or tropical disturbances in the vicinity of the islands. The trades are accelerated when passing through the channels between the islands, and this can make their transit unpleasant and sometimes difficult. The direction of the wind favors travel in a northwesterly direction up the chain; otherwise it is necessary to beat. Hilo, on the Island of Hawaii, is the most suitable departure or arrival point since travel to and from Tahiti requires the maximum easting. **Ports of Entry** include Hilo and Honokohau on the Island of Hawaii, Kahului on Maui, Honolulu on Oahu, and Nawiliwili on Kauai.

When traveling between Hawaii and the mainland of North America, the most important meteorological feature is the Pacific High, a high pressure area west of North America. Sailing routes skirt this high which usually migrates northwesterly to about 38°N, 150°W Longitude in July and August, then southeasterly to about 30°N, 130° W by January and February. This is a statistical generalization and daily movements may vary. The best times for travel to and from the Hawaiian Islands are from June to August. From North America the route swings south, then west around the high; return trips to the mainland go north and then easterly around the high. Cruisers with time to spare can take advantage of a favorable angle to the prevailing winds by making their landfall at Sitka, Alaska and then travel the protected waters of the Inside Passage and along the coast of British Columbia before proceeding further south.

For emergency services and navigation information call the United States Coast Guard on VHF Channel 16 and change to a designated channel as request by the radio operator.

Hanalei Bay

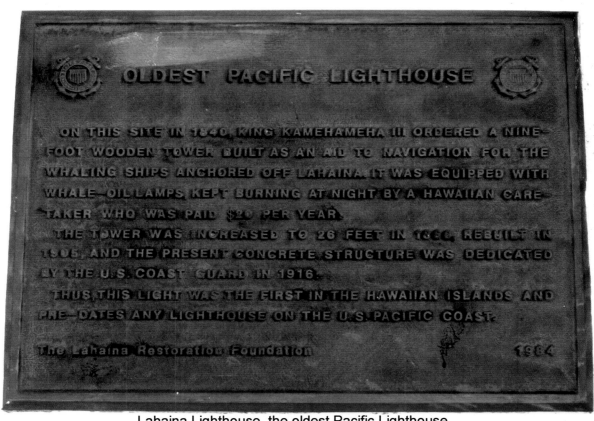

Lahaina Lighthouse, the oldest Pacific Lighthouse

Jo Russell

Somewhere (Kauai) Over the Rainbow…

Eric Lovett

Ala Wai fuel dock

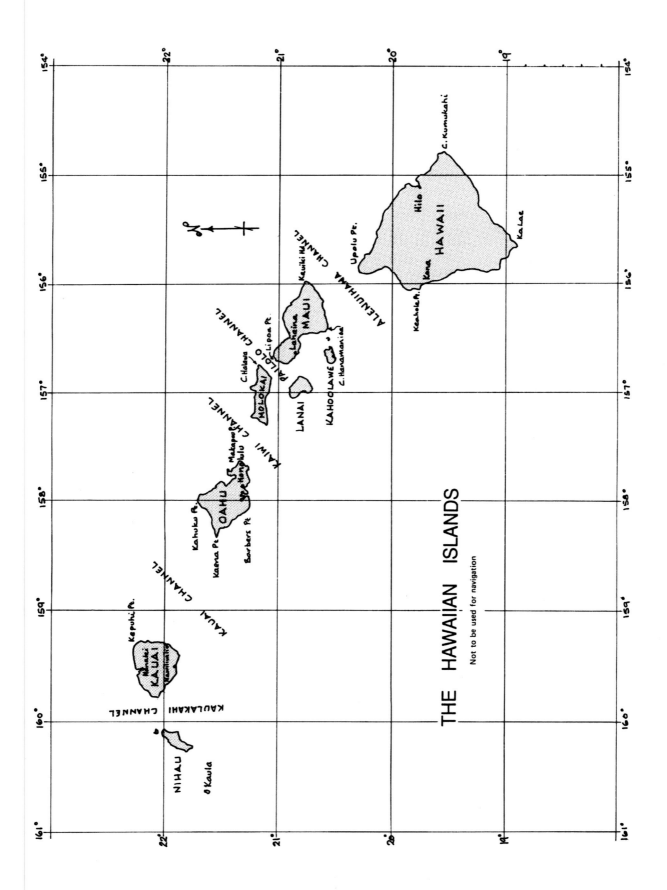

THE HAWAIIAN ISLANDS

Not to be used for navigation

154°

22°

21°

20°

19°

155°

156°

157°

158°

159°

160°

161°

C. Kumukahi

Hilo

HAWAII

Upolu Pt.

Kana

Keahole Pt.

Ka Lae

ALENUIHAHA CHANNEL

Kauiki Hd.

MAUI

Lahaina

Li poa Pt.

C. Hanamanioa

KAHOOLAWE

LANAI

C. Halawa

MOLOKAI

PAILOLO CHANNEL

KAIWI CHANNEL

Makapuu Pt.

Honolulu

OAHU

Kahuku Pt.

Kaena Pt.

Barbers Pt.

KAUAI CHANNEL

Kepuhi Pt.

KAUAI

KAULAKAHI CHANNEL

NIHAU

Kaula

194

THE ISLAND OF HAWAII (The Big Island)

This triangular island is the most attractive and interesting of the group. It has five volcanoes, three of which are dormant. Mauna Loa last erupted in 1975, but Kilauea's flank has erupted continuously since 1983. Bus tours operating out of both Hilo and Kailua-Kona visit Volcano National Park; this is a fascinating trip that also offers a good view of the countryside.

There is a distinct difference in climate between the two sides of the island. On the windward side, the regular rains give rise to lush green growth and create windy, cool and humid conditions. On the leeward side, it is dry, hot, and has gentle breezes, at times insufficient for sailing. In between lies the volcanic uplands with winter snow on the highest slopes. Sugar cane, ranching and tourism are the main industries. The island, however, retains a rural charm that is missing in others of the group, and the people, particularly in Hilo, are very friendly and helpful.

The three main capes of the island are each important features. Cape Kumukahi is the easternmost point and is a low lying, black lava mass behind which are cinder cones and several craters. A light is shown from a tall mast tower on the point. The trade wind tends to split at this cape with part going southwesterly down the lower eastern side of the island, and the rest going northwesterly along the upper coast. The offshore current behaves in a similar fashion. From Cape Kumukahi to Upolu Point at the northern end of the island is a distance of 75 miles. The intervening coast is steep and bold; an offing of 2 miles avoids all dangers. Hilo Bay is about 19 miles northwest of Cape Kumukahi and is the major indentation on this coast.

It is best to work your way up the west side of the Big Island to Upolu before heading across the Alenuihaha Channel to Maui. Ka Lae, the southern cape, is about 63 miles southwest of Cape Kumukahi. It is a windy area with disturbed waters due to the onshore current setting against the wind near the cape. Passage from Hilo to the Kona Coast generally means passing Ka Lae in the early morning hours. The cape should be given a berth of about 2.5 miles and the turn made in a slow, gradual fashion, as the seas allow, to avoid a knockdown.

About 22 miles northwest of Ka Lae and three miles north of Kanewaa Point is Honomalino Bay. This is normally a calm anchorage though it is exposed to westerly winds and southerly swell. Anchorage for about 6 vessels can be taken in 3 fathoms, sand.

Upolu Point is about 95 miles north of Ka Lae as measured following the island's western coast. It resembles many of the nearby bluffs, but can be recognized by the radio towers, buildings and aero beacon. South of Upolu Point is a small cove at Haena Point backed by a white sand beach. The cove is north of the light at Mahukona and can accommodate three or four vessels providing good holding in 5 fathoms, sand. It is reported to be an excellent anchorage as it is in the lee of the trade winds that blast the Alenuihaha Channel.

Alenuihaha Channel separates Upolu Point on Hawaii from the island of Maui, 26 miles to the north. When the trade winds are strong the crossing can be rough because the winds tend to accelerate at the channel's edges. An early morning departure is recommended so that part of the crossing can be made before the wind and seas build to uncomfortable levels.

Historically, Hawaiian consolidation occurred under Chief Kamehameha I from the Kohala area. Honaunau is a restored City of Refuge and National Historical Park. Equally significant is Kealakekua Bay, where Captain Cook anchored, died and was later buried at sea.

ISLAND OF HAWAII
(The Big Island)

Not to be used for navigation

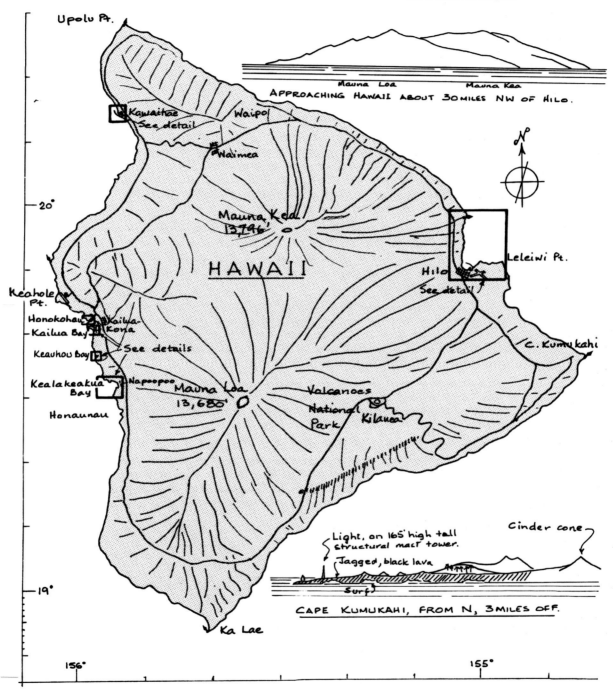

Upolu Pt.

Mauna Loa   Mauna Kea
APPROACHING HAWAII ABOUT 30 MILES NW OF HILO.

Kawaihae
See detail

Waipol

Waimea

N

Mauna Kea
13,796'

HAWAII

Leleiwi Pt.

20°

Hilo
See detail

Keahole
Pt.

Honokohau
Kailua Bay
Keauhou Bay

Kailua-
Kona

See details

C. Kumukahi

Kealakeakua
Bay

Napoopoo

Mauna Loa
13,680

Volcanoes
National
Park

Kilauea

Honaunau

Light, on 165' high tall
structural mast tower.

Cinder cone

Jagged, black lava

19°

Surf

CAPE KUMUKAHI, FROM N, 3 MILES OFF.

Ka Lae

156°   155°

HILO

This is a **Port of Entry,** the largest city and only port on the east side of the Island of Hawaii. If this is the vessel's first landfall in the islands, it is mandatory that entrance be made either at Hilo or at Honokohau before proceeding further on the Big Island.

Hilo Bay is the main indentation on the northeast side of Hawaii. About 1.5 miles north of the breakwater protected entrance is a lighthouse at Paukaa Point, another is about 5 miles further north at Pepeekeo Point, marking the northwestern point of Hilo Bay. The Port of Hilo is protected by a long breakwater built on Blonde Reef. A weak light is at the end of the breakwater and a lighted bell buoy marks the end of the reef.

Your first entry to Hilo is best undertaken during daylight since the number of lights in the area can be confusing. In rainy weather, visibility is often greatly reduced and even on a hazy day landmarks are not clear until the island is closely approached. The swell breaks heavily on the reef and breakwater, especially when the trade winds are strong. Buoys mark the passage into the harbor behind the breakwater. Transient vessels should proceed to Radio Bay as Reed's Bay is restricted to use by local boats.

The small boat harbor is in Radio Bay, beyond the piers and big ship facilities; it is the only dedicated transient facility in the State. Moorage is available Med-style to the south wall or you can anchor, as the holding is good. Though the harbor is subject to some surge, it is the safest place to moor during storms. Most boaters pull their vessel a little farther off the quay during heavy weather to avoid any backwash.

Only the skipper is allowed to leave the vessel to report to the Harbormaster, Agriculture officer and US Customs and Border Protection (located in a building just outside the port gates.) An entry fee per boat is charged to foreign and US vessels (which have been out of the country.) Opposite the US Customs and Border Protection office is a small store and shower facilities are near the docks. It is a pleasant walk to the downtown area where the fish market, a variety of stores, marine supplies and gift shops are conveniently located. After many days at sea one usually develops a longing for crisp green salads. Delicious meals with fancy desserts served in pleasant surroundings at the restaurants of Hilo don't disappoint. Charts and nautical guides are available at Basically Books at 160 Kamehameha Avenue. Two internet cafes are downtown, Surf Dog and Bytes and Bites.

The Harbormaster controls the basin and collects moorage fees. Rates are set by the State and there is a 15 day maximum stay in any State-run harbor, although time extensions are possible during the off season. A refundable $50 deposit is collected for keys to washroom and shower facilities.

Fuel may be purchased at service stations ashore and brought to the vessel in jerry cans. "Akin Petroleum" will deliver fuel to the dock if a minimum of 200 gallons is ordered. Several vessels may pool their needs and thereby avoid juggling jerry cans. Although equipment and repair facilities are limited, Honolulu and California can be contacted by telephone and needed items can be delivered by UPS, FedEx or DHL directly to Radio Bay or in care of the Hilo Harbor Office, which can also be used as a mail drop.

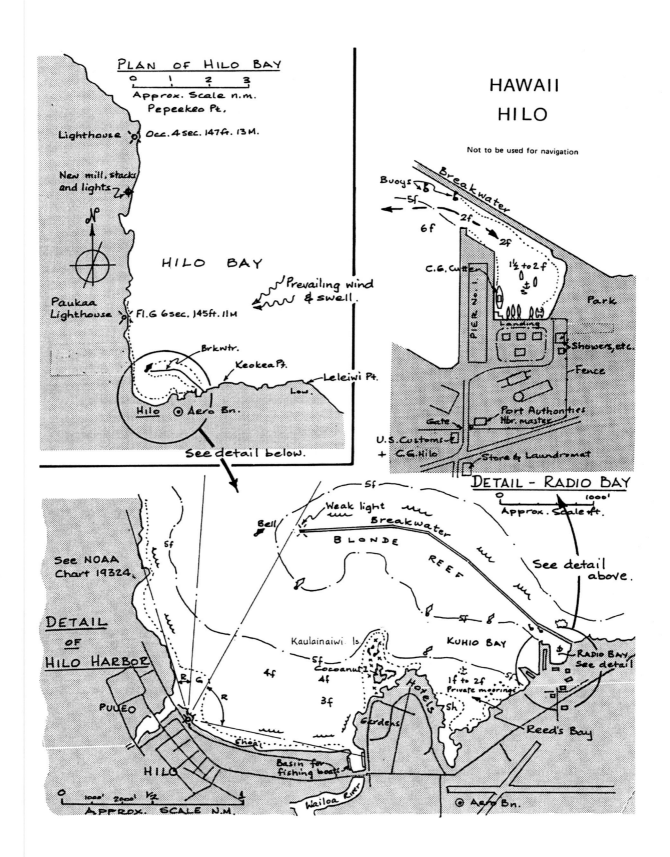

PLAN OF HILO BAY

0   1   2   3
Approx. Scale n.m.

Pepeekeo Pt.

Lighthouse · Occ. 4 sec. 147 ft. 13 M.

New mill, stacks and lights ·

N°

HILO BAY

Prevailing wind & swell.

Paukaa Lighthouse · Fl.G 6 sec. 145 ft. 11 M

Brkwtr.

Keokea Pt.

Leleiwi Pt.

Low.

Hilo ⊙ Aero Bn.

See detail below.

HAWAII
HILO

Not to be used for navigation

Buoys · 6

Breakwater

5 f

2 f

6 f

2 f

C.G. Cutter

1½ to 2 f

Landing

Park

PIER No. 1

Showers, etc.

Fence

Gate

Port Authorities
Hbr. master

U.S. Customs
+ C.G. Hilo

Store & Laundromat

DETAIL – RADIO BAY

0   1000'
Approx. Scale ft.

5 f

Weak light

Bell

Breakwater

BLONDE   REEF

See detail above.

See NOAA
Chart 19324.

5 f

DETAIL
OF
HILO HARBOR

Kaulainaiwi Is.

KUHIO BAY

5 f

Cocoanut I.

Radio Bay
See detail

R G

4 f

4 f

1 f to 2 f
Private moorings

R

3 f

Sh

Reed's Bay

PUUEO

Hotels

Gardens

Shoal

HILO

Basin for
fishing boats

Wailoa River

⊙ Aero Bn.

0   1000' 2000' ½   1
APPROX. SCALE N.M.

KEALAKEKUA BAY (Kealakekua means "Pathway of the God")

This wide, open bay is dominated by steep, high cliffs along its northern side and the volcano's gentle slopes come down to the sea beyond. The cliffs are visible many miles to the south as you travel northward on the Kona Coast in normally calm conditions. Because of its historical significance, the bay is included in this abbreviated guide to the Hawaiian Islands even though its use as an anchorage has been reduced by administrative decisions.

Much of the bay is a Marine Life Conservation District and Underwater Park and is divided into two zones. Though it is the best natural anchorage in the Hawaiian Islands, anchorage is no longer permitted inside the underwater park; visitors must anchor south of the park boundary. Two commercial cruise boats have permits to use the permanent moorings in Kaawaloa Cove near the Cook monument and commercial fishing boats belonging to a long established family have been granted special status in Zone B.

A concrete dock built at right angles to the beach allows easy access to the coastal road and village of Napoopoo where a walk up the hill leads to coffee plantations and mills. Dinghies must be lifted ashore or they bump heavily against the rough dock. Tourists snorkel off the dock but a better spot is in Kaawaloa Cove near Captain Cook's Monument, where a small dock allows shore access by dinghy. The nearby buoys are used by tourist boats from Kailua Pier and Keauhou Small Boat Harbor. Snorkeling from the concrete dock is easy in the calm, warm waters, where a variety of colorful fish can be found.

The paved road over lava beds to the south leads to the National Historical Park of Pu'uhonua O Honaunau, meaning Place of Refuge of Honaunau. A visit to this fascinating park is well worth the long, hot walk but with luck, a kind motorist may offer a ride. There are also tour busses that leave from Kailua. The informative presentation at the Park gives you an idea of what life was like on the islands prior to the arrival of Europeans in the 1700's. It is the site of a once sacred sanctuary for those who had broken the sacred laws (kapu) or were defeated warriors. Death was the price to be paid unless the accused could reach the refuge, where a brief ceremony of absolution was performed by a priest after which the offender could return to normal life at home. In the case of enemy warriors, they could wait until the battle was over and, provided allegiance was sworn to the victor, all was forgiven. A walk up the hill from Napoopoo leads to coffee plantations and mills.

CAPTAIN COOK'S MEMORIAL, KAAWALOA COVE

Kaawaloa Cove has a tragic history for it was here that Captain Cook was killed in 1779. A monument erected in his honor is in the cove. It was the unfortunate chance of his landing here on the festival of Lono, when he was associated with the god by the priests (for their own ends), that ultimately led to his death.

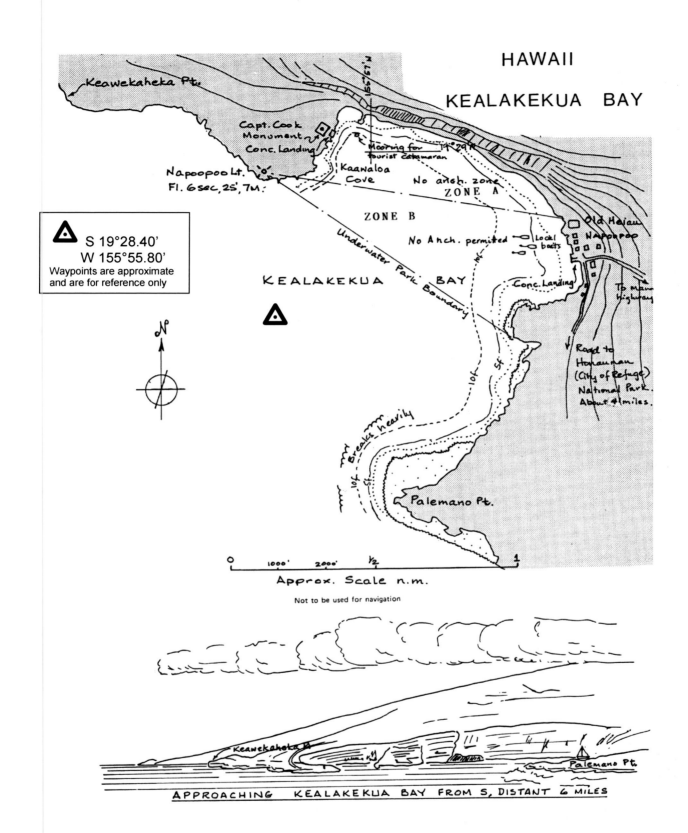

HAWAII

KEALAKEKUA BAY

Keawekaheka Pt.

Capt. Cook
Monument
Conc. Landing

Mooring for
Tourist Catamaran

19°29'N

Kaawaloa
Cove

Napoopoo Lt.
Fl. 6 sec, 25', 7M.

No anch. zone

ZONE A

ZONE B

Old Halau

Napoopoo

No Anch. permitted

Local
boats

Conc. Landing

To main
Highway

S 19°28.40'
W 155°55.80'
Waypoints are approximate
and are for reference only

KEALAKEKUA

Underwater Park Boundary

BAY

10f

N

5f

Road to
Honaunau
(City of Refuge)
National Park.
About 4 miles.

Breaks heavily

10f
5f

Palemano Pt.

0   1000'   2000'   ½   1

Approx. Scale n.m.

Not to be used for navigation

Keawekaheka

Palemano Pt.

APPROACHING   KEALAKEKUA   BAY   FROM S, DISTANT 6 MILES

KAILUA BAY and HONOKOHAU HARBOR

The "Gold Coast" of Kona, the tourist zone, commences soon after leaving Kealakekua Bay. About 6.5 miles to the north is Keahou Bay, a small cove with the Kona Surf Hotel dominating its southern point. The inner part of the cove is occupied by local boats, leaving only the somewhat exposed entrance for transient vessels.

Kailua Bay, 5.5 miles further north, is the site of the tourist Mecca of Kailua-Kona. The 'harbor' is frequently used by tourist vessels, and its long pier is mainly for their use. Other vessels may use the pier for up to one hour for loading. Occasionally one may be allowed to stay longer, after hours, with permission from the Harbormaster's office at Honokohau. A satellite harbor office is at the north end of the pier. In addition to many visitor facilities there are tackle shops, hardware and marine repair services. The only available area for anchorage is far from shore, exposed to the swell, and the holding is poor on rocky bottom therefore it is not recommended. Internet cafés are located at Zac's Photo and in the Scandinavian Shaved Ice shop in the center of town.

Two miles to the north around Kaiwi Point is the man-made harbor of **Honokohau** which was blasted out of the lava. The harbor is entered from an offshore buoy on a leading light, with a sharp turn to starboard into a wave dissipating basin; then turn to port through a short channel to the main basin. All slips are rented to local vessels, though the harbormaster rents space to transients on a temporary basis when space is available. Thus, reservations are not possible and transients must call the harbormaster on VHF Ch. 16 to check the availability of space. Fueling is best done in the early part of the day, because after 1700 the sports fishing fleet returns and the fuel dock area becomes congested. Above the fuel dock there is a small convenience store.

The building at the east end of the basin is shared by the office of the District Manager and the Harbormaster. The office is open Monday to Friday. For information call VHF Ch 16 or (808) 329-4215. Restrooms are located adjacent to the harbor and a small building on the south side has barrels for oil disposal. US Customs and Border Protection may be reached at (808) 334-1850 and the Agriculture Dept. at (808) 329-2828. An internet café is at the Hawaii Data Center at (808) 329-7371.

On the north side of the harbor is Gentry's Kona Marina which has an excellent reputation as a shipyard. Services include a 50-ton Travelift, painting, welding, refrigeration service, electronic repairs and hull repairs on wood and fiberglass vessels. This is the site of the only long-term dry storage in the state. For information on the availability of dry storage space or shipyard work, phone (808) 329-7896.

High-speed broadband service is available in the basin. An industrial park is nearby with additional services. Shops in the center have wide variety of boat supplies as well as groceries, fishing gear and tourist sundries.

Kawaihae Harbor is about 19 miles north of Honokau. It has a small boat basin within the breakwater and an anchorage area is outside. While getting there is usually easy, this is the area of the "Mumuku" winds. These strong trade winds funnel through the mountain gap at the valley of Waimea and blow with great velocity in a large area approaching Kawaihae. Usually lasting for a full day, these winds can reach 60 knots or more, making northbound travel impossible. In addition to the steep seas raised, a very strong north-flowing current is created along the coast.

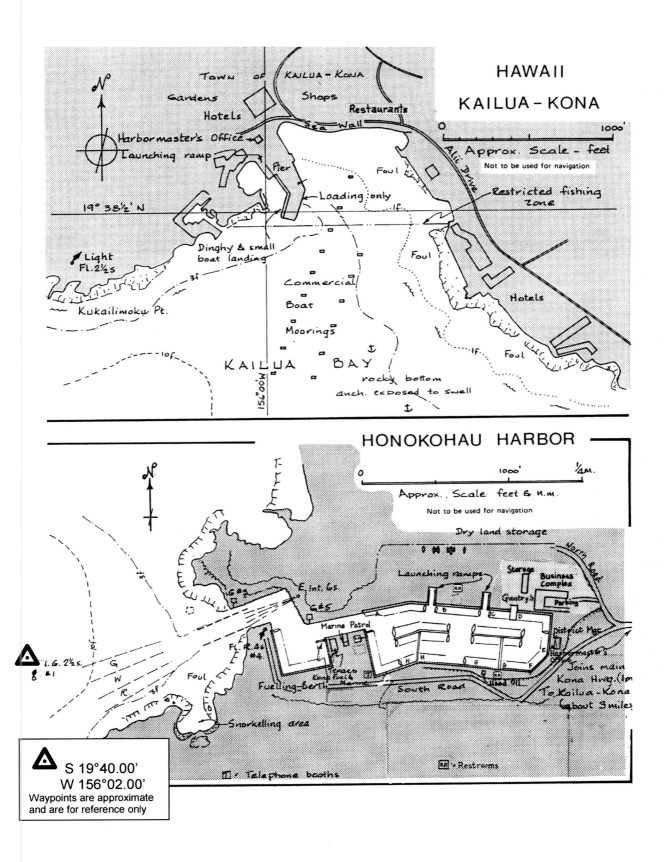

HAWAII
KAILUA - KONA

Town of KAILUA-KONA
Gardens   Shops
Hotels   Restaurants
Sea Wall
Harbormaster's Office
Launching ramp
Pier
Loading only
Foul

0 — Approx. Scale - feet — 1000

Restricted fishing Zone

Alii Drive

19° 38½' N

Dinghy & small boat landing
Light
Fl. 2½s
Kukailimoku Pt.

Commercial
Boat
Moorings

Foul
Foul
Hotels

KAILUA BAY
156°00'W
rocky bottom
anch. exposed to swell

HONOKOHAU HARBOR

0 — Approx. Scale feet & n.m. — 1000'   ¼ M.

Dry land storage
North Road
Launching ramps
Storage
Business Complex
Gantry
Parking
District Mgr.
Harbormaster's Office
Joins main Kona Hwy. (1m
To Kailua-Kona (about 3 miles

G #2
E Int. 6s.
G #5
Marine Patrol
Fl. R.4s #4
Texaco
Kona Fuel & Marine
South Road
Used Oil
Fuelling Berth
L.G. 2½s.
G #1
G
W
R   3f
Foul
Snorkelling area

— Telephone booths   — Restrooms

MOLOKINI and MAUI

Since most vessels proceed from the Big Island of Hawaii to the bright lights of Honolulu on the island of Oahu, they will cross Alenuihaha Channel, and can visit Molokini and Lahaina enroute. The channel crossing can be made comfortable by waiting for light trade winds. Staying in the lee of Hawaii until reaching Upolu Point achieves the best angle to seas and winds in the channel.

Once the vessel has passed Cape Hanamainoa on the southwest corner of the Island of Maui, the wind's strength is reduced. A short distance further is Molokini Island, a remnant of a crater, where a temporary stop may be made to enjoy the diving. Seventeen day-use moorings are available on a first-come, first-serve basis. Unfortunately, some cruise boats have been known to make cruisers feel like intruders. The island is a Bird Sanctuary and the waters are a Marine Life Conservation Area where fishing and coral collecting are forbidden. Charter boats and day cruisers operate out of Maalaea where a Coast Guard station is located.

Lahaina is about 17 miles northwest of Molokini. The entrance to the harbor has reefs on either side which are marked by privately maintained buoys. At the entrance there is a sharp turn to starboard which can be difficult to carry out in rough "Kona" weather. The small boat harbor is literally jammed from end to end with commercial and pleasure craft and space is seldom available for transient vessels. This is a crowded, tourist-oriented town, parts of which are maintained as a National Historic Landmark emphasizing its history during the days of whaling. Internet cafes are located at the Aloha Internet Center, Buns of Maui and Down-to-Earth (a health food store).

Most transient vessels anchor in the open roadstead off Lahaina, much as the whaling fleet did in the early 1800's. The designated anchorage area is too small and is filled with many permanent moorings. Vessels anchor over a wide area in about 9 fathoms, poor holding bottom, a little sand over rock or coral. Though summer trade winds are strong elsewhere, the anchorage is rolly but reasonably secure however it is not uncommon for vessels to drag. During Kona storms marked by southerly winds, the roadstead is exposed and unsafe.

An alternative anchorage is about 1 mile to the northwest, around Puunoa Point, off the remains of Mala Wharf. This is sometimes preferred to the outer limits of the Lahaina Roadstead since there are several good sandy spots. Landing and boat launching facilities are maintained by the State in the lee of the old wharf. It is about a 0.5 mile walk to Lahaina.

Though Kahului is a **Port of Entry** and the only deep water port on the island of Maui, cruisers are discouraged from anchoring here by the authorities except in an emergency. Before entering this busy commercial harbor contact the harbormaster on VHF Ch. 16.

The main attractions in Maui are its beautiful beaches and Haleakala National Park, the site of the largest crater in the world. This is an all-day trip by car up a steep and winding road to the crater's edge at an altitude of 10,025 feet. Interesting varieties of vegetation are seen on a hike to the higher altitudes and on a clear day the view is spectacular. Bring a heavy sweater as cold winds are normal at the summit.

Kahoolawe Island is controlled by the military and unless authorized, all vessels are prohibited from entering waters within two miles of the shore of the island.

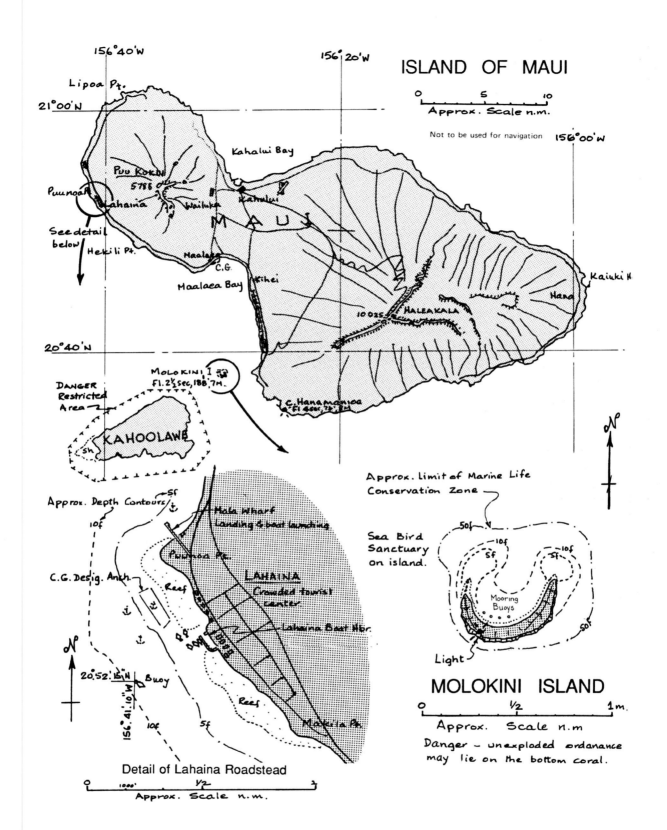

ISLAND OF MAUI

156°40'W   156°20'W

Lipoa Pt.

21°00'N

Puu KOKN
5788

Puunoa
Lahaina
See detail
below
Hekili Pt.

Kahalui Bay

Wailuku

Kahalui

M A U I

Maalaea
C.G.

Kihei

Maalaea Bay

Kaiuki H.

Hana

10 025
HALEAKALA

20°40'N

0   5   10
Approx. Scale n.m.

Not to be used for navigation   156°00'W

156°00'W

MOLOKINI I.
Fl. 2½ sec, 188' 7M.

DANGER
Restricted
Area

KAHOOLAWE

Sh

C. Hanamanioa
Fl 4 sec, 72' 7M

Approx. limit of Marine Life
Conservation Zone

Sea Bird
Sanctuary
on island.

50f

10f   10f

5f   5f

Mooring
Buoys

Light

N

MOLOKINI ISLAND

0   ½   1 m.
Approx.   Scale n.m.

Danger — unexploded ordanance
may lie on the bottom coral.

Approx. Depth Contours   5f

10f

C.G. Desig. Anch.

Maia Wharf
Landing & boat launching

Puunoa Pt.

Reef

LAHAINA
Crowded tourist
center

Lahaina Boat Hbr.

N

20.52' 15"N
156° 41' 10"W   Buoy

10f

5f

Reef

Reef

Makila Pt.

Detail of Lahaina Roadstead

0   1000'   ½
Approx. Scale n.m.

204

ISLAND OF OAHU

Separating Oahu from Molokai is the 22-mile wide Kaiwi Channel (Molokai Channel) where trade winds accelerate, with the strongest effects occurring near Molokai.

HONOLULU

The island of Oahu has less than 10% of the land area of the Hawaiian Islands but it is home for more than 80% of the population. The city of Honolulu, a **Port of Entry**, accounts for much of the population as it is the state center for communications, transportation, and business and includes Waikiki Beach, which is a major tourist attraction. When approaching Honolulu do not confuse Koko Head for Diamond Head. To be on the safe side, it is prudent to approach during daylight so as not to add to the list of vessels that have been lost by entering Maunalua Bay instead of Mamala Bay where Honolulu is located.

On the west coast of Oahu, 2 miles north of Barbers Point is **Ko Olina Marina** where clearance can also be arranged since U.S Customs and Border Protection and Agriculture officials come to the facility to handle entry for yachts. This luxurious marina provides first-class facilities and patrons have access to the hotel, spa, golf course and all amenities offered at the resort. For information call (808) 679-1050 or email harbormaster@koolina.com

Many cruisers come to Honolulu, where they may live aboard their vessel for up to 90 days if space is available and a permit has been issued. The two small boat harbors of Ala Wai Yacht Harbor and Keehi Lagoon have limited space for transient vessels. Kewalo Basin is a commercial basin and has fuel docks and repair yards where work can be done. A few small facilities are found outside Honolulu but these are usually filled with local vessels.

Ala Wai Yacht Harbor is 2.5 miles northwest of Diamond Head, a well-known landmark. The yacht harbor is entered through an angled channel. Within the main breakwater is a turning basin and fuel dock where one can complete check-in details and determine if any berths are vacant. A permit must be obtained from the Harbormaster, who also collects moorage fees. Transient moorage is limited to the outer one-third of Marginal Wharf in Basin #3. Mooring buoys line this wharf and vessels Med-tie to the wharf on a first-come, first-serve basis. There is a small repair yard in the harbor. Behind the Ala Wai Harbor offices is the huge Ala Moana Shopping Center where a post office and the Foodland supermarket is located. Easy access to an excellent bus system is on Ala Moana Boulevard, a major nearby thoroughfare. The fuel dock has a pump out station and laundromat.

Keehi Lagoon is a collecting spot for transient yachts since it is the only available large designated anchorage area and has good holding mud. Access is through the reef at Kalihi Channel where a daylight entrance is strongly advised. Moorage in the Lagoon is controlled by the State Marina which has offices opposite the anchorage. A fee is charged for dinghy docking and may also be assessed for anchorage. Negative aspects of a stay here are the noise of air traffic from the adjacent airport and the dust and dirt of commercial operations along the busy waterfront but as this is likely the only available place to moor, some discomforts will need to be tolerated.

A few miles to the west is the entrance to Pearl Harbor, which is closed to civilian traffic and navigation near the entrance channel is prohibited. Only retired military and those on active duty are allowed to moor at the Kaneohe Marine Corps Air Station (KMCAS) facilities.

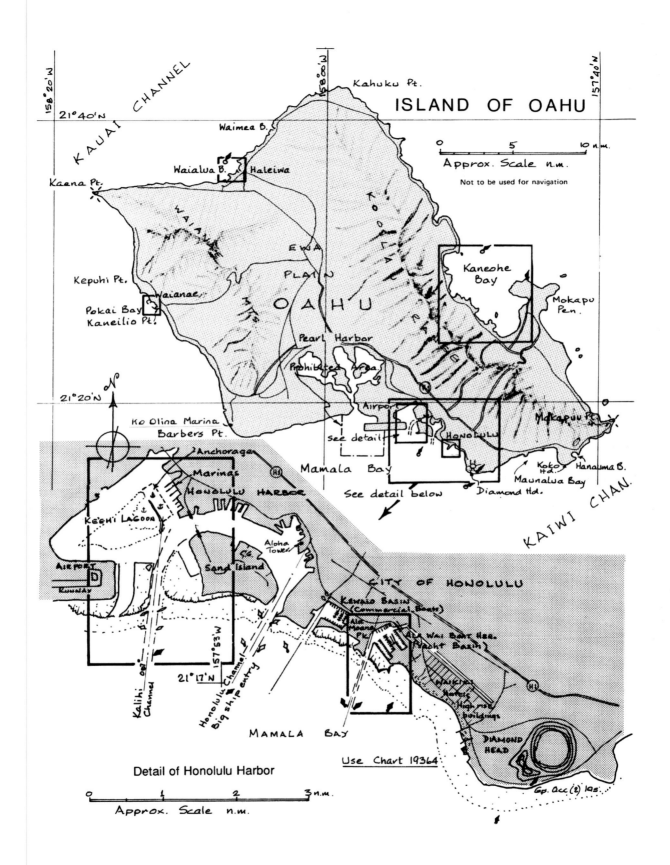

ISLAND OF OAHU

158°20'W
157°40'W
158°00'W
21°40'N
21°20'N

KAUAI CHANNEL

Kahuku Pt.

0   5   10 n.m.
Approx. Scale n.m.
Not to be used for navigation

Waimea B.
Waialua B. Haleiwa
Kaena Pt.

Kaneohe Bay

Mokapu Pen.

Kepuhi Pt.
Waianae
Pokai Bay
Kaneilio Pt.

OAHU

EWA PLAIN

Pearl Harbor
Prohibited Area

Airport
See detail
Honolulu
Mokapuu Pt.

Mamala Bay

See detail below

Koko Hd.   Hanauma B.
Maunalua Bay
Diamond Hd.

KAIWI CHAN.

Ko Olina Marina
Barbers Pt.

Anchorage
Marinas
HONOLULU HARBOR

H1

Ke'ehi Lagoon

Aloha Tower

AIRPORT
Kuulau

Sand Island

CITY OF HONOLULU

Kewalo Basin
(Commercial Boats)
Ala Moana Pk.
Ala Wai Boat Har.
(Yacht Basin)

157°53'W
21°17'N

Kalihi Channel

Honolulu Channel
Big ship entry

MAMALA BAY

Use Chart 19364

Waikiki
Hotels
High-rise
buildings

H1

DIAMOND HEAD

Gp. Occ (2) 10s.

Detail of Honolulu Harbor

0   1   2   3 n.m.
Approx. Scale n.m.

ISLAND of KAUAI

Kauai is 63 miles WNW of Oahu, across Kauai Channel. It is the northernmost major inhabited Hawaiian Island, only the tiny islands and rocks of the Northwestern Archipelago extend beyond it. It has a central high point of about 5,250 feet; the gentle slopes and gulches of the south and east become steep and rugged ridges on the north and west sides. The average annual rainfall at Mount Waialeale is 460 inches, yet the coastal areas get only a fraction of that amount.

The trade winds that bring the rain impinge on and divide along the northeastern side of the island, then follow the north and south coasts to meet southwest of the island. Thus at Waimea on the southwest coast, there may be calms or land breezes while strong trades are blowing offshore. The acceleration of the trades is most often experienced off the northwestern coast where they are pinched against the steep Na Pali coast.

Vessels cruising the Hawaiian Island chain usually make their first stop on Kauai at Nawiliwili Harbor. This is the principal port of the island and is located on the southeastern coast. The main town of Lihue is 2 miles away and the airport is nearby.

Beautiful Hanalei Bay is on the north coast and it is often the last, most northerly stop before vessels leave the Islands to sail to the mainland. When entering this open bay, give a wide berth to the extensive reefs off the northeastern corner. Anchorage in 5 - 6 fathoms may be taken off the old wharf, south of the massive Sheraton Hotel and Hanalei River mouth. To the west are the steep cliffs and narrow hidden valleys of the Na Pali Coast, offering amazing views and intriguing hiking trails.

On the south coast of the island is Port Allen, the second port of the island, located in Hanapepe Bay. A small boat harbor is located here. A few miles further to the northwest at Waimea Bay, is the open roadstead where Captain Cook made his first landing in these islands in January, 1778. Behind the bay is Waimea Canyon with steep walls, deep gorges, and many waterfalls.

NIIHAU

To the southwest, across 15 miles of Kaulakahi Channel lies Niihau, the Forbidden Island. The Robinson family owns and operates a cattle ranch on the entire island. They have forbidden intrusions for over a century in an effort to preserve the old Hawaiian way of life. Fewer than 300 people live on the island, while the Robinson family lives on Kauai on an estate surrounded by high barriers lined with bougainvillea.

Niihau has a 1,000 foot tableland at the center, with lower coastal strips on each end. The small, steep island of Lehua lies off the northeast end, while Kaula Island, a military area, lies 19 miles southwest of Niihau and is a military area. The southern tip if Niihau is a small, steep hill often mistaken for Kaula Island. There are no harbors on the island, nor is landing permitted though fishing boats anchor and rest in the lee of the island.

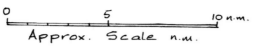

ISLAND OF KAUAI

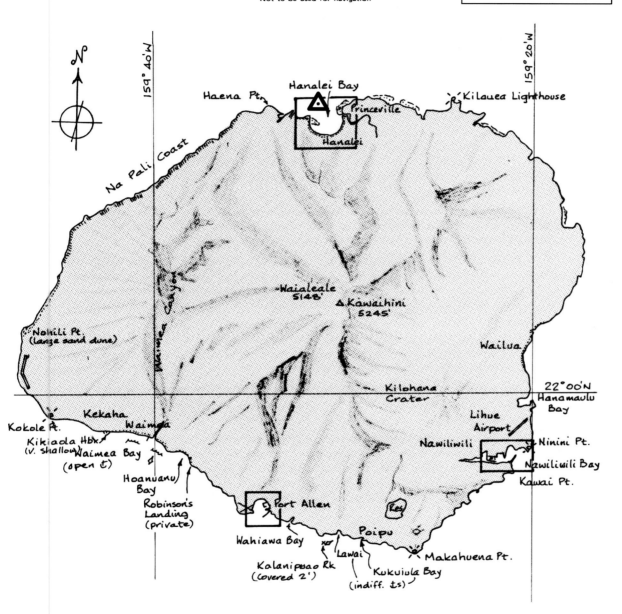

0   5   10 n.m.

Approx. Scale n.m.

Not to be used for navigation

S 22°13.00'
W 159°30.50'
Waypoints are approximate
and are for reference only

N

159° 40'W

159° 20'W

Haena Pt.

Hanalei Bay

Kilauea Lighthouse

Princeville

Hanalei

Na Pali Coast

Waialeale
5148'

Kawaikini
5245'

Nohili Pt.
(large sand dune)

Wailua

Waimea

22° 00'N

Kilohana
Crater

Hanamaulu
Bay

Kekaha

Lihue
Airport

Kokole Pt.

Waimea

Nawiliwili

Ninini Pt.

Kikiaola Hbr.
(v. shallow)

Waimea Bay
(open ℄)

Nawiliwili Bay

Hoanuanu
Bay

Kawai Pt.

Robinson's
Landing
(private)

Port Allen

Poipu

Wahiawa Bay

Makahuena Pt.

Kalanipuao Rk
(covered 2')

Lawai

Kukuiula Bay
(indiff. ℄s)

208

NAWILIWILI HARBOR

This **Port of Entry** is located on the southeast side of Kauai and has a part-time U.S. Customs and Border Protection officer, who can be called from the Harbormaster's office if a vessel is departing Hawaiian waters. The outer entrance to Nawiliwili Bay is between Carter Point and Ninini Point that is 0.75 miles to the northeast. The loom of the lighthouse at Ninini Point can be seen many miles at sea. The land runs westerly for 0.75 miles to Kukii Point, where a smaller light is located on the shelf below the bluff.

Kukii Point lies north of Carter Point. A rock breakwater extends northeastward from Carter Point making the harbor entrance about 0.2 miles wide. A light is exhibited at the end of the breakwater, where interlocking concrete bars give it a spiky appearance. Day range markers on two tanks within the harbor and a large buttressed warehouse on a bluff above the wharf are clearly visible. A low sea wall in front of the wharf appears to run across the opening, but once past the entrance, a sharp turn to the south, then again to the west (after rounding the tip of the sea wall) takes a vessel deep into the harbor. This reversed "S" turn is not difficult for small vessels but can be challenging for skippers of large vessels. Approval for mooring rests with the harbormaster who works from the State Harbor Office behind the wharf area. He may be contacted on VHF Ch.16 or by calling (808) 241-3750.

The small craft basin lies behind a second breakwater, about 0.5 miles into the harbor. The main pier with berths can accommodate up to 14 vessels, while multi-hulls and smaller vessels with shallow drafts can anchor in the wide space beyond.

Buoys for local charter boats are in line on the south side of the harbor, and vessels can also anchor behind them in Huleia Stream. Caution is needed in this area for the bottom shoals rapidly. When space is limited, a vessel may anchor in the bight north of the main breakwater, off the hotel and beach, though any place outside the small craft breakwater is subject to wind and surge.

Some shops, restaurants, and a small marine supply store are at the north end of the harbor. For major shopping or laundry and other services it is necessary to walk or hitch a ride 2 miles up Rice Street to the town of Lihue. The nearest internet café is Hanalei Bay Coffee Café in Kapa'a, about 15 miles distant. When traffic congestion is heavy this can mean a 20-minute trip via taxi.

The southern tip of Kauai at Makahuena Point is 7 miles southwest of Nawiliwili. A light is shown here and a tall tower is conspicuous. Avoid Koba Landing just beyond the point as it is not usable.

Kukuiula Bay, 3 miles west of Makahuena Point, has a small breakwater and can be used as an anchorage in good weather. It is affected by surge and is open to infrequent Kona storms from the south. Because seas break on the reef in front of and beyond the breakwater, on entry it is necessary to swing wide around it to keep to the center of the entrance. Local attractions are a blowhole and Lawai Bay, once featured in the old TV series, *Fantasy Island*.

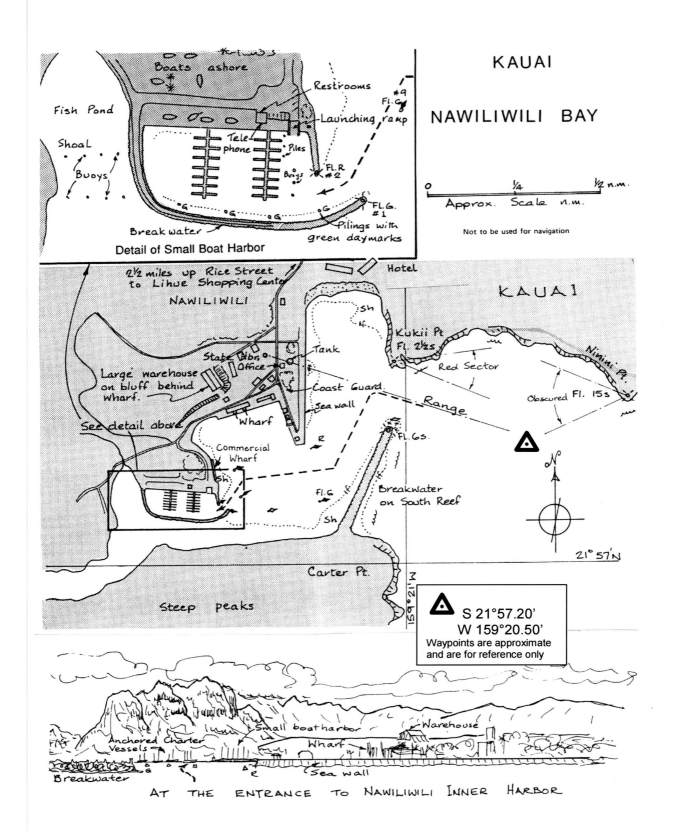

KAUAI

NAWILIWILI BAY

0   ¼   ½ n.m.
Approx. Scale n.m.

Not to be used for navigation

Detail of Small Boat Harbor

Boats ashore
Restrooms
#9
Fl. G
Launching ramp
Fish Pond
Tele- phone
Piles
Shoal
Buoys
Fl.R #2
Fl.G. #1
Breakwater
Pilings with green daymarks

KAUAI

2½ miles up Rice Street to Lihue Shopping Center
NAWILIWILI
Hotel
Sh
Kukii Pt Fl. 2½s
Tank
Red Sector
State Hbr. Office
Coast Guard
Sea wall
Range
Large warehouse on bluff behind wharf.
Wharf
Obscured Fl. 15s
Ninini Pt.
See detail above
Commercial Wharf
Fl. 6s.
R
Sh
Fl. G
Breakwater on South Reef
Sh
Carter Pt.
Steep peaks

21°57'N

S 21°57.20'
W 159°20.50'
Waypoints are approximate and are for reference only

Anchored Charter Vessels
Small boat harbor
Warehouse
Wharf
Breakwater
G
R
Sea wall

AT THE ENTRANCE TO NAWILIWILI INNER HARBOR

WEATHER FAX STATIONS AND FREQUENCIES

STATION	Countr	CALLSIGN	FREQUENCY
CHARLEVILLE	AUSTRALIA	VMC	2628 kHz, 5100 kHz, 11030 kHz, 13920 kHz, 20469 kHz
WILUNA	AUSTRALIA	VMW	5755 kHz, 7535 kHz, 10555 kHz, 15615 kHz, 18060 kHz
VALPARAISO PLAYA ANCHA	CHILE	CBV	4228.0 kHz, 8677.0 kHz, 17146.4 kHz
BEIJING (PEKING)	CHINA	BAF	5526.9 kHz, 8121.9 kHz, 10116.9 kHz, 14366.9 kHz, 16025.9 kHz, 18236.9 kHz
TAIPEI	CHINA	BMF	4616 kHz, 8140 kHz, 13900 kHz, 18560 kHz
KYODO NEWS AGENCY	JAPAN	JJC	4316 kHz, 8467.5 kHz, 12745.5 kHz, 16971 kHz, 17069.6 kHz, 22542 kHz
TOKYO	JAPAN	JMH	3622.5 kHz, 7795 kHz, 13988.5 kHz
SEOUL	KOREA	HLL2	3585 kHz, 5857.5 kHz, 7433.5 kHz, 9165 kHz, 13570 kHz
BANGKOK	THAILAND	HSW64	7395 kHz
KODIAK, ALASKA	USA	NOJ	2054 kHz, 4298 kHz, 8459 kHz, 12412.5 kHz
PT. REYES, CALIFORNIA	USA	NMC	4346 kHz, 8682 kHz, 12786 kHz, 17151.2 kHz, 22527 kHz
HONOLULU, HAWAII	USA	KVM	9982.5 kHz, 11090 kHz, 16135 kHz

Pacific Ocean Weather Fax Transmission Schedule

HONOLULU, HAWAII, U.S.A.

CALL SIGN	FREQUENCIES	TIMES(UTC)	EMISSION	POWER
KVM70	9982.5 kHz	0519-1556	F3C	4 KW
	11090 kHz	ALL BROADCAST TIMES	F3C	4 KW
	16135 kHz	1719-0356	F3C	4 KW

TRANS TIME	CONTENTS OF TRANSMISSION	RPM/IOC	VALID TIME	MAP AREA
0519/1719	TEST PATTERN	120/576		
0524/1724	SIGNIFICANT CLOUD FEATURES	120/576	03/15	D
0535/1735	CYCLONE DANGER AREA	120/576	03/15	E
0555/1755	STREAMLINE ANALYSIS	120/576	00/12	B
0615/1815	SURFACE ANALYSIS	120/570	00/12	C
0635/1835	EAST PACIFIC GOES IR SATELLITE IMAGE	120/576	06/18	G
0649/1849	SW PACIFIC GOES IR SATELLITE IMAGE	120/576	06/18	H
0701/1901	24HR SURFACE FORECAST	120/576	00/12	A
0714/1914	48HR SURFACE FORECAST	120/576	00/12	A
0727/1927	72HR SURFACE FORECAST	120/576	00/12	A
0740/1940	WIND/WAVE ANALYSIS	120/576	00/12	B
0753/1953	24HR WIND/WAVE FORECAST	120/576	00/12	B
0806/2006	24HR WIND/WAVE FORECAST	120/576	00/12	4
0816/2016	48HR SURFACE FORECAST	120/576	00/12	1
0826/2026	48HR WIND/WAVE FORECAST	120/576	00/12	1
0836/2036	48/96HR WAVE PERIOD,SWELL DIRECTION	120/576	00/12	1
0846/2046	rebroadcast/ 96HR SURFACE FORECAST	120/576	12/12	1
0856/2056	rebroadcast/ 96HR WIND/WAVE FORECAST	120/576	12/12	1
0906/2106	PACIFIC GOES IR SATELLITE IMAGE	120/576	06/18	5
0917/2117	SURFACE ANALYSIS (PART 1 NE PACIFIC)	120/576	06/18	2
0930/2130	SURFACE ANALYSIS (PART 2 NW PACIFIC)	120/576	06/18	3
0943/2143	TROPICAL GOES IR SATELLITE IMAGE	120/576	06/18	Y
0954/2154	TROPICAL SURFACE ANALYSIS	120/576	06/18	Z
1008/2208	24HR TROPICAL WIND/WAVE FORECAST	120/576	00/12	Z
1042/2242	CYCLONE DANGER AREA	120/570	09/21	E
1102/2302	48HR WIND/WAVE FORECAST	120/576	00/12	B
1115/2315	72HR WIND/WAVE FORECAST	120/576	00/12	B

TRANS TIME	CONTENTS OF TRANSMISSION	RPM/IOC	VALID TIME	MAP AREA
1128/2328	SEA SURFACE TEMPS	120/576	LATEST	F
1141/2341	rebroadcast 24HR WIND/WAVE FORECASTS	120/576	00/12	B
1154/2354	STREAMLINE ANALYSIS	120/576	06/18	B
1214/0014	SURFACE ANALYSIS	120/576	06/18	C
1234/0034	EAST PACIFIC GOES IR SATELLITE IMAGE	120/576	12/00	G
1248/0048	SW PACIFIC GOES IR SATELLITE IMAGE	120/576	12/00	H
1300/0100	SCHEDULE PART I	120/576		
1320/0120	SCHEDULE PART II	120/576		
1340/0140	SYMBOLS OR PRODUCT NOTICE BULLETIN	120/576		
1400/0200	24HR TROPICAL SURFACE FORECAST	120/576	00/12	Z
1410/0210	48HR TROPICAL SURFACE FORECAST	120/576	00/12	Z
1420/0220	72HR TROPICAL SURFACE FORECAST	120/576	00/12	Z
1430/0230	48/72HR TROPICAL WAVE PERIOD,SWELL DIR	120/576	00/00	Z
1440/0240	TROPICAL SEA STATE ANALYSIS	120/576	12/00	Z
1450/0250	rebroadcast 24HR WIND/WAVE FORECASTS	120/576	00/12	Z
1500/0300	48HR TROPICAL WIND/WAVE FORECAST	120/576	00/12	Z
1510/0310	72HR TROPICAL WIND/WAVE FORECAST	120/576	00/12	Z
1520/0320	rebroadcast/SEA STATE ANALYSIS	120/576	00/00	1
1530/0330	SURFACE ANALYSIS(PART 1 NE PAC)	120/576	12/00	2
1543/0343	SURFACE ANALYSIS(PART 2 NW PAC)	120/576	12/00	3
1556/0356	TROPICAL SURFACE ANALYSIS	120/576	12/00	Z

MAP AREAS:

A. 30S - 50N, 110W - 130E	B. 30S - 30N, 110W - 130E		HFO
C. EQ - 50N, 110W - 130E	D. 30S - 50N, 110W - 160E		HFO
E. EQ - 40N, 80W - 170E	F. EQ - 55N, 110W - 160E		HFO
G. 05S - 55N, 110W - 155E	H. 40S - 05N, 130W - 165E		HFO
1. 20N - 70N, 115W - 135E	2. 20N - 70N, 115W - 175W		OPC
3. 20N - 70N, 175W - 135E	4. 18N - 62N, EAST OF 157W		OPC
5. 05N - 55N, EAST OF 180W			OPC
Y. 05N - 32N, EAST OF 130W	Z. 20S - 30N, EAST OF 145W		NHC

HFO = Honolulu Forecast Office
OPC = Ocean Prediction Center
NHC = National Hurricane Center

RADIOFAX FREQUENCIES ARE ASSIGNED FREQUENCIES. TO CONVERT TO CARRIER FREQUENCIES, SUBTRACT 1.9 KHZ FROM THE ASSIGNED FREQUENCIES.

POLYNESIAN / SOUTH PACIFIC (REGION A) AIDS TO NAVIGATION

Note the color convention is the opposite of North American (Region B) marks.

IALA MARITIME BUOYAGE SYSTEM
LATERAL MARKS REGION A

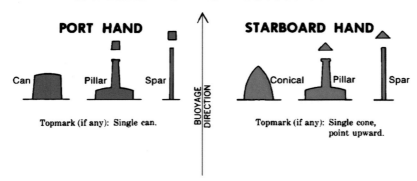

Lights, when fitted, may have any phase
characteristic other than that used
for preferred channels.

Examples
Quick Flashing
Flashing
Long Flashing
Group Flashing

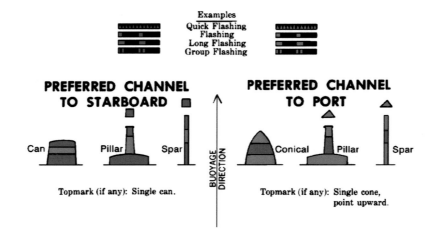

Lights, when fitted, are composite
group flashing Fl (2 + 1).

NORTH AMERICAN (REGION B) AIDS TO NAVIGATION

Note – the Aids to Navigation found in Hawaii follow this convention

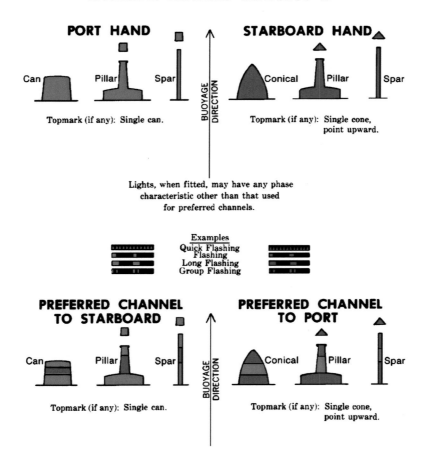

IALA MARITIME BUOYAGE SYSTEM
CARDINAL MARKS REGIONS A AND B

Topmarks are always fitted (when practicable).
Buoy shapes are pillar or spar.

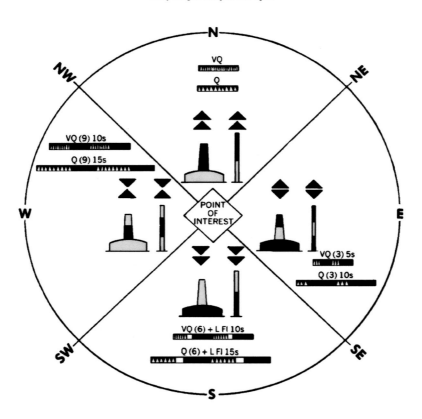

Lights, when fitted, are **white** . Very Quick Flashing
or Quick Flashing; a South mark also has a
Long Flash immediately following the quick flashes.

IALA MARITIME BUOYAGE SYSTEM
REGIONS A AND B

ISOLATED DANGER MARKS

Topmarks are
always fitted
(when practicable).

Light, when fitted, is
white
Group Flashing (2)

◻◼◻ ◻◼◼ Fl (2)

Shape: Optional, but not
conflicting with lateral
marks; pillar or spar
preferred.

SAFE WATER MARKS

Topmark (if any):
Single sphere.

Light, when fitted,
is **white**
Isophase or Occulting,
or one Long Flash
every 10 seconds or
Morse "A"

◻◼ Iso
◻◼ Occ
◼◼◼◻ L Fl 10s
◻◼◼ Morse "A"

Shape: Spherical
or
pillar or spar.

SPECIAL MARKS

Topmark (if any):
Single X shape.

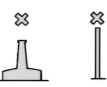

Light (when fitted) is
yellow and may have
any phase characteristic
not used for white lights.

Examples
◻◼ ◻ Fl Y
◼◼◼◼ ◼◼◼◼ Fl(4) Y

Shape: Optional, but not
conflicting with
navigational marks.

216

SKETCH SYMBOLS

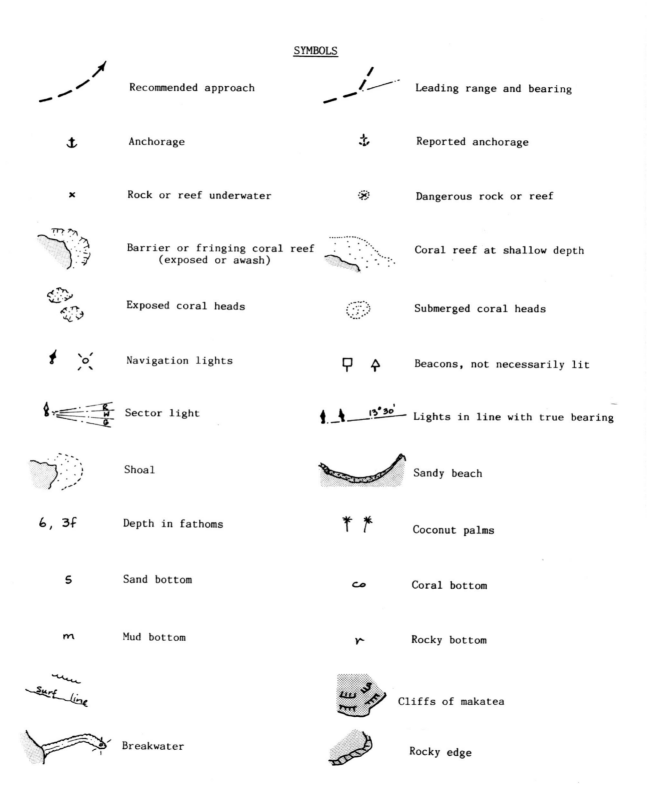

SYMBOLS

Recommended approach

Leading range and bearing

Anchorage

Reported anchorage

Rock or reef underwater

Dangerous rock or reef

Barrier or fringing coral reef
(exposed or awash)

Coral reef at shallow depth

Exposed coral heads

Submerged coral heads

Navigation lights

Beacons, not necessarily lit

Sector light

Lights in line with true bearing

Shoal

Sandy beach

6, 3f   Depth in fathoms

Coconut palms

s   Sand bottom

co   Coral bottom

m   Mud bottom

r   Rocky bottom

Surf line

Cliffs of makatea

Breakwater

Rocky edge

217